LOOKING FOR A FEW GOOD MOMS

Donna Dees-Thomases

founder of the Million Mom March

with Alison Hendrie

LOOKING FOR A FEW GOOD MOMS

How One Mother Rallied a Million Others against the Gun Lobby

RODALE

For Lili, Phoebe, Alexis, Isabella, and Brody. May gun violence be a thing of the past by the time you have your own children.

NOTICE: Mention of specific companies, organizations, or authorities in this book does not imply endorsement by the publisher, nor does mention of specific companies, organizations, or authorities imply that they endorse this book.

Internet addresses and telephone numbers given in this book were accurate at the time it went to press.

Printed in the United States of America

Rodale Inc. makes every effort to use acid-free ∞, recycled paper ♲.

Book design by Judith Abbate/Abbate Design

The excerpt on page 64 is reprinted with permission of International Creative Management, Inc. Copyright © 1999 by Anna Quindlen. First appeared in *Newsweek*.

Library of Congress Cataloging-in-Publication Data

Dees-Thomases, Donna.
　　Looking for a few good moms : how one mother rallied a million others against the gun lobby / Donna Dees-Thomases, with Alison Hendrie ; foreword by U.S. Senator Dianne Feinstein
　　　　　p.　　cm.
　　Includes index.
　　ISBN 1–57954–997–7 hardcover
　　1. Gun control—United States.　2. Gun control—United States—Citizen participation.　3. Violent crimes—United States—Prevention—Citizen participation.　4. Million Mom March (2000 : Washington, D.C.)　5. Dees-Thomases, Donna.　6. Mothers—United States—Biography. I. Hendrie, Alison.　II. Feinstein, Dianne, date. III. Title.
HV7436.D44　2004
363.33'0973—dc22　　　　　　　　2004000745

Distributed to the book trade by St. Martin's Press

2　4　6　8　10　9　7　5　3　1　　hardcover

CONTENTS

FOREWORD

In over a decade as a U.S. senator, I've encountered no lobby stronger than the gun lobby. Despite support for commonsense gun laws by an overwhelming majority of Americans, the National Rifle Association has largely tied up Congress and halted all sensible legislation regarding guns. Our last real victory came in 1994 with the enactment of the Brady Law and the passage of the Assault Weapons Ban.

Now the Assault Weapons Ban is under attack, and it could expire unless people like Donna Dees-Thomases can rise up once again and let their voices be heard.

I am convinced that if the NRA is ever going to be defeated, it will be by the mothers and fathers of this nation—parents who want a future for their children free of the violence and bloodshed sparked by the vast overproliferation of guns throughout our country.

These are the people who came together in the first Million Mom March. These are the people who will need to come together again and again and again, until the NRA is finally defeated.

These are the same people who I suspect will be interested in reading this book. It is a detailed story of how a group of mothers (and a few fathers, sons, daughters, grandmothers, and grandfathers) sparked by Donna Dees-Thomases' vision came together across our nation to say "Enough is enough" to the NRA and demand sane gun laws.

In our common struggle, we share the dream that one day the epidemic of death and bloodshed by gun that sickens American society will come to an end.

We share the dream of a nation where students can go to school without the fear of being shot; where parents can leave their children at day camp, feeling safe and secure; and where we can go to our daily jobs without concern that a disgruntled worker could charge down the hall killing innocent men and women with an assault weapon loaded with high-capacity ammunition magazines.

I do not believe that the Second Amendment of our Constitution consigns a well-regulated militia to the criminal, the hate-filled, or the juvenile. Let's be clear: The Constitution is not an umbrella for mayhem. The Bill of Rights is not a guarantor of violence. The Constitution is quite clear in its purpose to establish justice, ensure domestic tranquility, and promote the general welfare—and all of these goals are endangered when bullets fly.

The NRA likes to say "Guns don't kill people, people do," and then advocates for less regulation of guns and tougher sentences for those who commit crimes. But what do you do with a 5-year-old who takes a gun to school and kills his classmate?

There is no easy solution. We cannot legislate stronger families. But we can do something about the easy access to guns.

Never in the history of the United States have we seen the phenomenon of children using guns to kill as frequently as we do today. Never have we seen so many disgruntled workers, or loners, or those who feel in some way rejected, using weapons to kill as many innocent people as they can mow down.

No one needs an AK-47 with a 100-bullet clip in its magazine to go deer hunting. Such weapons are designed for one purpose and one purpose only—to kill large numbers of people in combat without having to reload.

But the NRA has gone on the offensive, and not just the Assault

Weapons Ban is in its sight. They want to pass sweeping immunity legislation protecting negligent gun sellers from lawsuits as well. And they won't stop there. Everything we have accomplished is at risk.

That's why it's so important that the dream that sparked the first Million Mom March not be extinguished.

We must stand together. We must march on Washington and in communities throughout our nation, telling the NRA and Congress: "Enough is enough! The time to protect our children and our families is now." There cannot be any turning back.

I ask you, as a reader of this book, as a mother or father or son or daughter, as a committed American: Do everything you can do to ensure that the dream that led to the first Million Mom March does not fade away. Help save the Assault Weapons Ban. Help ensure that gun manufacturers and dealers who flout the law can be held responsible. Help make the United States of America a safer, saner place in which to live.

—U.S. Senator Dianne Feinstein

When I became pregnant the first time, I didn't have a clue as to what to expect during the time leading up to the birth. So I boned up with all of the books I could find, including *What to Expect When You're Expecting.* This classic gave me every detail—great and small—about what was growing inside me, and it did so in an easy-to-follow month-by-month format.

When I first became incensed over kids being killed with guns in America, I wanted to march to Washington to protest the insanity—even if I had to organize it myself. But I was clueless as to how to make that happen. There were lots of books available on gun policy, but there was no book written on how to mobilize people on a grand scale. There was no *What to Expect When You're Expecting a Million Moms.*

I wasn't even sure, in those very early days, what I expected anyway. I knew I wanted to help make our world a safer place for my children. I suspected other mothers wanted the same thing. I wanted to help move sluggish (or nonexistent) legislation through Congress. I wanted to make a difference—but where was the primer on that subject?

Ironically, the only books that even touched on the power of people to make a difference were books about Martin Luther King Jr., himself a victim of gun violence, and the Civil Rights movement. King's words were certainly inspiring, particularly his belief that one way to stamp out evil is "through the marching of feet." So I searched for books on how to organize a march. There were none to be found.

I had only 9 months from the time I applied for a permit to pull together a march of a million moms for Mother's Day 2000. Without a guidebook to walk me through the mechanics, the logistics, and the politics of such an overwhelming journey, I kept getting lost and discouraged. There were many days that I felt I was taking more steps backward than forward. Often, I wanted to give up and go back to being "just a mom." But giving up would have meant giving in to the frightening fact that we live in a country where kids can buy guns almost as easily as Big Macs.

That was just unacceptable. And I'm not kidding when I say there were days I thought it would be easier to just move my family to Canada, where the law requires a 28-day waiting period and a thorough background check before a gun can be legally sold. There are no such federal laws on the books in our own country at this time.

Thankfully, every time I was ready to quit and call the moving van, some extraordinary ordinary woman would miraculously appear and do for me what good mothers do for their kids. When I stumbled, these women picked me up. When I made stupid mistakes, they corrected me with kindness and then encouraged me to go on. And when I hit a wall so big and intimidating that it paralyzed me with fear, these mothers helped me find the courage to climb over that wall and march on. To say I was inspired by these women would, quite honestly, understate their contributions. And it would oversimplify the adversity we faced— and we had plenty.

Working against me, on the other side of this issue, were the big, bad boogeymen from the National Rifle Association, who tried every way possible to discredit me and stop the Million Mom March. Why?

Because I was rounding up mothers—good and angry mothers—for a cause they believed in. In the end, all of the Million Mom March mothers proved to be tougher than the bullies from the NRA and more courageous than many members of Congress.

It was other mothers who helped create the guidebook on how to pull this thing off. I worked with dogged mothers who refused to take no for an answer; passionate mothers who were determined to protect their children; heartbroken mothers who had lost children to gun violence and who would not rest until there were laws in place to see that other mothers did not suffer what they had; and mostly, I was surrounded and supported by "ordinary" mothers: legions of good women who knew how to make a revolution happen, even while they made a mean peanut butter and jelly sandwich, juggled carpool schedules, and held down full-time jobs.

This book has been written to celebrate all of those mothers. I hope, too, that this book will help other mothers who want to make a difference—whether it is fighting for more nutritious lunches in public schools or getting a stop sign put in at a dangerous intersection.

Since I couldn't find the book, I decided to write it. My only wish for this book is that it helps others make a difference.

ACKNOWLEDGMENTS

In 1999, I was naive about the ferocity with which the gun lobby would come after me. So in 2003, when I wrote this book, I did so with eyes wide open, knowing that any unintentional misstatement of fact can and will be used by those who seek to discredit me, this book, or the cause by association. So I was not the easiest person to work with when it came to the writing of this book. I'd like to thank those who endured the painstaking, sometimes emotional writing process with me, including Alison Hendrie, Rachel Urquhart, Emily Heckman, and the copy editors at Rodale publishing.

A special thanks to Rodale publisher Sara Levinson for believing in this project, and to Tami Booth, Heather Jackson, Louise Braverman, and Amy Super from Rodale for their professionalism and enthusiasm.

Thanks to David Kuhn, my agent extraordinaire, who embraced this project as if he were my own mother, and to David's assistant, John Bennett, for his research.

I would never have met Sara Levinson or David Kuhn if not for the generosity of Ken Lerer. He has shared his office with me, his contacts, his passion for the issue, and probably most important, his assistant, Cristie Smith. (We should all be so lucky as to have a Cristie in our lives!)

Thank you to Maureen McEwan Tomlinson, whom I could always count on during my deadlines to feed my kids and the dog. And to my friend Richard Margolies, M.D., who has spent the last 20 years of our friendship feeding me during times of stress and deadlines—from the chicken soup during my graduate school exams to, most recently, the nourishment during the final 4 days of the editing of this manuscript. Thank you to Dan Rather for teaching me everything I know about sound bites and for not minding the abuse he took on my behalf from the right-wing media conspiracists simply because he was my boss years ago.

Publicists are always blamed when things go wrong, and rarely thanked when they go right—especially in the world of gun-control politics. A very special thank you to the top-notch communications team at the Million Mom March United with the Brady Campaign to Prevent Gun Violence, especially director Peter Hamm, as well as to the publicity department at Rodale publishing. And a thank you to Kim Izzo of *Late Show with David Letterman*, the show's director of publicity.

And finally, to the volunteers of the Million Mom March who are never thanked for what they do. I am in constant awe of the mountains you move every day. Without you, the world does not turn. I used to say I was just a mom until I met all of you. Thank you, thank you, thank you.

I don't know if a person becomes an activist suddenly or if it is a slow, gradual process that takes years. If it is the latter, and I had to try to pinpoint where in the past the seed for my activism was planted, then I would have to say it all started with bad tonsils. On November 22, 1963, I was home from kindergarten with tonsillitis, and I remember watching my father weep at the news that President John F. Kennedy had been shot in the head. *CBS News* reporter Dan Rather would be the first on air to pronounce the president dead.

I had always thought that moment had sparked a passion in me for journalism—certainly not for gun control. Unless a person is actually caught in the crossfire, I think most of us in America are oblivious to the gun-violence epidemic. For some reason, we tend to live our lives believing gun violence will never affect us, or we think the problem—and it is a huge problem—will somehow resolve itself. Some of us simply pack up and try to run away from it.

When I was growing up, my parents owned a pharmacy in New Orleans, in a relatively poor neighborhood. My father had trouble persuading other pharmacists to come work with him, because they feared the neighborhood. So my parents reluctantly gave up their lease in the Longshoreman's Building in downtown New Orleans and moved to Metairie, in the hopes of planting our family—and their business—in a supposedly safer place. But the suburbs were no safe haven. My father, who had never once been held up in New Orleans, was robbed at gunpoint numerous times in Metairie. Once a drug-addicted robber, desperate for a high, tied up my mother, put a gun to her head, and demanded that my father open his safe and give him all of the narcotics.

I don't know why I never considered that gun violence. Perhaps it was because neither of my parents were ever shot, were ever hurt physically. How naive I was then.

My parents rarely talked about those crimes, and rarely did they discuss guns. I do recall a time when one of my father's customers asked him why he didn't buy a gun and retaliate. "Because," I remember my father saying, "I want to live to see the next holdup."

There was one incidence of gun violence in my family, but it was rarely spoken about. My mother's younger sister was 28 years old when she killed herself with a handgun. She had four children, the youngest still in a bassinet. I probably wouldn't even remember this at all if it weren't for my chronically bad tonsils. I was 7 years old when she took her life. We were still living in New Orleans then. Aunt Margaret lived in Metairie, the "safer" suburb. I was supposed to go to the hospital that day to get my tonsils removed, but a phone call from my mother's other sister led to what at the time felt like a reprieve from an operation that was surely going to hurt. Aunt Margaret, my mother explained, had gone to heaven and so I would not have to go into the hospital, or even back to school that day.

After the funeral, *how* my Aunt Margaret committed suicide was never discussed, never mind the fact that she killed herself at all. Suicide, I suspect, is probably still not discussed in most families—at least in the South. But there is a lot of talk about guns, for sure, as the South is truly the cradle of gun culture in this country. In New Orleans, you can still pull up to the drive-through Daiquiri Store, buy a drink, and then go next door to the pawnshop and buy a handgun. Those of us from New Orleans actually laugh about this, only because it is so ludicrous. While we never had a gun in our own home, I assume members of our family did keep shotguns, because they lived in rural, isolated parts of Louisiana and Mississippi. I understood that feeling of isolation. We kept a summer house in Picayune, Mississippi, to be near my father's racehorses. All I remember about this house that was on 40 acres of swampland was that there weren't any streetlights or neighbors for miles. But there were lots of snakes and bugs, and fears about Charles Manson knocking on our door.

When I finished high school, I studied journalism at Louisiana State University in Baton Rouge. I think, at that time, I was more inspired by Dustin Hoffman and Robert Redford's version of Watergate in *All the President's Men* than by the real-life story. Journalism, at least as portrayed by Hollywood, is a business where the good guys take up the pen against the bad guys and work like dogs to make the world a better place. If Robert Redford could do it, so could I.

But the first job I had out of LSU, working as a reporter, shattered my idealistic belief that journalism was all about exposing corruption. As a reporter for a local Louisiana television news station, I covered things like frog-jumping contests and stories on the proper way to eat boudin.

A lucky assignment at a Rotary Club luncheon to cover U.S. Senator Bennett Johnston led to my leaving TV news for a few years to try my hand at public service. The closest I came to a place of power there was sharing my work space with the automatic signature machine. After a few months, I jumped ship and went to work for Senator Russell Long—the senior U.S. Senator from Louisiana, who was a true populist at heart. Senator Long was one of the most plain-speaking men I have ever met (despite being a stutterer). He was a master of the sound bite, and this was a gift he might have learned from his infamous uncle, Earl Long. Earl Long was committed to a mental institution by his wife while he was the active governor of Louisiana after having an affair with a Bourbon Street exotic dancer. He was able to talk himself out of that jam by convincing the state legislature to quickly pass a law that prohibits committing a sitting governor to a mental institution. If not from Uncle Earl, maybe Senator Long got his gift from his father, the late

U.S. Senator Huey Long, who was assassinated by a gun in 1935. Oddly, before I worked for U.S. Senator Long, I had briefly worked as an intern for a state representative while I was still at LSU, and part of my job then was to give his constituents tours of the state capitol in Baton Rouge. "See here," I would point out a spot to the tourists, "this mark is from the bullets that ricocheted off the walls during the shootout that killed Huey Long." I never once gave a thought to how it must have felt when bullets ripped through Huey Long's flesh, or that of his alleged assassin, who was shot and killed by the senator's armed bodyguards. In fact, I rarely gave guns a thought, period.

After a series of jobs here and there, I landed a plum one at *CBS News* in New York, where, ironically, I became Dan Rather's publicist 25 years after watching him cover the tragic assassination of JFK. This was strictly a coincidence, and I couldn't believe my luck, as Dan Rather embodied my ideal of a premier journalist. I didn't land this gig because of my journalism experience though, but because of my background working with Senator Long. Dan Rather was impressed that I had worked for the powerful senator, and he felt that, as a result of that training, I would have the skills to discuss difficult issues in plain language—just as Senator Long did. I did have experience making unsexy, complicated topics like oil taxes and gasoline royalties understandable to the layperson. If it meant that I had to understand these taxes in terms of how they would affect the price of mascara, well, then that was how Senator Long wanted us to talk about it.

My experience working for Senator Long apparently made me a better candidate for the job than recent graduates from schools like Harvard or Yale. I guess I had earned my degree from the Long family, where plain (and often corny) speaking ruled the day. And I shared the understanding of the effectiveness of plain Southern discourse with Dan Rather, who is himself a corny Southerner. And that's one of the reasons he's survived in the business for so long. Anybody who watched Dan Rather on election night 2000 knows what I mean. "The Bush-Gore race is closer than a too-tight bathing suit on a too-long ride home from the beach," Dan said, delivering the kind of line known at *CBS News* as the "Hey, Martha! Come out of the kitchen, and hear what Dan just said!" factor. If something was said in a way that got Martha out of that damned kitchen, then it was said well. Little did I know that learning to deliver information like this was the best activist training I would have.

While I definitely enjoyed some glorious moments of journalism at *CBS News*—the coverage of Tiananmen Square, the fall of the Berlin Wall—my job was mostly concerned with managing the petty dramas that come along with working in public relations for television news personalities. I started a year after Dan Rather was mugged and still would almost daily get a call from a gossip-page columnist wanting to know if the "Kenneth, what's the frequency?" mugger had been caught, or was there more to the story, like a jealous husband . . . Even I didn't believe Dan's wild story of being assaulted by a guy who delivered that now infamous line. (Unbelievably, and much to my shame, the details of this true story would be revealed to me during the Million Mom March.) After 7 years of countless PR crises, ranging from an on-air sparring between Dan Rather and then–Vice President Bush to our being scooped by CNN's live coverage of Desert Storm, the crisis that would put me on the ledge was the pairing of Dan Rather and Connie Chung as coanchors. From the minute she stepped foot on the set in her Prada shoes, I was inundated with calls from gossip writers who wanted to know things like, "Is it true that Connie secretly referred to Dan as Miss Clairol?"

It was clear that pairing Connie and Dan wasn't a great idea. In fact, it was terrible. Dan and Connie got along as well as a pair of squabbling siblings—and that was on a good day.

But I had other things on my mind. That same year, 1993, I married Jeff Thomases, a textile executive from Short Hills, New Jersey. With a new husband who didn't like me traveling with a globe-trotting anchor, I realized that I would have to leave my job sooner or later. And when I became pregnant, I knew that I could not work and take care of three children—Dan, Connie, and my own soon-to-be-born daughter.

I told *CBS News* in December 1993 that I would not be coming back to work after the baby was born the following February. I thought that was the ethical thing to do. After I gave notice, the powers that be wanted to keep me on for a while longer, but a *CBS News* bean counter trying to save a few bucks would agree to keep me on the payroll only if my extension was at minimum wage. Being 8 months pregnant and wildly hormonal, I reacted to this request by writing a scathing four-page memo that basically said, "Take this job and shove it!" I then sent the memo via interoffice mail (thankfully, I didn't have e-mail then) to a dozen or so executives at CBS, so that they could read, in gory detail, why I hated them and why I hated the network. Talk about burning bridges.

Burning bridges was the least of my worries then. I was trying to get used to the idea of moving out of New York City and into the suburbs.

Jeff had three sons from his first marriage, and though David and Danny were in their twenties and living on their own, Greg, Jeff's youngest son, was still in high school in Short Hills, New Jersey. I wanted to make Jeff happy by moving full-time into his New Jersey house (one he bought with his second wife) so that he could be near his son. In exchange, Jeff promised we'd move back to the city as soon as Greg went off to college.

The house was extremely beautiful, in a Frank Lloyd Wright kind of way, was set back in a wooded area, and was very isolated. It was the kind of house you would want to live in if you were a painter or a poet, or the Unabomber writing a manifesto, but I wasn't a painter or a poet or the Unabomber. And the house, having belonged to one of Jeff's previous wives, didn't feel like mine. But I was madly in love with Jeff, loved his kids, and wanted to make a go of life in northern New Jersey at least for the next 2 years. In December 1993, I made the move, and 2 years later, in 1995, with Greg on the verge of graduating from high school, I started skimming the *New York Times* real-estate section, plotting my return to the city. I hated the commute back into the city just as much as I hated the isolation of the suburbs. In 1995, we also welcomed our second daughter. Just after Phoebe was born, I landed a plum part-time job as a publicist at the *Late Show with David Letterman*. Ironically, I got the job because of that hormonally charged, four-page memo blasting the CBS brass I had sent just 2 years before.

I heard through the grapevine that Dave Letterman was looking for someone, but that he had rejected all of the candidates CBS sent over. I guess they were scraping the absolute bottom of the barrel because I— the memo writer—was called in for an interview. At that time, Phoebe was only 5 weeks old, and I was still nursing.

During the interview, Ken Lerer, the independent consultant for publicity, asked me if I had burned any bridges when I had worked at CBS before. Because of his question, I wrongly assumed he had heard about the memo. "Burned 'em? More like eviscerated," I volunteered, saying more than I really needed to. I think I mentioned something about calling a network executive a little weasel. There I sat, fat, leaking breast milk, knowing I had no shot at this job, when Morty's—then the *Late Show*'s executive producer—face lit up. He knew that Dave would be delighted by this, being the network "weasel whacker" that he is. I was hired on the spot.

As publicist for this comedy show, my job was mostly to promote gags such as how many *Late Show* staffers dressed in bunny suits could squeeze into an H&R Block office on tax day. It was a fun job. Not that hard. And the pay was okay. But the best thing was the hours. I only worked 1 day a week, Monday, so I got to spend most of my time with my kids, while still keeping my hand in the work game. It also gave me the chance to meet with city real-estate agents to find my dream apartment.

It was now 1996, and Jeff and I were close to signing a deal on an apartment when suddenly and tragically, the mother of my stepsons passed away. Even though Greg was living away at college at this time, now that his mother was gone, I felt that it was important to keep a home for him in New Jersey—at least for the time being.

So I put the plan of moving back to the city on a back burner once again. Greg would graduate in 1999, and so I would wait until then before calling any more realtors. But as a gesture of hope, my husband and I decided to start planning for the day when our girls would no longer have a backyard, and we built a vacation house on Fire Island, New York, where we were already spending our summers as renters.

I loved summertime then, as the show would often be in repeats and I would stay out on Fire Island with nary a care aside from getting a sunburn. And the summer of 1999 looked like it was going to be the best ever. Jeff put down a hefty deposit on a Tribeca apartment, and I was elated. When summer was up, I would be going home! Or so I thought. I had no idea that, before the summer was out, a latent, fierce, maternal instinct would be unleashed in me, and everything in my life would turn upside down.

"There's been a
shooting here . . .
He shot up the whole
damn place. Oh my God."

—A CALLER TO A 911
OPERATOR ON AUGUST 10, 1999,
GRANADA HILLS, CALIFORNIA

AUGUST 1999

If there is such a thing as a moment
being ripe for a revolution, then I
would have to say the summer of
1999 was about as fertile as a warren
of rabbits. We're talking egg counts
that would put Perdue to shame.

Up until then, I was not an activist. I was just a mom.

My family and I were spending
that August much as we had spent
the last five summers—vacationing
on Fire Island, an idyllic 31-mile-
long barrier island off the coast of
Long Island that, culturally, seems
to be stuck in a wonderful kind of
1950s time warp. And that's why
we like it so much. Cars are banned
on the island for most of the
summer, and kids on bikes compete
for sidewalk space with adults
pulling groceries in little red
wagons.

Life in our town of Seaview is like life in *Leave It to Beaver* land, and this summer was no different—even if it was one of the hottest, driest summers on record. I did not mind the drought. A drought meant our beach house guestrooms would be filled with friends who needed to flee the sizzling streets of New York City, and I loved having company, because the rest of the year, we lived in an isolated, northern New Jersey suburb, in a beautiful home stuck way off-road, abutting a forest reservation. Other than the occasional lost hiker, rarely did anyone drop by. Like a lot of isolated, suburban moms with small kids, I relished the weekly playgroups where we moms would get together to discuss who was the "best" pediatrician, or which were the "best" schools, or whether or not we had been to the newest store at the Mall at Short Hills. In other words, what we talked about was Stepford mom stuff. Rarely would we talk about ourselves or "unsafe" subjects such as religion or politics. And never did we discuss the more taboo ones like the politics of guns in America. But all of this was about to change.

The afternoon of August 10 should have been no different than any other lazy beach day, but that day I got a call from Robin Sheer, one of my New Jersey playgroup moms. Robin's daughters Elizabeth and Claudia both attended the same Jewish Community Center nursery school as my two daughters, Lili and Phoebe, and so I assumed she was calling so we could catch up on the girls. But this wasn't a social call. "Are you watching CNN?" Robin asked, sounding frantic.

No, I wasn't. Nor did I want to. Since leaving my full-time job at *CBS News* years before, I had happily traded in Dan Rather and Connie Chung for Barney, Elmo, and Big Bird. I didn't feel the compulsive need to always be tuned in to an all-news channel waiting for the latest, breaking story about some horrible catastrophe—unless it had something to do with mindless trash, like the Monica Lewinsky scandal. Then I was glued to the tube. Since I had had children, I found the news to be, frankly, too full of bad news.

And Robin was calling about bad news. A Jewish Community Center in California had just been shot up; the kids attending day camp there were injured, maybe even dead. I clicked on the TV, saw the hovering helicopters, and the BREAKING NEWS headline, and immediately thought, "What mother in her right mind wants to watch this stuff?" Then I turned the TV off. Before I hung up with Robin, I probably "thanked" her for calling, and then I went back to one of my preferred sources of news—the *National Enquirer*, or maybe it was the *New York Post*.

As on most summer weekday nights, I was on my own with the kids because Jeff stayed in New Jersey so he could be within easier commuting distance to his office in the city. I missed him on these nights, but the trade-off was that I got to have the TV remote control all to myself once I put the kids to bed. On this August night, I settled in to have a few laughs at Seinfeld, and then at 11:35 P.M., I began to channel surf backward looking for Dave. The show was in repeat, but I liked to see what it felt like to watch Dave like a regular viewer instead of seeing him at 5:30 P.M., the time the show was usually taped. As I surfed backward through the channels, toward Channel 2, home of Dave and the *Late Show*, I stumbled onto Channel 7, home of Ted Koppel and *Nightline*. My remote finger froze.

The entire program that night was devoted to what had happened in Granada Hills, California, that morning. The North Valley Jewish Community Center there was stormed by a gunman while a summer day-camp program was in session. This ws what Robin called about earlier in the day. It seems that this guy just marched into the place and started shooting. Ted Koppel had just introduced taped footage of terrified children being led out of and away from the center by armed police. Good Lord, I wondered, how will those kids ever recover from that? How will they ever sleep again, having watched their friends be shot full of bullets? My heart was in my throat as I watched that chain of children, hand in hand, being led to safety. Something was terribly wrong with this picture. This was no daisy chain of happy, innocent children who were blissfully unaware of the evil in the world, safe on the grounds of their camp—this was a string of survivors being led away from a death trap. And those children could have been mine.

I was immobilized with shock. I stayed with the program and watched in horror as the television camera zoomed out to show the powerful images of SWAT teams leading these preschoolers off to safety.

The program then cut to two law-enforcement officials, one from Vancouver, the other from Seattle, who tried to apply reason to this insanity. Handguns and assault weapons, they both said, were much too easy to get in this country, especially compared with Canada, where the laws are much stricter. The Vancouver policeman talked about how strict the gun laws are in Canada, unlike those in America, where they are loose, lax, and riddled with loopholes. But it was the Seattle police chief, Norm Stamper, who made me sit up in bed and listen.

Norm Stamper: I think the registration of all firearms seems to me a sensible step for us to take. The licensing of all owners of firearms seems sensible. Ensuring that every owner of a firearm is made to understand that he or she has to prove proficiency in the use of the firearm and safe handling of that firearm as well. Those seem to me to be reasonable steps for us to take as a society.

I couldn't believe what I was hearing. Didn't we already require registering all firearms in this country? Weren't all gun owners licensed? This blew me away. It was hearing this that transformed me from a carefree mother into a mother who cared.

Norm Stamper: . . . I am reminded of a statement made by then-Senator Barry Goldwater some . . . 27 years ago that . . . it would take 50 years to reach a level of responsible gun control that would have the desired effect. And I think if that prophecy were true, and if, in fact, we had had the political will to follow up on it in those days, we might be at half the gun violence problem we have today some 25 or so years later. I think we ought to be ashamed. I think we ought to be embarrassed as we compare our gun violence and homicide rates against those of other countries . . . If we don't develop the will now to do something about it, what will this picture look like 5, 10, 15, or 20 years from now? How many more children will, in fact, meet a sudden, violent death at the hands of a firearm if we don't act now?

I was lost for a moment until I realized that he was referring back a quarter of a century—nearly 30 years—to the assassinations of John Kennedy, Bobby Kennedy, and Martin Luther King Jr. What he was saying, in effect, is that this debate about the lack of meaningful gun legislation had been dogging our country for decades—since the time I was in grade school. I was stunned. And now I was mad.

So much for my taking advantage of my children being asleep and my husband being out of town that night. Instead of going to bed after *Nightline*, I went online, and what I found there not only shocked me, it scared me. After entering the search words "gun control," I found myself wandering into chat room after chat room overflowing with viciously worded, hate-fueled diatribes from gun-loving "Americans" who happened to hate other Americans who were Asian, African-American, Jewish, Latino, and, in some cases, women. The only thing they appeared to love more than their guns was making a profit by selling guns to other gun nuts like themselves. There was a lot of hate poorly camouflaged as patriotism in those chat rooms. It made me want to find an American flag and give it a good cleaning. Fast.

Apparently, events like the tragedy of Granada Hills prompted these gun nuts to come out of hiding and log on. I read the words of kids paying homage to Eric Harris and Dylan Klebold, the two teenagers who had gone on a killing rampage at Columbine High School only 6 months before. Columbine! That previous April, I shut off that news coverage even faster than I had tried to shut off CNN earlier on this day. I was more concerned with little girls in pigtails carrying their baby dolls than I was with teenagers in trench coats carrying semiautomatic weapons. Was this because I was insensitive? Or was it because today's horror happened to children so similar to my own? Whatever the reason, I felt ashamed. Ashamed that I had somehow convinced myself that this wasn't my problem. And I felt sick.

Now that I was focused on the issue, and I was online, I read about shootings I should have taken more interest in. Just that past Fourth of July weekend, I had somehow glazed right over the news of the shooting death of former Northwestern basketball coach Ricky Byrdsong. I had gone to graduate school at Northwestern. I wasn't much of a basketball fan, true, but now that I thought about it, the one and only time I did go to a collegiate basketball game was on March 30, 1981—the day President Reagan and his press secretary, James Brady, were shot. I certainly remembered that shooting, but other than making a mental note not to stand too close in public to my then-boss, Senator Long, I didn't think much about the facts of the shooting, except that I knew that it had to do with some nut trying to impress the actress Jodie Foster.

Now, because of the JCC shooting, for the first time I was really curious to know just how these nuts manage to get their hands on guns at all.

In the case of Ricky Byrdsong, the shooter, Benjamin Nathaniel Smith—a member of a white supremacist hate group who had a history of violence and who was under a court restraining order secured by an ex-girlfriend—bought a gun through a classified newspaper ad and went on a Fourth of July killing spree in Illinois and Indiana. He targeted African-Americans, Jews, and Asians. In the end, he killed two people and wounded another nine. Smith shot people in Chicago, two of its suburbs, three other Illinois cities, and Bloomington, Indiana. In addition to Ricky Byrdsong—who was shot while walking with his children through their Skokie, Illinois, neighborhood—Smith killed Won-Joon Yoon, a South Korean doctoral student at Indiana University.

As I surfed the Web that night, I read about gun laws in this country, and I was shocked at how bad—or nonexistent—they are. There are only six federal laws concerning gun control, and they have such giant loopholes that I could drive my minivan through them. Outside of these six very skeletal laws, there are a mishmash of roughly 300 state and local laws that have been cobbled together in an attempt to put a stop to this very real public health crisis.

The stronger state laws would work better if only they were uniform across the states. For example and hypothetically, a college student down South who needs to finance his spring break vacation can legally purchase guns in bulk in a state with poor laws, load them into his SUV, drive up I-95, and make a killing (literally) by selling them illegally to teenagers in New York City. Apparently, scenarios like this were playing out every day in this country.

One solution, offered by former presidential candidate Bill Bradley, was to make it illegal at the federal level to load up on all of these guns in the first place. But the gun lobby pooh-poohed that by saying that limiting gun purchases to only one a month would put an unnecessary burden on gun collectors. Well, let's weigh that for a moment, shall we? The burden of burying children versus the burden of having to wait a month to add a new gun to the gun rack. Which side did Congress pick? The kids? Or the collectors?

It is hard to say, because bills like this never make it out of committee, much less to the floor for a roll-call vote. As I read on, it sounded like a lot of these congressmen must be getting drunk at gun-lobby parties, because their reasons for not pressing for these laws were so ludicrous. Thankfully, a few members of Congress did sound sober and were trying to change things. But not with a whole lot of success.

In fact, the Byrdsong shooting came on the heels of Congress utterly disrespecting the mothers and fathers of the dead kids at Columbine when it failed to close the lethal "gun-show loophole" when it had the chance—a loophole that enabled a private seller at a gun show to sell a gun legally without even being required to check a photo ID, much less run a background check on people who shouldn't own guns, such as kids like the 18-year-old girl who bought guns this way for the Columbine killers.

To be honest, I didn't even know then what a gun show was. The Violence Policy Center Web site described them as "Tupperware parties" for the criminally insane. That was enough to catch my attention. Certainly not everyone who attends a gun show is a Timothy McVeigh. Even my dentist later told me he likes to go to them. But it sure sounded like any teenager or terrorist who couldn't buy a gun legally from a law-abiding licensed dealer could just go to a gun show and buy one from a private dealer who is not held to the same federal laws requiring background checks as is his licensed counterpart.

Why was I so outraged now? Did I write to my congressman after Columbine and demand action? I did not. What, I wondered, would I do now?

When Buford Furrow surrendered to the FBI a day or two after Granada Hills, I, and the rest of the country, learned that he was a convicted felon with a history of mental illness. He should never have been in possession of a gun, but he walked right through a loophole, bought guns, and shot at children, all the while claiming that his actions were "a wake-up call to kill Jews." Well, he woke me up, although not quite as he had intended. I still wasn't sure—now that I was awake—what I was supposed to do. I have to admit, my first thought was to pull my kids out of the Jewish Community Center. I had enrolled Lili and Phoebe in a local JCC nursery school to help educate them in the faith of their father, half-brothers, and probably most important, my Jewish mother-in-law. But I wouldn't keep them there if it meant making them targets for mentally disturbed anti-Semitic gun nuts, like the Buford Furrows of the world. Maybe they should be raised instead as Southern Baptists, which is what my mother was, or as Catholics, like my father and me, especially since I had never heard of anyone shooting up a Baptist or Catholic Church—at least not then.

After August 10, 1999, I felt I needed to make some hard decisions in my life. But I wasn't sure at the time what those decisions would be, except that I would damn well stop reading the newspapers only for the gossip pages and start taking notice of the stories about gun violence. And there were plenty. The first to catch my attention was about the drive-by shooting death of an 11-year-old choirboy from Brooklyn. His name was Kelvin, and based on his picture, he was adorable. Apparently, he was also a wonderful kid who was beloved by many. The article quoted a police lieutenant named Eric Adams, who was a member of an organization called 100 Blacks in Law Enforcement. Lt. Adams was clearly shaken up by Kelvin's death, as he was by the many unnecessary gun deaths he had seen in his Brooklyn neighborhood. He used his chance to speak up in print to beg Americans to end their love affair with guns. Too many kids were getting killed, he said.

I decided on the spot that I wanted to meet Eric Adams, and so I called his office. Maybe he would be able to tell me, a formerly apathetic American citizen, what I could do to help. It would be days before Lt. Adams returned my call. In the interim, I became a voracious Web surfer, hungry to learn as much about the policy side of the gun issue as possible. I read about initiatives to childproof guns that were derailed by the gun lobby, probably for the same reasons that the automotive lobby tried to block the mandatory installation of airbags and seat belts. Taking safety measures at the manufacturing level costs money and may take pennies from profits, was the thinking of many lobbyists. Was saving lives worth so little, I wondered?

I logged on so much to the Web site of Handgun Control Inc. (HCI) that if they rewarded me with frequent flier miles, I could have flown around the world at least a dozen times. Their Web site and those of the other national gun-control groups, like the Violence Policy Center, were extremely informative. But none showed me how to get directly involved in the issue beyond donating money or writing a letter to my congressman. I resolved to do both, but it just didn't seem like enough.

I called directory assistance in Washington, D.C., and asked for the phone numbers of the gun-control organizations. I specifically wanted to reach HCI because I knew that Sarah Brady, the wife of James Brady, President Reagan's wounded press secretary, was their chairwoman. She was the most well-known gun-control advocate in the country at that time. She was also a mom.

But the number for Handgun Control Inc. wasn't listed. I assumed (correctly) that this was probably a measure taken to prevent gun nuts from harassing the staff. I tried to contact a few other of the national gun control groups by phone but came up against the same roadblock. How hard would I have to work, I thought, to find an organization I could give my time to?

Then I heard about a group in my home state of New Jersey that focused on gun control. It was called Ceasefire, and it was attempting, but without much success, to get a law passed in New Jersey mandating state-of-the-art technology to childproof all new handguns sold in the state. It sounded like a good organization to me. Through a crazy, circuitous, time-consuming amount of calls, I finally tracked down their number. I called and left a message. Nobody called me back. So I left several more messages, and still, no one called me back.

Now I was really starting to get annoyed. I was a person who returned calls, and I was used to getting my phone calls returned. Three days after the Granada Hills shooting, I had left half a dozen messages, but no one had returned my call. Maybe I was going to have to leave my beach retreat, head back to the mainland, get in my minivan, drive to Washington, and just show up on Handgun Control Inc.'s doorstep. In fact, I did start mulling over the idea of getting a caravan of minivans and driving to Washington, D.C., to protest, like the farmers who rode into Washington on their tractors in the 1980s. But I let the thought slip away.

The weekend came and went. By Monday morning—the only day I worked—I had put the idea of volunteering on a back burner while I got myself ready to get into the city. I got up early that morning so that I could catch the 7:35 A.M. ferry from Fire Island to Bayshore, Long Island. But, just my bad luck, I had spent so much time the last few days trying to be an overnight expert in public-health policy, I forgot to make my reservation for a seat on David's Taxi, a shuttle service to the city from Bayshore. All the van seats were filled, so I was forced to take the Long Island Railroad, cramped with beach commuters like me from up and down all of Long Island.

The seat right next to me was the only one free, and a man who looked curiously like Buford Furrow plopped himself into it. His arms were emblazoned with swastika tattoos and, most worrisome, he carried an army duffel bag that bulged with something that was eerily shaped like a rifle. Oh my God, I thought. Was he a disciple of Furrow's, heeding the "wake-up call to kill Jews?"

A woman with two small children seated across from me was apparently thinking the same thing. She caught my eye and gave me a long look that said, "Lady, I've only got one body to throw over these two kids if this guy starts shooting. What are you going to do to help me out here?" Would I have the courage to throw myself over someone else's children? I hoped so. But I didn't want to find out or think too much about it. I quickly picked up my *New York Post* and tried to distract myself with something a tad lighter, so I began to read an article about how to create a Web site and register a domain name.

————

Someone once said that inspiration is really nothing more than all of life's experiences colliding at the same moment. And for me, this collision took place on the LIRR. Most people who have been inspired to take action rarely feel the need to explain how they got from point A to point B, but because so much disinformation has been spread about the creation of the Million Mom March, I feel the need to set the record straight. What I want to tell you is this: It wasn't because I had worked on Capitol Hill for a few years, or that I had worked in television or for *CBS News*, or because I was a publicist that I wanted to take action, though all of this experience would come in handy once the Million Mom March was a reality (especially being a publicist). The experience that had given me the organizational skills—and the courage—to decide to take a stand and get involved in gun control was simply this: my time as a mother.

So much gun violence surrounds us, and unless we're caught in the crossfire, most of us don't pay much attention to it. But if you stop to think about it, you'd be surprised to see where guns may have, however remotely, touched your own life. Only after I decided to get involved in gun control did it occur to me that a random pattern of gun violence runs through my own life. There was my father, terrified but resilient, staring down the barrel of a gun behind the counter of his pharmacy; there was Senator Russell Long, for whom I'd worked on Capitol Hill, who had lost his father to an assassin's bullet. (Even Dan Rather, my longtime boss at CBS, had had a bizarre run-in with a gun nut—but more about that later.)

Despite all of these bullets whizzing by, it wasn't until a man named Buford Furrow urged other gun nuts like himself to target children just like mine that I decided that a mother's got to do what a mother's got to do.

Sitting on the train that day, with a wary mother and her two kids sitting across from me and a threatening-looking man toting a bag that carried something in it that looked suspiciously like an assault rifle, I took out a pen and an old manila envelope—the only paper in my bag— and started to write. And what I wrote was a simple one-page plan on how I might get myself and other moms to stand up, speak up, and make gun control a reality. Those few words on that torn manila envelope were the rough draft for what became known as the Million Mom March. How did I come up with this name? Just that day, in the *New York Post*, there was an article about a controversy on a permit dispute for the Million Youth March. Being a good publicist, I realized that this "Million March" brand had built-in news value. So I decided to borrow the name.

I then pulled my calendar out of my bag, shuffled through the pages, and picked a date: May 14, 2000. It was Mother's Day. That had a nice ring to it. I counted back from that date to today's date, and it was almost exactly 9 months. I couldn't believe it. It was the gestation period known and universally understood by all mothers! There is a god, I remember thinking, and she's not only a publicist, but she's also a mom!

The train pulled into Penn Station. The scary, tattooed man stood up to disembark and unzipped his bag. The other mom and I held our breath. Out came an umbrella, its spokes all broken and tangled. "Guess I won't be needing this anytime soon," he said to no one in particular. He then stuffed it into a trash bin on the platform. Clearly this man was not the neo-Nazi maniac with an assault weapon I had imagined him to be. But what about next time? And, more important, why do we have to live in fear of a next time?

By the time I reached my midtown office that morning, I was no longer just a mother and part-time publicist. I was a woman on a mission. When I had a break in my work, I logged on to www.register.com, the company mentioned in the article I had read on the train, and I— a card-carrying technophobe—easily registered the new Web site: www.millionmommarch.com.

I then called the Capitol Hill Police in Washington, D.C. (I knew the capitol switchboard number by heart from my stint with the senators back in the 1980s.) Officer Raymond, who answered, was very polite. He didn't even snicker when I asked for an application to march on Washington next Mother's Day, and he promptly faxed me a permit application. I filled out the details with as much information as I had, which, at this point, was very little. All I recall writing was that I was going to lead a rally of mothers in support of sensible gun laws. There was a line on the application for the estimated attendance for the event. Hmmm. I didn't know. Maybe 10,000, I wrote.

I faxed it back and waited 15 minutes. Then, impatiently, I called back.

"So, did you get it?" I said, my foot tapping on the floor.

"Yes, I got it," Officer Raymond replied, matter-of-factly.

"And?" I asked.

"And, we're passing this baby around like one hot potato." He sounded like he meant this.

"Why?" I asked.

"Because," he said, "we all know that our own mothers will be there."

At first I didn't understand what he meant. But I learned, soon after that conversation, that two Capitol Hill police officers had been shot and killed while on duty the year before. I realized that Officer Raymond was probably remembering this senseless crime and his fallen colleagues when he made that comment. Of course their mothers would be there. Maybe 10,000 wasn't such a pie-in-the-sky figure after all.

Next I called my husband, Jeff, at his office, to give him a heads-up. I tried to sound as nonchalant as I could. "Honey," I said. "I'm planning to organize a march on Washington." And then, almost as an afterthought, I asked him, "Is that okay with you?" I thought Jeff would laugh, but I guess he knew me better than I knew myself. He didn't seem to doubt for a moment that I was serious. But he was concerned. "Going against the gun lobby? That sounds kind of dangerous." And, with that, he fled to Peru. Okay. He didn't actually flee to Peru; he went there on a business trip. But in the 6 days he was gone, the Million Mom March completely overtook me, the kids, the house, the neighborhood—it was like the blob, only pink (our official color), and it was oozing over everything.

The next call I made was to Jeff's sister, my sister-in-law, Susan Thomases, one of the smartest people I know. And, yes, she is the Susan

Thomases who is a friend of Hillary Clinton's. Susan gave me the best advice I would ever get: Find a good lawyer and get a good accountant. She also suggested that I track down an event planner named Isabelle Tapia and hire her. Little did I know that this name would haunt me for some time to come. Other than this sage advice, I never asked Susan for anything—including access to Hillary (or Bill) Clinton—nor did she offer it.

I had made the mistake of asking Susan a few weeks back to help me get the first lady booked on the *Late Show with David Letterman.* Instead of just asking her for me, Susan roped me into going to a $1,000-a-person fundraiser, where I stood in line for an hour to get the chance to invite her myself. But when I asked the first lady if she'd agree to do the show, she looked at me as if I had just asked her to agree to a root canal. That reaction probably had something to do with the funny, merciless beating Dave was giving her husband on the show about the Monica Lewinsky scandal. While I didn't write the jokes, I did have my hand in publicizing one of his funniest Top Ten Lists, called Presidential Jobs That Sound Dirty. The list ranged from Polishing the Presidential Podium to Unwrapping the President's Big Mac. The first lady, however, was clearly not amused.

Given this experience, I knew that if I wanted the first lady involved in the Million Mom March, the request should probably come from someone other than me.

I left my office at the *Late Show* that night and went back out to Fire Island where the kids were still on summer vacation. I wasn't sure what my next step should be, so I did what all women do when they know they need to get something done, but they're not sure where to start: I called my five closest friends. And I was very blessed because my five closest friends also happened to be professionals in promotions, public relations, and marketing.

If there is such a thing as a recipe for launching a modern revolution, I would say it would require the following ingredients: promotional items, slogans, corporate sponsors, and a well-written press release. That's what, as a public relations professional, I knew I needed to get started. As a mother, I knew how much more quickly things get done when you enlist the aid of other mothers. Amy Putman—mother of three—created the logo and slogans for the T-shirts while holding down a full-time job to pay for the health insurance her son Jacob, who was born with only one lung, needed. Amy was the model of tirelessness, working on our advertising campaign in the middle of the night when her kids and husband (an on-call doctor) were asleep. Julie Levi—mother of two—created the T-shirts. Debbie Taffet—mother of two—found our first corporate sponsors, who paid for the T-Shirts, and Debbie's friend, Alison Hendrie—mother of four—put the final touches on the press release, mission statement, and all of our clever mom gimmicks that would make mothers and the media take notice of us. And there was Robin Sheer, who convinced her husband, a clothing store owner, to buy $5,000 worth of our T-shirts to sell and give away. (The Sheers also provided the venue for our first—and most important—press conference.)

In less than 3 weeks, these remarkable women, who were all working and raising families, built what became the foundation of the Million Mom March.

It was happening. It was becoming real. Now we needed a date to launch this thing. The only possible choice, in my mind, was Labor Day. Not only was saving our children from gunfire a labor of love, but Labor Day is a traditionally slow news day, when producers can only hope for something horrific to happen like a 30-car pileup on the Long Island Expressway. This may sound cold, but that's how the news business works. They also like kickers, those fun, upbeat stories to end the broadcasts so that everyone leaves with a warm, fuzzy feeling about the anchors before switching to *Jeopardy*. I figured we'd probably be the kicker if it were a slow news day. And possibly part of the lead if there were a major shooting over the holiday weekend. I know news. What I didn't know was how to get people to commit to showing up at a news conference. I figured I needed at least 10 moms. Might be tough, because Labor Day was a day when parents are usually returning from vacation and getting the kids ready for the first day of school.

For the next few days, I was a mother on a mission to find 10 other mothers who would be willing to show up on Labor Day. I would worry about finding the other 999,990 later.

I also began pestering ivillage.com, the first Web site founded by and for women, to help me with our Web site, and they generously put us in touch with Abstract Edge, a startup of brilliant twenty-something Web designers who worked out of a basement in Roslyn, New York. The MMM would be their second client; their first was a nonprofit organization for anorexia nervosa sufferers. Somehow, while it wasn't an exact fit, at least they knew how to work with women.

The next item on my agenda was finding a spokesperson, a spokesmom, for the group. I was half-tempted to call Susan, my sister-in-law, and see if she couldn't run this by her friend Hillary, as it would certainly get us publicity if we had the first lady on board. But I had a gut feeling that I should try to find someone who wasn't so obviously for the cause. I even thought I should look for someone who was pretty conservative politically.

But did I know anyone like that? Or, more important, did I know anyone conservative that I liked? I looked through my Christmas card list, and the first Republican who popped up that I was fond of was Millie Limbaugh, mother of Rush. I once gave her a tour of the *CBS News* studio. I dialed her up at her Missouri home, hoping she would remember me.

Millie answered right away and couldn't have been warmer. As I started to explain what I was up to, Millie jumped in and told me she was a member of the NRA. Hmmm. Even better, I thought. A card-carrying member of the NRA and the mother of the most conservative talk-show host in America—no, make that the world—as an endorser of the Million Mom March. Would she, could she help us? In a chipper voice, as if she were going to tell me she was leaving for Florida in a few weeks, she gave me her sad news: She was dying of cancer. She sounded apologetic, as if this cancer was a problem only because it inconvenienced others. Then she moved on to happier news about her grandchildren and before hanging up, she said sincerely, "I wish you gals luck."

Heartbroken for Millie but undeterred, I then tried Donna Hanover Giuliani, the wife of New York City Mayor Rudolph Giuliani. But her aide informed me that she was too consumed with pressing family matters to participate. This was quite the understatement, I would later learn.

So I went back to my Rolodex. I stopped at Sherrie Rollins Westin, a communications director in the first Bush White House, who was now a vice president at the Children's Television Workshop. Sherrie was a mother. She was also beautiful and articulate and politically well-connected. Although she seemed to be sympathetic to our cause, Sherrie declined, hinting that her involvement could put funding for CTW in jeopardy. From what I later learned, the gun lobby once even went after funding for the Centers for Disease Control and Prevention in Atlanta because they dared try to gather statistics on gun deaths in America to prove that it was indeed a public-health crisis. (The gun lobby has also tried to cut funding for the Bureau of Alcohol, Tobacco, and Firearms because of its work in tracking down bad gun dealers.) Now here was Sherrie trying to gently tell me that if she combined her roles as vice president of CTW with spokesmom for the Million Mom March, Big Bird might be a dead duck.

Getting someone famous or connected or Republican was now clearly a long shot due to our time crunch and, frankly, the sheer newness of such a potentially controversial project. So I turned to Julie, our T-shirt mom. Julie is bubbly and bouncy and very enthusiastic, and she graciously agreed to be our representative in the first round of media interviews prior to our Labor Day news conference.

It's funny, but I didn't realize then that failing to find a high-profile spokesmom and using "regular" moms who cared passionately about the cause to speak on our behalf turned out to be the best thing to happen to the MMM. I don't know why I didn't realize it at the time, but I should have, particularly since I was working for David Letterman then, and Dave's credo was that only real people matter. Only real people are Nielsen families; therefore, only real people can sit in Dave's audience. I know—I once had to tell the sportscaster Greg Gumbel that he could not have tickets. Don't be fooled by the occasional celebrity you see sitting in Dave's audience in the Ed Sullivan Theatre. If Paul Newman is in the audience, you can be sure it's just for a joke, and the minute the camera is off him, he gets bounced from the seat for a real person. Of course the Million Mom March needed a real person to be our "face."

In the meantime, I finally tracked down the elusive but very real Bob Walker, then president of Handgun Control Inc. Because I wanted to be sure of our facts, I faxed Walker a copy of our press release, certain he'd now get back to me. He did, and when he spoke to me, he was very nice. But I could almost hear the sound of his eyes rolling as I told him I was serious about this march. It was David Bernstein, who was in the press department at Handgun Control Inc., who would cheer us on. I guess I shouldn't have been surprised by this, because David is a publicist, and he saw us as a major news story waiting to happen.

Our Web designers at Abstract Edge, Eric, Scott, and Marcel, also embraced the Million Mom March mission: Get it done, and get it done fast. "Perfection is the enemy of good" would be our motto for the Web site that would be a work in progress for the next 9 months. I wanted it to look fifties, as if we were the Harriets to the Ozzies of those up-standing but boring gun-control groups. "Would you like flowers on it?" Eric would ask. Yes. Flowers. The Abstract Edge boys created a flower with petals that, when clicked on, would lead to something else—from gun-policy facts to where to buy our T-shirts. And we had them create a "Time-Out Chair" in honor of Alison's cute but naughty 2-year-old daughter, Tess. Our Time-Out Chair would be used for public figures who behaved badly (i.e., those who didn't take a stand for gun control), and this became the most popular feature on the Web site. The only problem with the Time-Out Chair was who to put in it first: so many people to choose from, so little space.

As moms, we knew we had to find a way to reward good behavior too, but with what? We decided on a wholesome, all-American apple pie. I couldn't bake one if my life depended on it, but my stepchildren's mother could. Now deceased, Liz fed the homeless, and in her spare time, I was told, she baked the best apple pie in the world. Before, I had been a little jealous of this, but now we honored Liz by creating the Million Mom March Apple Pie Award. And I'm sorry that Liz wasn't around to see how, over the next months, those pies of ours were in such hot demand!

Next, I put my own media skills to work. I called *CBS This Morning* first to see if I could book Julie for an interview. Why CBS first? Because this is the morning show everybody calls last. Historically, it attracts fewer viewers than the other two big network morning shows, and I thought we'd have our best shot there. My hunch was right, and a pro-ducer called me back. At first, she seemed a little skeptical about me and my motives. But when she heard my 3-year-old in the background screaming impatiently from the bathroom, "Mommy, come wipe my tush NOW!" she—obviously a mother herself—assured me that she would hold, and when I returned, she enthusiastically took down Julie's number for the preinterview.

Life went back to normal briefly, and that Saturday, September 4,

By **now,** the Jim and Sarah Brady story is a familiar one, at least for those of us over 40.

Jim was the press secretary to Ronald Reagan at the time of the assassination attempt against the president in March of 1981. A bullet meant for his boss tore through Jim's head, causing severe injury and permanent brain damage. The shooting sentenced Jim to life in a wheelchair. Sarah became his full-time caregiver. It was a devastating event for the entire nation, and Jim was correctly hailed as a national hero.

Though Jim's injuries inspired Sarah to learn more about the issues of gun control, it was a child—her son, Scott, 6 years old at the time—who spurred her to action. While visiting family in Illinois, Scott found a handgun sitting on the front seat of a truck he'd climbed into and pointed it at his mother, thinking it was a toy. It wasn't. Scott had picked up a fully loaded .22—the same caliber used by John Hinckley to shoot his father in the head. It was at that moment, a potentially life or death moment, that Sarah made it her mission to get Congress to enact sensible gun laws and keep lethal weapons out of the hands of children and criminals.

When I began to research a march on Washington, I was warned about the nasty, hateful tactics employed by the gun industry, and the examples most often cited were how they vilified Sarah Brady, calling her an evil fascist and a mental head wound, and wishing her every heinous death imaginable.

Undaunted by such personal attacks—if anything, more resolute than ever—Sarah devoted her significant talents to putting the gun issue on the American agenda and forcing legislators to address it for the first time since 1968, when the first major gun law was passed following the assassinations of Dr. Martin Luther King Jr. and Senator Robert F. Kennedy earlier that year. It wasn't until 1993, after years of struggle and battling the bad guys of the ubiquitous gun lobby, that the next substantial gun-

1999, we celebrated Phoebe's fourth birthday. Although we lived in the New Jersey suburbs, where birthday parties bordered on the obscene, we always celebrated Phoebe's on Fire Island, where simplicity rules. The only thing she wanted for this birthday was to have water-balloon fights and a pie-eating contest. I gave the kids MMM T-shirts as party favors. I couldn't help myself.

By late afternoon, Jeff was off to Kennedy Airport for a business trip safety legislation was passed. The Brady Law, named for James Brady, required feder-ally licensed firearms dealers to run a background check on any potential buyer that must flow through law enforcement databases and which mandated a 5-day waiting period before a gun can be sold. (Sadly, the 5-day waiting period has since been elim-inated.) Since 1994, the Brady Law has stopped more than 600,000 felons from pur-chasing firearms. However, because of that infamous loophole—in which only federally licensed dealers must comply with the law—there are still many gun sales by unli-censed or so-called "private sellers" that do not require any buyer background check at all. The more persistent criminal can find guns by crossing state borders and going to gun shows or by getting a straw purchaser to buy the gun for him or her. And without required registration or ballistics fingerprinting, the straw purchaser can be difficult to identify.

In 1994, when everyone told Sarah that it would be impossible to go back to Congress to demand a ban on assault weapons, Sarah and countless other selfless ac-tivists rolled up their sleeves and went back to work. The bill was signed into law by President Bill Clinton. But it wasn't a perfect law. It would expire after 10 years, in 2004. Without a renewal by Congress and another presidential signature, AK-47s and Uzis will be legalized and back on our streets again in late 2004.

Sarah's words to me when we finally connected were comforting and inspiring. She told me it was people like us moms, the heart of the nation—citizens who vote—who capture the attention of Congress, and if we converge on Washington, they will listen. Sarah Brady's endorsement was a huge boon to our march, but her dedication to the cause and her ongoing efforts turned our march into a movement.

Over the next 9 months, I would awkwardly attempt to walk in Sarah's footsteps. But I would discover that this was one road that was filled with many roadblocks, land mines, and detours. I could never imagine that I'd walk it successfully, and never while also pushing my husband in a wheelchair.

to Germany, and I felt the familiar pang of loneliness that I always felt went he left on a trip. But for the first time in years, I also felt sur-rounded by a family of friends. The founders of the Million Mom March were—to me—the kind of women that myths are made of; these were the women who could lift a 2-ton car off a child pinned under-neath. In my mind, these MMM women were lifting an 18-wheeler off too many children pinned underneath. The massive truck was the gun lobby, and its weight was crushing our children's hope for a future free of gun violence.

———

The Friday night of Labor Day weekend, the phone rang at my beach house. Our babysitter yelled out to me that a Mrs. Brady was on the phone. My kids often pretend to be deaf when I speak to them, but— and this is true for all moms—the minute I get on the phone, they are all over me. This is what is known as the "phone magnet" to moms. This call was of special interest to the girls, because they thought it was Carol Brady, the mother from *The Brady Bunch,* calling. (They knew who she was from watching nonstop repeats on Nick at Night.) Now I stood over them, shushing them while I was also trying to get the phone to my ear.

"Donna," said the voice at the other end of the line. "It's Sarah Brady." Sarah, the chairwoman of Handgun Control Inc. Sarah Brady, wife of Jim Brady, gun violence victim. Sarah Brady, my hero. Sarah had that easily recognizable deep smoker's voice—sexy, but authoritative. As far as I knew at that time, she was the only person in this country fighting for our right to live free of gun trauma. (I would find out over the course of the next few months that there have been many dedicated people who have fought for the same right—they just didn't do it as effectively as Sarah.)

And here she was calling me to tell me how important and instrumental it is for mothers to get involved in the cause. In fact, she told me that she credits the PTA moms for pushing through the Brady Law in 1993. "They weren't paying attention to me," Sarah would say about Congress. "But when the PTA moms showed up on the steps of the U.S. Capitol, they began to listen." It was a "you-go-girlfriend" kind of remark. She asked if there was anything she could do for us, and I told her I was sure there'd be something, but for now, we were okay.

As I hung up, I looked at the girls. Their mouths were wide open, and to this day, they still think I know Florence Henderson.

After my brief conversation with Sarah Brady, I thought about how brave she was, given that she had been, literally, a target for the wrath and ridicule of the gun nuts. Gun nuts—not to be confused with law-abiding, responsible gun owners and hunters—are those borderline psychopathic people with some kind of sick Freudian relationship with their guns. I got a quick education on just how sick these gun nuts were when a mutual friend of Sarah Brady's and of my sister-in-law, Susan, called me one day, warning me what I was in for. He told me about one gun-nut Web site selling T-shirts with Sarah's photo inside a bull's-eye. The caption read: "WE SHOT THE WRONG BRADY!"

After Phoebe's birthday, I left the kids on Fire Island with their god-mother and returned to New Jersey, mostly because there were no Kinko's copy centers on Fire Island. I needed to print up press releases for the next day's news conference. Alone at home in my suburban Short Hills living room, I downloaded the last revised press release and our mission statement, and I took them to the Kinko's in Union, New Jersey, which would become my home away from home. I knew our original mission statement by heart. It had been vetted by our original corps of sponsors, our mother-in-law focus groups, editorial writers (some of whom worked for conservative newspapers), and, of course, many moms. While this statement evolved and changed over the course of the next 9 months, I still love this first draft that Alison Hendrie wrote with such raw passion. I've added some corrections here, to show that, though we might not have had all of our facts straight when we wrote this, our hearts were in the right place.

ORIGINAL MISSION STATEMENT
September 1999

MILLION MOM MARCH MOTHER'S DAY 2000 is dedicated to the mission of educating our children and our country about the life-threatening danger of guns.

Although simplistic and seemingly self-evident, this mission is in direct conflict with a powerful, heavily financed cultural and political juggernaut which justifies misuse of guns with references to freedom, liberty, and the American Dream.

We, the mothers, know that life is the first pursuit promised by our Constitution. *(My mother-in-law, a former teacher, had to point* *out that the Constitution doesn't guarantee life—that would be the Declaration of Independence. Oops.)* Our children's lives far outweigh the right for just anyone, especially juveniles, to carry a semiautomatic assault weapon or a Saturday Night Special.

While we acknowledge that guns may be necessary for hunting, law enforcement, and national security, the proliferation of firearms intended for one purpose only—killing another human being—has become untenable.

We believe that it is only common sense for individuals who want to exercise their Second Amendment rights to be required to submit to a sensible waiting period and background check before they are permitted to purchase a gun from any person or place. *(We had to change this after a supporter wrote to our Web site and very gently suggested that we read the Second Amendment. We did, and oops again: The Second Amendment doesn't actually guarantee individual rights. This would be corrected in the next edition.)*

We believe that every responsible and law-abiding gun owner should welcome legislation requiring safety locks on all handguns sold in the future. *(We had to add the words, "built-in safety locks" because as it was explained to us, a detachable trigger lock is more likely to end up in a junk drawer. We learned that the technology does exist to make built-in locks, and it works in much the same way as the childproof bottle caps created by aspirin manufacturers.)*

We call on all officers of the law to assume a no-nonsense approach in enforcing existing gun laws and to join us in our mutual crusade for stronger legislation.

We call on all child-friendly, nonviolent stores, companies, and corporations to sponsor us in these pursuits by advertising our message that guns—in the wrong hands—are simply unacceptable. In turn, we, the mothers, promise to patronize all child-friendly, nonviolent sponsors who join us in this mission.

We call on the like minded to work with community law-enforcement agencies to offer swaps of meaningful goods and services for guns. We call on the proper authorities to then destroy the repossessed weapons.

Our aim is to recruit—from all walks of life—mothers, grandmothers, stepmothers, godmothers, foster mothers, future mothers, and all others willing to be "honorary mothers" in this crusade. Our goal is to educate and mobilize the mothers of America to this cause. Our commitment as voting citizens is to realize our goals by Mother's Day 2000.

The Labor Day press conference was going to be held on Columbus Avenue in Manhattan, in front of our first sponsor's store, New Frontier, which was owned by Robin Sheer and her husband, Howard. They had dressed the mannequins in the store window in Million Mom March T-shirts. In the world of publicity, backdrops are everything, and so this would be priceless. I checked the *Weather Channel* Sunday evening to find out the next day's forecast: rain. Ah, in the world of signs and omens, I wasn't sure if this was good or bad. But I'd have to worry about that later.

Eric of Abstract Edge called me some time around 10 P.M. that night. It was time to go live with the Web site to check for problems. Was I ready and standing by? Yes. I crossed myself, and with this blessing, www.millionmommarch.com went live. I slowly opened my eyes to see. I gasped. The marching mommy stick figures on the site were RED!!! Not pink. RED!!! We looked like marching communists. Commie Mommies. I called Eric in a panic. "Check your monitor setting, Donna," he said patiently. Oops. I was working on my old computer. A quick adjustment and the marching mommies were pink. Eric was a genius. I plopped into bed that night around midnight, exhausted, exhilarated, frightened, and nervous—a state I would find myself in for the next 9 months, but for a host of different reasons.

CONCEPTION

2

"My sister was shot and killed by her husband in front of two NYC police officers in a Brooklyn subway station. I had to sit down and tell my nephew that mommy was never coming home."

—FELICIA IN FLORIDA

SEPTEMBER 1999

The morning of Labor Day, September 6, 1999, got off to a very bad start.

Not only was it supposed to rain, but I was scheduled to be on *CBS This Morning*, and the car service that was to take me from my Short Hills, New Jersey, home into Manhattan at the crack of dawn was late. I called the dispatcher in a panic, who then, in turn, called the driver. I was told he was waiting outside my house, but here I was, standing outside on my front steps, and all I could see was a pile of garbage strewn around from a bag ripped open by our resident raccoon, who always managed to leave this kind of present for me on the busiest days of my life.

"He says he's right outside your mailbox," the dispatcher insisted.

My mailbox is way down at the end of my winding driveway—it feels like half a mile away on a cold morning—and the driver didn't realize he should come down the road, which ran parallel to a pretty steep ravine. (When my youngest stepson, Greg, first learned to drive, I would worry that he would drive too fast, miss the curve, and plunge right off the 100-foot drop-off.)

I met the driver at the mailbox, and I could tell that he was slightly embarrassed for not venturing up our challenging driveway. He made a comment on how isolated my house was, and then he added, "Hope you own a gun."

I admit that I often thought of buying a gun when I first moved to this house. Coming most recently from Manhattan, I shared Woody Allen's fear of the country, believing that the woods were full of lunatics with chainsaws and drifters with big hunting knives. At least in the city, I thought, someone would hear me scream as an intruder banged his way into my apartment via the fire escape. To get a gun legally, I would have to be willing to get a license and register the thing (New Jersey is one of the few states to require this). This would not be a problem. I was even willing to go for a safety-training course, although this isn't even mandatory in most states.

But as a practical matter, I had children. I instinctively knew that having a gun in the house was a bad idea. While arming myself with statistics for the morning's media blitz, I stumbled across a study publicized in the 1998 *Journal of Trauma* that concluded that it was statistically far more likely that a gun I owned would be used against me, rather than helping me stop a would-be Ted Bundy. And a gun in a home was even more likely to be used in a domestic spat, a suicide, or in an accidental shooting.

I'm sure other people would feel comfortable about locking up or hiding a gun in their home. But I was operating under the "Lili Lipstick" principle: It didn't matter where I put my lipstick, that kid would find it and apply it all over herself, the furniture, and her sister.

People who bought guns for self-defense were even prone to using them unwisely outside of their homes, I would learn over the next months. I even read about a case of road rage in Alabama that involved two women drivers. It ended with one of them being shot and the other being tried for murder. In court, the shooter sobbed to a jury that "She spit on me, and I killed her." Her victim was unarmed. Although the shooter expressed remorse at her trial, it didn't make the other woman any less dead.

——————

Since it was a holiday, we made great time through the Lincoln Tunnel, and I probably could have slept in for another 30 minutes. With the queasiness I was beginning to feel, I was tempted to ask the driver to turn around so that I could go back to bed and forget I ever started this thing. I was scared. I wasn't so much afraid of my message—which would be a very public declaration to the NRA and all of the gun lobbyists in the country that they were about to be taken on by a group of mothers—as I was nervous about being on live television. I never liked live TV. I had worked briefly at a small TV station in Lafayette, Louisiana, right out of college, where most of my assignments, like covering the Breaux Bridge Crawfish, were taped. But it was my first live on-air experience—coincidentally on a Labor Day—when I was forced to cohost the local cut-ins to the Jerry Lewis Telethon—that made me dread today's show. It was a nerve-racking experience for me, and a bit humiliating, especially when one caller offered to donate money to the cause if I took some speech lessons to rid myself of my harsh New Orleans accent.

It had been many years since I had lived in New Orleans, but now I felt certain that my native accent would come pouring out of me once the cameras were rolling and I opened my mouth.

God, I hoped I wouldn't freeze up on air and ruin this precious opportunity, this moment of airtime, which, to use a mommy metaphor, was a bit like the brief time of ovulation: I knew I had to catch the moment while I could. But instead of a cold glass of chardonnay and warm scented candles to help get me in the mood, I had to rely on a hot cup of Starbucks and the cold studio of *CBS This Morning.*

Though I was nervous, my motivation remained clear—1999 was a bloody year for our children, and not just because of highly publicized cases like Columbine and Granada Hills. At the time we were launching the Million Mom March, 12 children were dying because of guns every day in this country.

One NRA official even tried to claim that the Centers for Disease Control and Prevention, whose research turned up this statistic, were misleading the public, because, of the 12 children killed each day, how many of them were virtually adults, being 15, 16, or 17 years old? Was this guy joking? Does he think the mothers of these kids don't grieve for them just because they might have been in high school?

I got to the CBS studios sometime before 7 A.M. to meet Julie Levi, the T-shirt mom, who would be appearing on the show with me. At exactly 6:57 A.M., I glanced at the clock, and like every Labor Day since 1995, I savored the precise moment my daughter Phoebe was born.

Like the CBS greenroom where I now sat, the operating room at St. Barnabas' Hospital in Livingston, New Jersey, was cold. I was in labor most of the night and almost fully dilated, but the baby went into distress, and I was rushed into the OR for an emergency C-section to save Phoebe from strangling to death from her own umbilical cord. Phoebe, a fighter, survived her difficult birth.

Now, 4 years later, here I was, waiting in a television studio to send out the message that we do everything to give our children life, and then somebody like a Buford Furrow with far too easy access to a gun tries to take it all away, and that this must stop. Phoebe, my Labor Day baby—and every American child—deserved better than this.

It felt a little weird to do the first interview at CBS, my former workplace. I knew many of the people who were there that morning, and as I prepared with a woman named Harriet Kaufman (whom I didn't know), who would be interviewing us on air, I got a hearty high five from Dave Dorsett, a cameraman for the *Late Show* who was filling in that morning for a vacationing colleague. I was happy to see him. My first day at the *Late Show* a few years back, he helped me make the awkward transition from news to comedy—two completely different beasts. At *CBS News*, he said, if a plane goes down, we work late, order in, and have a few laughs. In network comedy, if a joke falls flat, we work late, order in, and sit around at the postmortem, woefully wondering, "Why did this happen? How could this happen?"

I hadn't worked for *CBS News* in 7 years, but when I did, it was rarely for *CBS This Morning*. Only once could I remember being called in during a PR crisis for the morning show when Andy Rooney of *60 Minutes* fame was assigned to cover the 1988 Democratic Convention in Atlanta for the program. Andy—never one to mince words—made an unfortunate comment on air (now better left forgotten) that became the focus of a media frenzy. Everyone on the morning show went berserk—

everybody but Andy who, completely unrepentant, brushed off the incident with the comment that "controversy can be good for a struggling broadcast." It's funny what sticks with you over time, but that piece of wisdom has stayed with me for years. And I hoped this credo would hold true today, as we went live on *CBS This Morning* to announce to the rest of the country that we moms were mad as hell, and we weren't going to take it anymore!

I glanced at the monitors and admired how adorable Julie looked in her Million Mom March T-shirt that featured Amy Putnam's logo of a gun with flowers sprouting out of the barrel. It was very sixties, very pro-peace. My daughter Lili, then 5, was the one who added the scribble through the gun, which was her way of showing that kids and guns don't mix—a brilliant, if I may say so, stroke of genius that solved the dilemma of how to convey that we were about saving kids' lives and not for banning guns from the hands of responsible, law-abiding Americans. This was a hugely important distinction to make, and it is one that bears repeating. We Million Mom Marchers were not radically opposed to the responsible, well-regulated sale and ownership of handguns. We were (and are), however, utterly committed to making sure that the laws surrounding gun sales and ownership are strong enough to protect our kids.

I checked myself out in the monitor and thought, "Holy moly!" Take a few extra baby pounds (okay, so the baby was now 4) and add those so-called 10 TV pounds, and I looked like a "before" picture in a Jenny Craig ad. When Julie designed this T-shirt, I was certain we'd have a celebrity spokesmom in place, and she would be sitting here instead of me. If I had imagined for 1 minute I'd actually have to wear this baggy white T-shirt myself, I would have insisted Julie design something slightly more flattering, preferably in black and with a control top.

Even with Julie sitting there next to me, my heart was pounding. I felt sick at the idea that I was about to go on live television to announce a march for which I had no funding, no staff, and no clue about how to organize. What I had so far was a one-page press release, a campy Web site, and the absolute confidence that we mothers could pull this off. At least that was the impression I was hoping to convey to a television audience of more than a million.

The cameramen moved in to get a close-up of the back of one of our T-shirts, which bore our slogan: "Looking for a Few Good Moms." Amy,

Logo Mom, almost changed the slogan at the last minute to "Because I Said So . . . ," which is clever but not as effective. She was concerned that the U.S. Marines might sue us. That perked me up. Sue us? A bunch of moms? I only hoped we'd get that lucky, I told her. As a publicist, I could see the value of a cease and desist letter from the Marines. We'd hold a news conference, apologize profusely, and then unveil our new slogan. The publicity would be priceless. So we stuck with our plan.

The interview went better than I expected. I surprised myself with how much I knew about the federal gun laws in this country—all six of them—and suddenly I was no longer afraid of live television. I was on a roll. Julie was on a roll, too.

Julie: We want moms to get involved. We want moms on the grassroots level to go out there and form community efforts to get involved. Visit our Web site, buy our T-shirt, support our cause. All the proceeds will go to making the Million Mom March happen on Mother's Day 2000.

Harriet Kaufman: You are saying don't lobby your congressman?

Julie: Lobby your congressman's mother, his wife, his sister, his mother-in-law—maybe more will happen that way.

We were able to make every point and pitch our Web site. The interview was a home run.

When we were done at *CBS This Morning*, Julie and I raced over to MSNBC for another live interview that came our way at the last minute. The producer there insisted that I do the interview solo, so Julie acted as my Lamaze coach, reminding me to breathe . . . breathe, and give out the Web address. I said something like, "If we can make babies in 9 months, surely Congress can pass laws to protect those babies in the same amount of time." Yeah. You would think.

When we wrapped that up, off we went to Columbus Avenue for our official press conference. We got to the store, New Frontier, where we were holding the event. No one was outside. Not a soul. It had stopped raining, so where were the moms? I found them inside the store shopping for leather pants. Talk about multitasking! One of the moms made the executive decision to move the news conference inside, and it was the right call. It looked packed, with 25 moms dressed in T-shirts who gave up their last day of summer to help us launch our march. Among the supporters were our five founding moms, including Amy the Logo Mom, Debbie the Corporate Sponsor Mom, and Alison, Writer Mom— whom I met face-to-face for the first time, despite being in touch with her constantly via e-mail for the past 3 weeks.

We were not all moms, of course—we wanted men to participate too, and I had finally connected with Lt. Eric Adams from 100 Blacks in Law Enforcement, who was thrilled that moms from suburbia were ready to take this on. He became our first "honorary mom" and joined us at our press conference. Lt. Adams brought a sense of realism to our cause, because kids in his community were dying every day. Eric also brought with him Sgt. LaPrena Kingwood, a mom and police officer from Long Island who told me her heart skips a beat every time she pulls someone over and he reaches inside his pocket. At the time, I had no idea how many law-enforcement officers die each year from a bullet (41 in 1999 alone). I couldn't imagine having her job and being a mother too.

It never occurred to me to ask anybody I knew if they had ever had a brush with gun violence. I assumed, incorrectly, that most people don't have a tale to tell. But there were devastating tales even among our own moms: Elise Richman, who was with us on Labor Day, had lost her father when he was shot at a backyard barbecue by the jealous husband of the hostess. The bullet was intended for the shooter's wife—not Elise's dad, who was an innocent bystander. To make it all the more tragic, this murder was witnessed by Elise's teenage sister. Elise was initially sheepish when she approached me to attend the news conference, because she had been a close friend of my husband's first wife, and she had learned about the march through her husband, Michael, who worked for my husband, Jeff. Maybe she thought that connection might be a little too close for comfort. Would it be alright with me if she came? Absolutely! Now I only had to recruit 999,975 more moms.

We had our moms gathered for our press conference. Would the media come? One by one, the New York television news crews, including CNN, showed up. Now there was no turning back.

Before we could high-five each other, a mom wandered into the store and hit us with a cold splash of reality as to why our mission was so important. Nancy, a tourist from Raleigh, North Carolina, was strolling by and saw our bright pink posters in the window of New Frontier. She rushed in and told us a horrible story about her son David who had been shot in the face by a friend while helping him move. The friend picked up the gun to show David it was not loaded. But it was, and the gun went off accidentally. David survived, Nancy told us with the heart-wrenching details only a mother could, but his face was almost destroyed.

Being new to this issue, I didn't think to ask her about the gun, but along my journey, I would hear similar stories from so many mothers that it became second nature to ask key questions like: "Did this gun have a chamber load indicator?" Apparently, some guns still hold a round of ammunition even after the clip is removed. But since gun manufacturer is one of the least-regulated industries in this country, correcting this kind of safety defect is nearly impossible. As hard as it is to believe, toy guns are better regulated than the lethal real thing. Nancy left before I could get her full name, phone number, or e-mail address. I wanted to kick myself, and from that moment on, I was determined to keep an accurate record of everybody who contacted the Million Mom March, and this became the cornerstone of our philosophy: Everybody is important, and everybody can do something.

Like those early days when you've conceived and you feel the wisps of new life fluttering in your belly, well before a pregnancy test can provide confirmation, I returned home that night certain that the Million Mom March had taken. But just to make sure, I stayed glued to the local news. Then the phone started to ring. Somebody just saw us on NY 1! Somebody just saw us on Fox TV . . . in Atlanta!

I flipped the channels and stopped on *WNBC-TV News* in time to catch anchorwoman Michele Marsh reading from the teleprompter.

> *First there was the Million Man March. Then the Million Youth March. Now there's another Million Member March . . . this time, mothers!*

As Michele uttered these words, it was like hearing from the gynecologist that the rabbit died. This thing, this Million Mom March, was now out there in the universe. I was exhausted but proud that I was finally using my public relations skills for something more than getting celebrity names in—or out of—the newspapers.

I began returning e-mails and phone calls to interested moms, and I was determined to make the Million Mom March a model of open communication like the Butterball Turkey hotline: You call us, we'll call you right back!

One of the first moms to contact me was a woman in Arkansas, Regina Kaut, the aunt of Brittany Varner, who was shot and killed on March 24, 1998, at the age of 11. Brittany died with three other young girls and a teacher in Jonesboro, Arkansas, at the hands of two shooters who were 11 and 13 years old. Before the shooting stopped, 10 other children were injured.

I hadn't paid much attention to the Jonesboro shooting. I was probably too wrapped up at the time in the Monica Lewinsky/Linda Tripp drama. Regina filled me in: According to police reports, the two boys accused of the killings stole the guns they used from the home of one of their grandfathers. The families of some of the victims believed that their children would still be alive if built-in trigger locks were on those guns. This simple safety precaution, which would be easy for gun manufacturers to implement, still hasn't happened. I know. It is insane. Built-in trigger locks would allow gun owners to disable their weapons so that no one else could fire them. This simple measure could, in and of itself, have a huge impact on the number of gun deaths in this country each year.

Brittany's family reached out to the likes of Congressman Asa Hutchinson (R-Arkansas) for help in making sure that this kind of tragedy wouldn't happen to anyone else. But like me, Congressman Hutchinson was apparently more concerned with Ken Starr's report on Monica Lewinsky's thong underwear and had no sympathy or patience for Brittany's family. He had no interest in making the gun industry childproof its guns. Perhaps he believed that criminals don't want childproofing, and it is the criminal market that keeps the gun industry going.

Regina Kaut was mad as hell, and she wouldn't take it anymore. She wanted in, and she signed up to act as the Arkansas state coordinator for the Million Mom March.

I next heard from Lisa Laursen-Thirkill. Lisa was mad as hell, too. As the legislative director for the Oregon State PTA, Lisa said gun-violence prevention was on the top of her state PTA's agenda. "Obviously," she told me, "because of Kip Kinkel." I resisted asking "Kip who?" but vaguely remembered something about a shooting in Oregon. Was it this year? Or last? Lisa went on with the details: On May 21, 1998, Kip

Kinkel, a 15-year-old freshman at Thurston High School, arrived at school armed with a .22-caliber rifle, a .22-caliber handgun, and a Glock semiautomatic handgun. He shot and injured 22 kids and killed two students, including 17-year-old Mikael Nicklauson, who had just enlisted a few days before to serve in the Oregon National Guard. (Again, as I later learned, the gun nuts would dispute deaths like Mikael's, claiming a 17-year-old should be counted as an adult.) Kinkel's father bought him one of the guns. (I'm not sure if Kinkel used that gun to kill his father, but he also shot both of his parents to death.)

I did a little research online and learned that a similar shooting almost took place the same day in St. Charles, Missouri, but it was thwarted by police. A few days before that, an honor student in Fayetteville, Tennessee, opened fire in the parking lot of his high school and killed a classmate. In April of the same year, a 14-year-old shot to death a science teacher at a school dance in Edinboro, Pennsylvania.

In December of 1997, another 14-year-old boy killed three students and wounded five others at a morning prayer circle at a West Paducah, Kentucky, school. Two months before that, in Pearl, Mississippi, a teenager murdered his mother and then killed two students and wounded six others at school.

It would be these last two shootings that made Rene Thompson of Kentucky mad as hell and decide she didn't want to take it anymore, either. Rene e-mailed me saying she was sick of the senseless violence, and she wanted to do something so that her 2-year-old son, David, would not have to grow up in a world where kids have such easy access to guns.

Trouble was, Rene didn't get out much—she was agoraphobic. What could she do from the confines of her home? I suggested she organize the state of Kentucky. "I couldn't possibly do that," she wrote back. At least that's what she believed then. So she decided she would write to her congressman about the gun-show loophole.

————

While I got lots of e-mail from concerned mothers—and more than a few dads—I also got a lot of mail from gun nuts. Gun nuts should not be confused with the law-abiding citizen who acts responsibly with his or her gun and doesn't make thwarting sensible gun laws a full-time hobby.

I started to create categories for the gun-nut mail. Some seemed like they were paranoid psychopaths, the kind of people who think their dentist is really a secret government operative who wants to implant microscopic listening devices into their teeth. David Koresh was this kind of a gun nut. He was also responsible for introducing us to another kind of gun nut: the gun nut mother. These were the moms of Waco who preferred that their children die in an inferno to simply giving up their guns. There is no arguing with these people. There is no sense in trying to debate them. We certainly shouldn't elect them to Congress, but we should also make sure that their votes and voices aren't the only ones counted or heard.

I heard from people who were victimized by what I call "unenlightened" law-abiding gun owners. These are the otherwise good people who fall for the hysterical—and often erroneous—direct-mail campaigns of the NRA. And within that category are gunslingers who feel they need to carry their gun everywhere with them, like the grandpa who went to visit his grandchildren, left his loaded gun on the coffee table, and fell asleep. His 3-year-old grandson picked up the gun and shot himself. I heard this from a mom somewhere in the Dakotas. I was getting the impression (which turned out to be correct) that this type of thing happens *every day* in America because some people think they have a right to be stupid with their guns.

Then there were the e-mails from hard-core gun enthusiasts. They seem a bit more sociopathic than the gun nuts and don't necessarily care about the politics of guns. They just like the machismo and the thrill of high-powered firearms. It's one of those Freudian things, if you know what I mean. These are the guys who, if they could live out their fantasy, would become mercenaries featured in *Soldier of Fortune* magazine.

Unfortunately, hard-core gun enthusiasts occasionally go berserk, too, like the one who shot and killed Joey Bennett, a 4-year-old Tampa boy, in 1998. Apparently, killing an innocent child wasn't enough of a thrill for this guy, because he also shot two veteran Tampa police detectives and a rookie highway-patrol trooper. This guy was a habitual felon whose friends described him as being "in love with automatic weapons."

Of course, there are the educated and responsible gun owners and hunters who *adamantly* believe that guns need to be regulated, and these folks wrote to me, too.

"I think that the NRA has gotten out of control in its influence over legislators. My husband is a hunter, but he too supports responsible gun legislation. As a teacher, the increase in gun violence in schools frightens me."

—BETH in Texas

A poll conducted by Celinda Lake concluded that a majority of Americans support gun regulation, even the majority of gun owners. But there are also a powerful 4 percent of gun owners who ONLY vote on gun issues, which means that they don't care about any other legislation. This 4 percent, which presumably is made up of gun nuts and hard-core enthusiasts, should have far less political power than they do, if we tie gun legislation—or the lack of it—to the epidemic of gun violence in this country.

What can we do about this? It doesn't take a rocket scientist to figure out that the problem begins and ends with Congress. Too many of our elected officials hide behind the distorted (and inaccurate) interpretation of the Second Amendment that the gun lobby lives and dies by. I too believe in the Second Amendment—the one written by our forefathers that provides for "a well-regulated militia" in this country. It doesn't allow for every Tom, Dick, or Nuthead to buy a gun and give it to his kid. Here is what our forefathers wrote.

"A well-regulated militia, being necessary to the security of a free state, the right of the people to keep and bear arms, shall not be infringed."
—AMENDMENT II, U.S. Constitution

Well-regulated. That's what they wrote.

———

I tucked my own kids safely into bed that night. School was to start in a day or two, and the week was going to be crazy busy with back-to-school stuff. By midnight, I had the courage to go back online and check the e-mail that was bounced to me from the Million Mom March Web site. And there, like some petri dish full of eggs multiplying exponentially, were moms . . . and more moms. They had all heard about the Million Mom March and wanted in.

"I have no story about a gun-related death . . . I want to keep it that way."

—MARGARET in Michigan

"We cannot wait for the next Columbine massacre to take some action on the escalation of gun violence in this country!"

—REGINA in Wisconsin

"We have been quiet for too long. I'm tired of watching the NRA dictate arms control. I think there are more of us than them, and we need to get more vocal about it."

—STEPHANIE in New York

"My son was recently gunned down while on vacation in Chicago. I want to help."

—CARMEN in New Hampshire

"I'm a mom. I want to be there when a million other moms help me send a message to Congress that they will ignore at their peril."

—LAURIE in California

"As a former ER nurse, never once did I see a robber shot by a home owner! All of the shootings were by people who knew each other."

—IVY in Pennsylvania

It was overwhelming—but in a tragic way—that so many people wanted to get involved. Some estimate that 1.1 million Americans have been killed by a gun since 1968, the year Bobby Kennedy and Martin Luther King Jr. were shot down. Now this was no longer a statistic to me. Here were all of these people who had lost someone to gun violence reaching out to join our march.

It was also reassuring to hear from so many people who had wanted to plan their own march on Washington but just did not know how to do it. I went to bed about midnight that night, knowing I wasn't sure how to do it, either. But hopefully, by Mother's Day, we'd have figured it all out.

I awoke the next morning with a jolt. Oh, my God! What had I started? It was like the awakening one has after realizing there is more to getting pregnant than buying cute new maternity clothes. My phone started ringing off the hook. My voice mail quickly filled up. I had so many people to call back. And after I checked our post office box the next day, I had so many letters to answer. I didn't know what to do. My husband saw what I was up against and offered to pay for an assistant for me—out of his own pocket. He was generous—and realistic—as he knew that the amount of work I was looking at would kill me if I didn't have some help. So I hired a woman I met while handing out fliers on the playground.

The march could have miscarried right then and there simply from the weight of too much interest and too little infrastructure. But just when it seemed the whole endeavor would collapse, along came the next tier of women who turned that simple one-page plan into the beginnings of a national volunteer campaign. Without them, the march would have been a good idea, but nothing more.

Spring Venoma was one of those women. She was the first person to write to our post office box, and she was mad as hell in Michigan. Her father-in-law was shot and killed by a mentally ill woman who had too easy access to a gun. Spring, who came from a family of deer hunters, said she had wanted to do something for years but didn't know where to get started. I called her and asked her if she could help. I figured she could start with something small. "Spring. This is Donna Thomases. I'm glad you want to be involved. Are you willing to organize the state of Michigan?" Spring gasped. No. She was too shy, she said. Couldn't she just post fliers or something? Like legions of other moms I've met along the way, Spring got over her initial shyness and summoned the courage to become our Michigan state coordinator.

Jane Vandenburgh, a novelist from Washington, D.C., wrote me and sent $20 with a note saying her daughter's beloved babysitter had been shot and killed by a jealous boyfriend.

Hilary Wendel was mad as hell in New York City. Hilary, a stay-at-home mom, saw the mannequins dressed in Million Mom March T-shirts in the window of New Frontier on Columbus Avenue and ran home to e-mail me. I didn't want to scare her off (as I feared I nearly did Spring) so I asked her to start even smaller. Trying to sound as nonchalant as possible, I asked if she'd be willing to organize the city of New

York. "Sure," she answered. "When do I start?" Was this woman nuts? No, I learned soon enough—just incredibly confidant, smart, and organized.

I heard from Greta, Elizabeth, and Lou (whom we affectionately referred to as Grandpa Lou) Pare in Massachusetts, and Victoria and Dawn in California. There were Kelly and Johnneymae in Brooklyn, Joan in Queens. Annie, Debbie, and Christine in New Jersey. I heard from hundreds of mothers who were willing to sign up for our risky, untested, and completely by-the-seat-of-our-pants venture.

But it would be Dana Quist—mad as hell in Florida—who was the key to bringing the Million Mom March to the next level. Dana was the first mom to recognize a fundamental flaw in the Million Mom March plan, and that was this: Essentially, we had no plan. Other than a one-page press release, a Web site, a post office box, and a ton of news coverage from our Labor Day efforts, I didn't know what the heck we were supposed to do next. I did have a notebook and kept a "To Do" list, and at the top was a note to myself to find Isabelle Tapia, the event planner who remained lost to me. Dana knew we had to do something, that we couldn't wait around for a professional event planner to miraculously show up on our doorstep. So she created a "Recipe for Grassroots Organizing" which we posted on our Web site, and which we've included in the appendix of this book. We lived by this document for the next few months, as it instructed new recruits on the essentials like how to create a database of family and friends; how to organize small meetings that focused on a specific agenda; how to delegate tasks; and, crucially, how to facilitate the growth of the group. Dana's recipe was so good because it kept things concrete while also providing guidelines to help the group scale and grow. We added a few ingredients—like our (888) 989-MOMS number—as we progressed from a few moms in our basements to a couple of hundred moms across the country working around the clock to recruit more like-minded women and men.

Hilary Wendel, who was in charge of mobilizing New York City, was also the queen of organizing a meeting, and she gave us this practical advice: Delegate small tasks and set realistic deadlines. As soon as you have a core group of three to five volunteers, expand outward again.

Later, John Shanks from Handgun Control Inc. added his sage and safety-conscious advice to the plans, particularly for moms from rural areas: If it is an "invited-all" meeting, make sure you meet in a public place, and ask for security if concerned. And save all gun-nut mail for the FBI.

It was women like Dana, Hilary, Debbie, and Amy—and all the others—who created the identity of the Million Mom March. Most organizations, like most companies, develop a distinctive personality, a unique culture. The Million Mom March culture was like that of Rosie the Riveter: We attracted people with a can-do attitude. The e-mails started to pour in, and the only way to sort through them was to delete the "You should be doing . . ." messages and contact those who used magic words like "I am going to do . . .." It seemed we recruited the kind of people who were doing everything themselves anyway—in other words, mothers, handy dads, the best and brightest college students, and concerned single working women with no kids.

The you-should-be-doings mostly wasted our time, but the I-am-ready-to-helps like Dana and Hilary figured out fairly quickly that if we were going to recruit like-minded people, as outlined in our Mission Statement goals, we would have to figure out a way to reach other moms. Since we couldn't always depend on national TV, Dana and Hilary found a way to combine old-fashioned grassroots organizing (fliers) with a little modern technology (computers), and they helped us figure out how to create and use downloadable fliers. This seems like it should have been a no-brainer, but for people like me who were over 30 and new to e-mail, this was rocket science. Dana and Hilary came to the rescue. Dana also clued me in to the etiquette of e-mail, advising me to stop using all caps all the time. "Why are you SHOUTING?" she'd write. "I AM NOT SHOUTING," I'd respond. E-mail etiquette was something I needed to work on—and still do.

———

When Amy first designed the flier, we managed to move it around the country by copying it and faxing it from one Kinko's to another. With the help of Eric, one of our Web guys, Hilary figured out how to put it up on our Web site, and the next thing you knew, the Million Mom March flier was downloaded and posted on bulletin boards across the country. So easy was this process that for weeks, a mom in Mississippi, Betsy Griffith, did this on her own, without letting us know she had joined the team. Betsy became the model volunteer. She didn't need recognition. She didn't demand a pat on the back. Just get me the damn fliers, and I'll get the job done.

Rene Thompson was the first to prove this. She got back to me a few nights later to share the letter she had written to her Congressman, Ken Lucas (R-Kentucky). Actually, Rene decided to write to Congressman Lucas's mother instead.

Dear Mrs. Lucas,

Do you know what Kenny has been up to? Those Columbine kids got their guns because of a loophole in the Brady Law. Kenny had the chance to close that loophole on June 18. But did he? No. He voted against closing it! How many more kids are going to have to die before Kenny does something about this?

I hope you have a good talking to your boy.

She signed it Rene Thompson, and like a good schoolmarm, she perforated an edge of the page and instructed Mrs. Lucas to sign it and return it as proof that she got the note and that Kenny didn't toss it in the trash on his way home from Congress.

Before going to bed that night, inspired by Rene, I wrote my own congressmen—something I had rarely done since leaving Capitol Hill. I wrote to Senators Torricelli and Lautenberg demanding to know what they had done to stop gun violence in this country. It didn't have the same zing as Rene's, but I felt it was effective nonetheless.

I left the computer on, and around midnight I heard this strange beepy noise. It was my first Instant Message! It so startled me that I jumped out of bed. On the screen in the top left-hand corner was a message from GoPowers, a moniker that would aptly describe the sender, I would later learn.

"Are you the woman organizing the march on Washington?"

It took me a minute to figure out how to answer this.

"Yes, who are . . . ?"

"My name is Gail Powers. My son attends the JCC in Granada Hills."

"I've been trying to reach . . ."

"I'm yours. At your disposal. What do you want me to do?"

The life-and-death gun issue has an enormous impact on the American people, on the economy, on healthcare, and on the very fabric of our culture. Perhaps no politician recognizes this more than Congresswoman Carolyn McCarthy.

On December 7, 1993, a crazed gunman named Colin Ferguson, an avowed racist who hated white people and Asians, boarded a commuter train on the Long Island Railroad carrying a cache of assault weapons. Then he opened fire on the packed train. When he was finished, five people lay dying, including McCarthy's husband. Her son Kevin was also critically injured. Kevin survived, despite tremendous odds against him. Almost immediately, Carolyn, who was a nurse and a housewife before then, was thrust into the national spotlight.

Shocked and grieving, Carolyn spent her days and nights nursing Kevin—who had been shot in the head—back from the brink of death. The severity of his head wound meant that Kevin had to relearn how to do almost everything. Six months after the shooting, while he was still in a rehabilitation hospital, Kevin began to regain his cognitive awareness and speak again. One day he turned to his mother and asked a question she'd asked herself over and over since the massacre: "How did this happen?" She had no answer for him. But this question haunted her so much that she made it her mission to not only seek out answers, but to prevent this from ever happening again. Carolyn joined New Yorkers against Gun Violence at a time when the group was actively lobbying then-Governor Cuomo to pass an assault weapons ban in New York, at the same time President Clinton was trying to do so on a federal level. And that, she told me, was her first experience with politicians.

The Instant Mail thing was too fast for me. I felt like George Jetson walking Astro on that crazy conveyor belt. Jane, get me off of this crazy thing!!

That night, Gail Powers volunteered to be the California state coordinator. But it took her a few weeks to feel comfortable enough with me to share her memories of the Granada Hills violence. Her 4-year-old son, Nathan, had watched his friends be gunned down. Even though he was still too young to read and write, he had dictated a note to his mother and asked her to give it to his rescuers: "Thank you, policemen, for saving us from the gun because you're our friend."

Gail had heard about the Million Mom March from a source I didn't even know we'd reached—Senator Dianne Feinstein from California.

Because so many of her colleagues in the gun-control movement were victims themselves, she got a firsthand look at how they were treated by politicians—and she didn't like what she saw. "I thought it was terrible, that here we were, the people they represented, and they just didn't want to see us," she recalled.

She never imagined that she herself would become a politician until the anniversary of her husband's death. The assault-weapons ban had been signed into law in 1994, and a year later—on December 7—Congress was threatening to repeal it. "We were going to have a memorial, a candlelight ceremony at the railroad station that evening, and I got a call about the assault-ban issue that morning. I flew down to Washington with survivors and victims from the train massacre to try to do something." Congress postponed the vote that day, but it came up again soon.

This time, Carolyn's own congressman, Dan Frazier, voted to repeal the ban, and her fury at Frazier's stance led her to run for his seat—which she promptly won.

"I just got really mad, and I said I don't think he's representing us well. He certainly can't be listening to people in the area, and that's when I decided to run." Carolyn McCarthy is now in her fourth term and is still fighting to pass legislation that will reduce gun violence in America.

"Not a day goes by that I don't know why I'm here in Congress," she observes. And not a day goes by that gun-safety advocates aren't grateful that Carolyn McCarthy— Congresswoman McCarthy—decided to go into politics.

Gail's friend Karyn had met with Senator Feinstein that day demanding to know why people were not protesting gun violence in the streets. Senator Feinstein handed her one of our fliers and told her a bunch of East Coast moms were already on it. Without even meeting us, Senator Feinstein believed we were credible. She got it.

I probably should have known that she would be a natural ally. While on the San Francisco County Board of Supervisors, she had watched as her colleagues, Mayor George Moscone and Supervisor Harvey Milk, were gunned down by a madman who blamed it all on Twinkies. I also heard back rather quickly from both Senators Lautenberg and Torrecelli. Their replies were tersely worded but polite, and I was able to read between the lines, where they basically said, "Where have you been, you idiot? We've been championing this cause for years!" Senator Lautenberg's letter also went on to mention that he had authored a bill to close the gun-show loophole and that it had passed the U.S. Senate— but not the House of Representatives—and so had failed to pass in Congress on June 18th, 1999, just 2 months after Columbine.

I should have checked the Thomas.gov search engine (http://thomas.loc.gov) before writing to them. Senator Lautenberg had been trying to close the gun-show loophole well before Columbine happened. Two months after the Colorado tragedy, he still couldn't make it happen. Readers may find it helpful to see how their own elected state officials voted on this issue. We've added this vote count (courtesy of the Thomas.gov search engine) to a section in the back of the book called "Just the Facts, Mom" on page 221. I encourage you to find out how your representatives voted on these bills and let them know how you feel about it.

It was good to know that many leaders like Senators Feinstein, Torricelli, and Lautenberg were on our side. What was surprising is that some officials would only tell us "we're pulling for you" off the record, as though they were too cowardly to publicly take a stand against the gun lobby. I was getting pretty annoyed at this seemingly all-powerful, yet illusive Wizard of Oz–like group that was known as the gun lobby. I thought that perhaps they really were like the wizard—all smoke and mirrors, just a cranky old man behind a curtain trying to control everyone by pulling a lot of levers. Or maybe they were just a bunch of high-paid lobbyists who were afraid of losing their jobs and their livelihoods if they made any trouble for the gun industry. I couldn't help but wonder how brave these off-the-record officials— or their friends the gun lobbyists—would be if they had to stare down the barrel of a gun.

I certainly don't want to make it seem like there weren't a lot of brave politicians working on this issue. I wrote to Congresswoman Carolyn McCarthy of New York the same day I applied for a permit to march. It would be weeks before I would hear back from her, and when I did, her first reaction to the Million Mom March was, "I want in!" Unlike a lot of the secret "well-wishers" we ran into, Congresswoman McCarthy had, literally, stared down the barrel of a gun—at least by proxy—when she lost her husband (and almost her son) to random gun violence.

Congresswoman McCarthy was a bit concerned by the overwhelming logistical obstacles we faced in executing the march, but that didn't stop her from believing in the power of us moms. So far we had only signed up 149 marchers, but it was a start. Carolyn quickly became what we called a working marcher, meaning that for the next 9 months, she lived and breathed the Million Mom March and did whatever she could to help us make it happen.

"My name is Judy Harper. I lost my 13-year-old son. I want to help."

—E-MAIL TO OUR WEB SITE
DURING OUR FIRST 3 MONTHS

There were days during our first 12 weeks when I would cry for no reason. Other days, I felt so nauseous that I thought I was going to throw up. And when my mood wasn't swinging from the extremes of cranky and giddy, I was just plain fatigued.

But these symptoms are normal when new life is taking hold. And the Million Mom March was growing, within me and within the larger community of moms who were working to make certain this baby came to term.

As in the first trimester of a pregnancy, I was acutely aware of how fragile our organization was in those early months. After our Labor Day launch, our operation blossomed from being a handful of local moms concerned with gun violence to a national network of working marchers who wanted to change gun policy in this country. But this was no smooth, effortless period of growth. Like the development of a fetus, our growth was explosive and often chaotic. At times, things were very touch-and-go.

What carried me—all of us—through those early months was a core group of moms. This group consisted of the handful of women who emerged from the ranks of the volunteers early on. This core group was immediately identifiable, available, and strong, and they became the nucleus of the organization, the cell around which everything else developed. The core moms would also help define our corporate identity and establish the "voice" for the movement.

Million Mom Marchers typify the ability of women to get things done and to get them done well. And I believe the core moms brought the art of multitasking to a new level.

The conversations we had often sounded like sitcom shtick and went something like this.

Dana: Why pay full price at (*Trent, don't stick that Cheerio up your nose*) Kinko's? With all the printing we're doing, we should able to get a discount (*Trent!*), don't you think?

Donna: Because we can't get the discount without a federal ID. (*Lili, stop. Mommy will get off the phone in a minute.*). We either wait a few months for Jeff Berger to get us our 501(c)(3) status or (*Phoebe, you're going to fall off that . . .* CRASH!). Oops. Gotta run!

Somehow, amidst the chaos—or maybe because of it—we understood each other and got things done: Gail Powers from California, Dana Quist from Florida, Hilary Wendel from New York, Rene Thompson from Kentucky, Spring Venoma from Michigan, and Lisa Laursen-Thirkill from Oregon were just a few of the core moms who unified our efforts across the country. We communicated mostly by e-mail, or we'd pick up the phone when the loneliness of working at our computers got to be too much. But we never wasted each others' valuable time on idle chitchat, other than maybe one or two side conversations about kitchen tiles and appliances. Jeff and I were in the middle of a major construction project for our new Tribeca apartment, and sometimes for efficiency's sake, I'd ask a Million mom or two for some quick advice, such as which is a better stove—a Viking or General

Electric? Dana, in addition to working full-time to organize the South, was studying to get her license in interior decorating, so I would sometimes end an MMM call by asking her for decorating advice.

We worked with amazing efficiency. We were all about identifying problems and working to find solutions for them. And there were lots of problems. So fragile was our ragtag organization in those early weeks that there were times that I feared it would fall apart. Bizarrely, almost every time our group threatened to break apart, it usually had something to do with a man. The first guy to come along and hassle us was named Floyd—Hurricane Floyd, that is.

It was the middle of September, 1999, and I was so consumed with the Million Mom March that I barely took notice of a storm that was packing 150-mile-an-hour winds and making its way toward the coast of Florida. It was Dana who finally brought my attention to the storm— but not because she was overly concerned about it—even though she was in Florida! Dana, who always answered her e-mail or phone calls immediately (this was her great strength as a grassroots manager) called to apologize for being out of touch for half a day. As it happens, Dana and her family were holed up in a hotel that was being used as an evacuation center. While half of the state was scrambling to batten down the hatches, Dana, along with other storm refugees, sat in the lobby of the hotel. She sat working away on her laptop, all the while recruiting as many moms from among the hotel-bound as she could. This woman is obsessed, I thought, as if I should talk. Even as we spoke, Floyd was tearing his way up the East Coast toward New Jersey. We lived inland, which gave me a false sense of security. In a matter of a few hours, the water in the creek behind our property was rising so fast that it was threatening the retaining wall that was the only thing between our house and the ravine. That was the bad news. The good news (at least from my husband's point of view) was that we had just sold our house.

As the water began to rise, Jeff began to move valuables from the living room to higher ground. (By valuables I mean his Yankee memorabilia.) I instructed the girls to run to their rooms and pack a few clothes for an emergency sleepover at Debbie's (our Corporate Sponsor Mom and a neighbor just up the road).

I continued to talk on the phone to Dana while I packed a bag for myself. But we weren't even talking about Floyd. We were talking about how best to distribute our fliers and logo to new recruits. Dana urged me to go back to Kinko's and ask my new friend, "Mr. Second Amendment," to help me download the PDF files we now had. Mr. Second Amendment, as I called him, was very helpful and supportive, but he would end every conversation by letting me know I was going to have to take his guns from his cold, dead hands. I had no intention of doing that, I'd reassure him. I just needed him to help me with the fliers.

Just as Dana and I seemed to agree that it was best to put the logo and flier on the site to be downloaded directly by our grassroots recruits, a gigantic tree in our yard that must have been 50 feet tall fell over, just missing our house. I barely blinked and kept on talking to Dana on the portable phone. Jeff looked at me as though I were some insane woman who had wandered off the street into his house. His look said, "Who are you? And what have you done with my wife?" It seemed like Jeff looked at me more and more as though an alien from another planet had taken over my body. And not just because I was so consumed by the march. I had also recently announced to him that I was now having second thoughts about moving back to the city, and this really made me sound like a crazy woman, given that for all the years of our marriage, I couldn't wait to get back to New York.

What had caused my change of heart? Just a few days earlier, I had gone into the city, down to the neighborhood we planned to move into, to visit P.S. 234, the school my girls would attend. I looked up at the immense dark silhouettes of the twin towers, which loomed over the playground. Standing there, I was suddenly seized by a terrible repressed memory from my high-school days. I remembered the day when our school was locked down because of a sniper shooting from the rooftop of a nearby Howard Johnson's hotel. Before the shooting was over, a few police officers and some bystanders were dead. We could hear the gunfight from our school.

I may sound like I was turning into someone as paranoid as "Cowboy Mike," one of my gun-nut pen pals, who feared that the government was about to swoop down and confiscate his gun and TV satellite dish. But ever since Buford Furrow had made that call to action to "kill all Jews" a month earlier, I didn't feel like my kids were safe anywhere. Maybe my recalling this shooting from my school days was a premonition of what was to come. Whatever the reason, the material thing that I had wanted so desperately—a New York City apartment—was now the last thing I wanted. Especially one so close to the World Trade Center.

But all of this was difficult for me to explain to Jeff—probably because I was always on the phone or online, or out posting Million Mom March fliers all over New Jersey.

The kids and I stayed at Debbie's the night Floyd raged around us, while Jeff stayed home to keep an eye on things. While the children slept, Debbie worked up a strategy for getting corporations to sponsor us. We were a marketer's dream. Moms with kids who consume products they sell. She made a list of all of the companies she'd contact, from The Right Start to Dannon Yogurt.

The next morning, the kids and I went home to find that our house was still standing—barely. Sometime during the night, that retaining wall did give out and was swept away by the rushing water from the creek. We were staring at almost $200,000 worth of uninsured property damage, including the loss of that wall. I hate to admit it, but this turned out to be a blessing in disguise because I was secretly thrilled when the new owners of our home wisely backed out of the deal.

It gave me some breathing room to talk to Jeff about things, like where we ought to live. I don't know if it was because of the fatigue, the stress, or just too much coffee, but I was very confused and felt completely incompetent to make such a life-altering decision at that time, especially in terms of how such a decision would affect our kids.

With the burden of the financial crisis hoisted on us courtesy of Hurricane Floyd, I wasn't sure how much longer I could finance the Million Mom March on the family Visa card. Jeff had been patient and generous, but he had his limits. So did my Visa.

In the midst of all the drama caused by Floyd, Rene called me to alert me to the latest shooting. Rene was the Million Mom March town crier, giving us a heads-up when shootings were in the news. Competing with Floyd for the headlines was a man named Larry Gene Ashbrook who had a history of mental instability and who had walked into the Wedgwood Baptist Church in a quiet middle-class neighborhood in Fort Worth, Texas, and opened fire on a crowd of about 150. The church was packed with mostly teenagers, who were there singing hymns as part of a special youth gathering. Ashbrook walked in and opened fire on the parishioners, shooting dozens of people in the back and killing seven. Then he shot and killed himself. He had come to church carrying a Ruger 9mm pistol and a .380 pistol—both of which he had acquired legally at a flea market (despite his history of mental problems).

First a Jewish Community Center, now a Baptist Church? If I were serious about shopping around for a safer faith—and I had given it some thought—then, perhaps, the only religion left for us was my father's Catholicism. I had never heard of anybody barging in and shooting up a Catholic church. At least not yet.

The reactions to the Fort Worth church killings bordered on the surreal. Around this time, Congressman Tom DeLay (R-Texas) essentially told newspapers that, despite the recent tragedy at a church in his home state, the House of Representatives would continue to worship at the altar of the NRA when he proclaimed, just days after the massacre, that the U.S. Congress is "pro-gun"! I suppose this wasn't surprising, given the incredibly insensitive and stupid remarks he'd made following the Columbine massacre: "Guns have little or nothing to do with juvenile violence," Congressman DeLay pontificated. Instead he blamed school shootings on the teaching of evolution in the schools and working mothers who take birth control pills. After learning of these comments, and despite her self-imposed seclusion in Kentucky, Rene Thompson took action. She sent me an op-ed piece she wrote in response to DeLay's comments. I don't know if it was ever picked up by any newspaper, but we posted it on the front page of our Web site (www.millionmommarch.com).

In Roll Call last week, the Honorable Rep. Tom DeLay announced that "This House is pro-gun." Thank you sir, for reminding us. We were under the impression that the House of Representatives was a pro-constituent House.

According to the Gallup Polls done in August 1991, 66 percent of Americans (including 52 percent of registered Republicans) favor commonsense gun laws, but this doesn't seem to matter to the very Honorable Mr. DeLay, who, incidentally, is accompanied everywhere by a bodyguard whose salary is paid for with our tax dollars. DeLay reminds us that "This House is pro-gun," even after Paducah, Columbine, Granada Hills, and Fort Worth, and despite the growing numbers of dead and wounded children across this country. This House, claims Mr. DeLay, "refuses to yield to the whims of the populace."

We owe you a great debt, Mr. DeLay, for telling us in a recent article in the New York Times *that this House has been bought and paid for by pro-gun lobbyists.*

Since you've been honest with us, we would like to be honest with you. Here's what matters to the majority of Americans: We believe there should be mandatory gun-show background checks, safety locks on guns, and the registration of all firearms. In fact, these things matter to 66 percent of us, and we vote.

Stand by your guns, Mr. DeLay. Come Mother's Day, we mothers will stand together on the steps of Capitol Hill to remind your PRO-GUN House that on election day, the voters will stand by our children.

Sincerely,
R. Thompson

Rene's letter was great—except for the part about standing together on the steps of Capitol Hill. Right around this time, I got word that our permit had been yanked, due to an oversight on my part. Apparently, another organization had applied for a permit for that same piece of Capitol Hill real estate for the same weekend as our Mother's Day march. I don't mean to male bash, but a guy I'll call Karl, one of our male volunteers, was supposed to follow up on that permit application. And, despite numerous claims that he was on top of it, I was surprised one day to find out that he had not followed up at all. The Police Memorial had booked it for the day after Mother's Day and so needed our Sunday to set up. While I was certain we could work something out, "Karl" was busy alienating any friends we might have among the cops by accusing them of being too cozy with the NRA. Oy vey.

I still hadn't found Isabelle Tapia, and this latest screwup—which was my fault because I had delegated this very important task to the wrong person—really shook me up.

Between this mishap and Floyd, I didn't know if I could take much more bad news.

But the bad news just kept coming. A good friend and college mentor from LSU called me with a heads-up I had been half-expecting. Dan B. is well connected in Louisiana politics and had heard from a high-placed friend at the NRA that the organization planned to come at me with guns blazing.

According to Dan B., the NRA was planning to somehow use the fact that my sister-in-law was a friend of Hillary Clinton's to portray me as a "secret Democratic operative." Dan B. also figured that they'd throw in my brief time on Capitol Hill as further evidence that I was some kind of highly placed—yet secret—Democratic insider. Though this sounded kind of glamorous, in a Charlie's Angels kind of way, my time on Capitol Hill was anything but glamorous. In fact, it bordered on the comical. Besides sharing an office with the automatic signing machine, the closest I had come to wielding power was as the Louisiana Congressional delegation's "Yambassador," a job that gave me the power to dictate which yam recipes would be served on Yam Day in the Senate Dining Room. What I took away from my Capitol Hill experience, besides knowing by heart the general Capitol phone number was this: Yams will never be as popular as white potatoes on the hill. I had no idea how the NRA would use this very damning information against me. It would be interesting to see.

In the meantime, I had more important things to worry about. The permit situation signaled to me once and for all that it was crucial that we find and hire a professional organizer as quickly as possible. The closer we came to march day, the less we could afford any more amateur blunders. So my main goal became to raise cash so we could hire the person who would get us to Washington in one piece—if I could ever find her.

To add to my string of luck—so far, all bad—I heard from David Bernstein, the friendly and very helpful publicist in the communications department at Handgun Control Inc. Initially, I was delighted by his call as he told me that HCI planned to highlight the Million Mom March on their Web site. Not only that, but they were also talking about taking out a full-page ad in *USA Today* and featuring us prominently there, too. I couldn't believe what I was hearing! This was too good to be true.

And, of course, it was too good to be true. I made the mistake of crowing about this promotional coup to our entire grassroots by encouraging everyone to pick up a copy of the newspaper and use the full-page ad as a poster. HCI did run a full-page ad in *USA Today*—but it didn't even mention the Million Mom March, let alone feature us. Instead, it announced the formation of a new organization called "Mothers Against Senseless Shootings." The ad featured a huge photo of the Granada Hills children being led to safety. After the ad ran, my credibility plummeted among the ever-growing legion of working marchers—those moms who were working 24/7 to get the word out about us. David Bernstein called me, sheepishly, to apologize and to tell me that the top brass at HCI had made the final decision to create this new "in-house" mothers organization. I think the ad cost them $75,000, give or take, but a few weeks later, still no one knew who they were or what they were about. I couldn't help wondering, looking at our dwindling funds, what that $75,000 would have done for us.

On top of all this, the volunteers were getting antsy. Moms working from their homes in isolation needed a constant stream of news to keep them motivated, and all I seemed to have for them was bad news. We needed something—anything—to boost morale. And out of the blue, it came when Carolyn McCarthy called. Her press assistant had set up an impromptu press conference to announce the Million Mom March on the steps of the U.S. Capitol. The congresswoman, probably weary from getting nowhere in Congress on the issues of gun control, looked at us moms as if we were the troops landing on the beaches of Normandy. Carolyn McCarthy, congresswoman extraordinaire, officially became Mom #150 that day. With her help, I had no doubt that we would find the other 999,850.

Congresswoman McCarthy's press conference went off smoothly, except for one minor mishap: Three boxes of T-shirts that Julie had sent by UPS were missing in action until I ran into one of UPS's chief lobbyists, Marcel Dubois, the husband of a friend from LSU, who happened to be walking the Congressional grounds with conservative Congressman J.D. Hayworth of Arizona. Marcel immediately got on his cell phone to track down our shirts, and in no time, a nice young man in cute brown shorts delivered them to the Capitol just before the press conference. While Marcel was taking care of this, I tried to convince Congressman Hayworth that he should support us. He was a large, gregarious man who suddenly looked trapped. He looked down at me and stammered, "I like moms, I have a mom, my wife is a mom," and then he beat a hasty retreat. (It's interesting to note that the NRA would later boycott UPS—without any success—for making the moral and ethical business decision to stop shipping guns by land and only ship them by air in order to stop guns from being stolen off their trucks.)

Since our main goal was to recruit people to our cause, McCarthy's press conference brought us a huge infusion of new volunteers, including people like Pat Thomas of Virginia who had lost a son to gun violence and who had vowed—in honor of her son—to show up anywhere, anytime, any place, to prove that people care about gun violence in America.

But not every one of the new volunteers was so well-intentioned. In his bestselling book, *The Tipping Point*, Malcolm Gladwell writes that, in all groups, there is a certain point at which every organization will be challenged and things will get a little wiggy, particularly if the infrastructure is weak. Gladwell postulates that the health of any organization tips with the 151st member. I couldn't believe how precisely Gladwell nailed this! Here we had Carolyn McCarthy, working marcher #150, who had arrived like an angel. The minute numbers 151 through 154 walked through the door, we had trouble. These moms became known as the 151s. Though the 151s may have arrived with the best of intentions, they immediately focused all of their energy, time, and talent on trying to divide the Million Mom Marchers by gossiping, manipulating, and generally spreading a considerable amount of ill will.

These women had my home phone number, and they called me morning, noon, and night. The only place I could go to find refuge from this small band of malcontents was to my tiny *Late Show* office, and then only on Mondays—the one day a week I worked for a job that I relished. The only Million Mom Marchers who had my work number were Hilary Wendel and Dana Quist. On one particular Monday, Dana called me. I wasn't that busy, having nothing more to promote that day than the Top Ten Ways the Y2K Will Affect Your Dog. So I spent a considerable amount of time hearing her argument for why we needed to rethink using the words "gun control" on the Web site. "It's killing me down here," Dana pleaded in her singsong Puerto Rican accent. She had been going to Mommy & Me classes with her son Trent to recruit moms, and she kept hearing the same thing: Southern women were for gun safety but *not* gun control.

Dana's call came on the heels of an e-mail from the well-known security expert, Gavin DeBecker, who urged me to drop the word *control* as well. Nobody wants to be controlled, Gavin explained. To many people, control seems synonymous with banning. That was Dana's opinion, too. The NRA had done an effective job of convincing its members, through hysterical direct-mail campaigns, that gun control was really a liberal conspiracy, headed by Sarah Brady, to storm their homes and confiscate their guns.

Up to this point, I'd been fairly adamant about not futzing with the Web site too much, mainly because it was simply too expensive to overhaul it every time someone didn't like something—and somebody always didn't like something. But Dana had good instincts. So I sent an e-mail alert to our core group before I left work that day, telling them that we'd be changing one of our key slogans from *Mobilizing for Commonsense Gun Control* to *Mobilizing for Commonsense Gun Laws.* I had no idea that changing one word could cause such a stir. Volunteer #151 sent an e-mail *to our entire database,* now at a few hundred working marchers, blasting this move as our "giving in" and backing away from our stance. The tone of the e-mail was militant and uncompromising and completely unsympathetic to Dana's very real concerns about alienating the Southern states.

By the time I got home that night and logged on to the computer, the damage had been done. Our Connecticut organizer was the first to quit. This was a real loss, because she was a committed activist whose daughter, an editorial writer for a conservative newspaper, was also on board. Both mother and daughter had been early and passionate supporters of the MMM.

"I want nothing to do with this obnoxious group," the Connecticut mom wrote before she quit. The Illinois organizer walked out right behind her. "I want to change the laws and save lives. Not debate how we word this or that. What a waste of time." It would be months before we were able to find replacements for these women, but eventually, Beth and Linda signed on to organize Connecticut. And Steve Young, from the Bell Campaign, a grassroots organization of gun victims, eventually took over Illinois for us. Like so many other dads I would meet during this time, Steve had lost his son to a gun.

If there was anything I learned from this messaging experience it was this: It is crucial to protect your e-mail database. That send button, like a trigger on a gun, is just too easy to press. Other than that small handful of volunteers who reacted so badly, the rest of the volunteers agreed that the word *control* should be taken off our Web site, and the matter was settled.

The 151s quieted down for a while after that. But apparently they only went away to regroup, because they came back with a vengeance—this time demanding paying jobs. Pay? With what? My Visa card? I guess someone forgot to tell them that we were an all-volunteer organization.

The only person we had budgeted for a paying job was an experienced event planner. And the name Isabelle Tapia, which I had heard in the very first days of the MMM, kept coming up. But I still couldn't find her, and I was getting lots of questions from the grassroots that I couldn't answer. No one seemed to know how or where to reach her.

We may have lacked the professional planning we needed to pull off the big day, but our moms were masters at recruiting. They were out there, adding to our roll call on a daily basis, hanging posters, and arranging meetings with local civic and church groups. In fact, our *Looking for a Few Good Moms* slogan (which was on our flier) became the "Kilroy Was Here" of the gun-control movement, thanks to Mr. Second Amendment, my friend from Kinko's.

Our reach was even beginning to extend into the heartland—even into Oklahoma. My husband wrote a letter about us to a customer of his in Tulsa who, in turn, gave the letter to his wife, Jan Finer. And Jan, a medical doctor and mother of four, came down with Million Mom March fever overnight and took it upon herself to organize the Million Mom March/Oklahoma in her spare time.

Jan did what all secure, bright women do when they want to change the world: She called her closest friends, including Randee Charney, a lawyer, and Alice Blue, a social worker. Together they scheduled a Million Mom March meeting for Columbus Day, 1999, at a Unitarian Church in Tulsa. They wanted to have a gun-control expert speak at their meeting, so I called a few of the national gun-control organizations, begging them to send someone to Tulsa. Sorry. Budgets are too tight, I was told. Joe Sudbay of Handgun Control Inc. tried to help by giving me the phone number of his one and only Oklahoma contact—but it turned out the number was no longer in service. So I flew to Tulsa myself and met Jan at her house. She had just gotten in from work, and I watched as she fed her four kids, typed a quick speech, and drafted an agenda for the meeting. We were out the door in a flash. Halfway down the driveway, her husband, David, yelled out to her—she'd forgotten the speech in her printer. She whipped back around, rolled down the window, grabbed it from his hand, and sped off as she simultaneously called in a patient's prescription to a drugstore on her hands-free cell phone. I've never seen someone so busy in my life, and I couldn't believe she was also agreeing to organize a local event in Tulsa for Mother's Day.

Most of the Million Mom March meetings I organized galvanized 5 or maybe 10 people, so when I walked into the Unitarian Church and saw more than 65 in attendance, my mouth dropped. But Jan was disappointed with the turnout and apologized, saying, "Maybe if we didn't hold it on a holiday, we could have gotten more people." More? This was the biggest Million Mom March meeting I had attended so far.

The crowd in Tulsa was diverse and included the Democratic mayor of Tulsa, Susan Savage, as well as Nancy Inhofe, daughter-in-law of NRA best friend Senator James Inhofe. Nancy was an emergency-room doctor, and she told me that if her father-in-law would only see the bloody carnage she sees, then maybe he'd be less inclined to vote with the gun lobby, lock, stock, and barrel.

Only one protestor, a pawn-shop owner, showed up and tried to disrupt our meeting. He started yelling about how it was his God-given right to make a buck by selling guns and that our intent was to put him out of business. We just ignored him, but he was persistent, demanding rather loudly, "I want my right to have a say!"

A tall, buxom blonde by the name of Sharon rose up like a goddess and said in a sexy, husky voice, "You've already had your say. Now it is *our* turn. So go away." She then shooed him away like Dorothy shooing away the Wicked Witch of the West.

We all watched him deflate like a truck-flattened snake on a scorched highway. I turned to the lady sitting next to me and asked, "Is it my imagination, or did he just shrivel up and disappear?" She nodded, and in her most proper church-lady voice, she snickered, "I bet you he has something else all shriveled up. And that's why he loves his gun." Those Tulsa moms sure have a way with words.

At the last minute, I did manage to secure a speaker for the event. She was a woman named Mary Leigh Blek, the president of the Bell Campaign—the new organization started by victims of gun violence. Mary Leigh flew in from Orange County, California, to give the Tulsa crowd some facts and statistics.

The local Tulsa media covered the church meeting, and I was surprised when Jan Finer gave out her home phone number while the news cameras were rolling. That was brave, I thought. I stayed at Jan's again that night, and following the local news, her phone began to ring. I answered for her.

"Hello?" I said, afraid I was going to get an earful from some gun nut. The caller had a very sweet Oklahoma accent: "I'm calling about that Million Mom March on Mother's Day." Here we go, I thought and braced myself. "I'm sick and tired of all of these guns. I plan on marching if you think there will definitely be a march here in Tulsa. I can't go to Washington, because I cook Mother's Day dinner for my entire family. But I can march while the turkey's in the oven!" I took down her name and number and added her to Jan's growing roster of supporters. Of the 10 or so calls that came in that night, all were supportive except for one caller who used the time to vent her frustrations about President Clinton. "I don't like the man. I don't. Never did. And I don't like his uppity wife, either!"

Mary Leigh Blek tried to persuade Jan, Randee, and Alice to consider moving their Mother's Day event from Tulsa to Oklahoma City, the state capitol, but they knew Tulsa women would want to be home for Mother's Day. There was also some apprehension about going to Oklahoma City after the 1995 bombing of a federal building by gun nut Timothy McVeigh. McVeigh was an NRA member who liked to boast that only law-abiding citizens *like himself* would be affected by gun regulations. McVeigh was also said to be a frequent visitor to gun shows, where he allegedly sold weapons and anarchist literature under an assumed name.

———

Right after I returned from Tulsa, I heard about a minimarch (literally) being organized by a man in Manhattan. It was to be a Children's March. Bob Kaplan from the Workman's Circle wanted to round up our children and take them to Washington, D.C., to show Congress the precious commodity we should do our best to save. He scheduled the Children's March for late October. I wanted to show my support, plus I knew nothing about organizing buses to Washington, and I figured this

Maureen King, an upbeat mother of five, was the type of activist who would board any bus, anytime, to protest gun violence in this country. But she hadn't always been that way. Maureen is a family person, one of 12 children herself, whose life revolved around caring for her children. Pat, her husband, was a police officer and a deeply committed father. She worked during the day, and Pat, a 21-year veteran of the Long Branch police department, worked nights so that he could be with his kids during the day. But late one night, while he was on a break, Pat was shot and killed waiting for takeout at a Chinese restaurant. A career criminal with a stolen handgun saw the uniform and pulled the trigger twice, shooting Pat once in the back of the head and once in the neck—execution style. Pat never had a chance. "The only saving grace for me is that he didn't suffer and was killed instantly before he knew what was happening," Maureen told me.

After Pat's death, Maureen went numb. And she became angry. It seemed like every time she turned around, she heard about another policeman being shot. Just when she felt she couldn't take it anymore, she got a call from her local congressman, and something in her shifted. Congressman Frank Pallone, a Long Branch native himself, had made a point of checking in with Maureen after Pat's death, to make sure she and the kids were alright. He always offered to help in any way possible. During this particular call, when he asked Maureen if she needed anything, she blurted out, "Yes, I need your help. What are we doing about all these school shootings?"

That moment marked the birth of an activist. Maureen joined Ceasefire New Jersey, a state gun-control group. When she heard about the Children's March, she was among the first on board, and in fact, she had helped organize the very bus I met her on.

It was a ride that really opened my eyes to how we not only take our police officers for granted but how we take their families for granted, too. Maureen reminded me that police officers are not only on the front line, they *are* the front line. And their wives and children worry about it every waking moment.

Her husband, Pat, was the sweetest person you could meet, she told me with a smile, and she went on to say that people teased her that he was too nice to be a cop. She bristled at that. Cops *are* nice, she'd say, they're supposed to be nice! He was also very safety conscious, especially at home. He always kept his gun locked away in the safety box with the ammunition locked up separately. Maureen believes that killing someone with a gun is the most cowardly act imaginable.

would be a great way to find out. So I reserved a seat on the bus for my girls, myself, and *People* magazine.

A *People* writer, shopping for his kids' shoes, had contacted me about doing a piece on the MMM, thanks to a strategically placed flier in KellyShuz—a kids' shoe store in Milburn, New Jersey. So I invited the *People* reporter and a photographer to join us on the bus to the Children's March.

As we boarded the bus, the *People* photographer started snapping my picture—and this was at 6 A.M. If I had known I was going to be featured, I would have made more of an effort to gussy up. As it was, I was tired and sleepy, just like everyone else on the bus.

Our bus made a stop at a toll booth in South Jersey to pick up a passenger. I watched as a woman with a bright and cheery face got on. She had a certain kind of energy that prompted me to make a beeline for her. Her name was Maureen King, and she was the wife of a slain New Jersey police officer. Until I met her, I don't think I gave much thought to how the trauma of gun violence affects the wives and families of police officers. That morning, Maureen King helped open my sleepy, baggy eyes.

When Maureen isn't busy with her kids, her work for Ceasefire, New Jersey, and riding buses to Washington, she manages Fallen Officer, a license plate program—the first program of its kind in the nation—in honor of her husband, Pat. She runs it from her home, and all the proceeds go to funding scholarships for the children of slain police officers. And, she'll proudly tell you, it's the third bestselling plate of all the 16 specialty plates available in New Jersey. This was one woman who was definitely busier than I. Maureen taught me that morning that it is possible to be busy and still be nice. I vowed I was going to try to live by her example, as soon as I got some sleep or another cup of coffee.

———

The Children's March attracted about 1,000 people—it was a weekday when most kids were in school and most parents worked. Bob Kaplan, who organized it, did a Herculean job of lining up a dozen or so buses to go to Washington to lobby our congressmen for sensible laws. (I learned from him that the most important person in any activist organization is the person willing to organize a bus. It is a thankless but absolutely crucial job.) Bob was deeply troubled by the shootings at the Granada Hill Jewish Community Center. He was a grandfather, and he couldn't imagine one of his grandkids being shot.

When we arrived on the mall, I heard a big, booming voice calling out for me. "Anybody here know Donna Dees-Thomases? I'm looking for Donna Dees-Thomases." I waved the woman over, wondering who was looking for me, and an outgoing African-American woman maybe just a little older than me came over to introduce herself. It was Connie Rucker from the outreach department at Handgun Control Inc., and she came bearing gifts of HCI T-shirts (a woman after my own heart). Connie said, "Honey, I'm telling you, this Mom's March is going to be big. Big, I say." I hugged Connie. It was so nice to hear somebody from the institutionalized world of gun control express so much faith in our group.

Another woman wandered over, well-dressed and attractive, about my age. "You're Donna?" she asked in the longest, slowest Southern drawl I've ever heard. "I was supposed to find you." Rachel Smith from Raleigh, North Carolina, who was studying to be an ordained minister, looked me up at the suggestion of Lisa Price from North Carolinians against Gun Violence (I had called several of the state gun-control groups looking for volunteers for the MMM), and now here was Rachel, volunteering to organize North Carolina—a state where a 12-year-old can legally possess a rifle or shotgun without the consent of his or her parents. I hugged her, too. And I felt relieved that we now had a solid contact in North Carolina. I was still kicking myself for letting that woman from North Carolina I only knew as Nancy get away from us on Labor Day. Not long after I met Rachel Smith, another North Carolinian named Marcia Owens contacted our Web site. I put her in touch with Rachel, and together they formed an incredible team. Both were Christian women who looked at gun violence as an affront to their religious beliefs.

I got back to New Jersey just in time to dash into Manhattan for one of Hilary Wendel's meetings. The *New York Times* New Jersey edition had learned about us when a reporter sat next to one of our moms on a bus coming through the Lincoln Tunnel. Amy Putman was that mother, and they even sent a photographer to cover Hilary's meeting. (*Newsweek*'s Jonathan Alter also learned of our march from Amy on the same commuter bus, and whenever we needed a boost in publicity, we'd ask Amy to *get back on that bus*.) I'd initially hoped for the national edition of the *Times*, but it turned out to be a good thing the story only appeared in the regional edition: About 100 people signed up on our Web site as a result, and Annie, my database assistant, and I called and wrote back every single one of them. (This is how we recruited some Pennsylvania moms, including Nancy Gordon, who became our Pennsylvania state coordinator.)

One of our biggest media coups, a mention in Anna Quindlen's *Newsweek* column, came about by sheer luck. In late November, I'd convinced a publicist friend to let me riffle through her Rolodex, and I found Anna's home number. An hour after I left her a heartfelt (I hoped) message, she returned the call saying she'd been talking about the march over lunch and was actually trying to find me. This was pure Kismet—with a bit of moxie and elbow grease thrown in.

Anna interviewed me briefly, and I forwarded her several e-mails, including one from Judy Harper, a mother from Athens, Georgia. Judy's 13-year-old son "got into things," she wrote, including his stepmother's stash of loaded guns. While visiting her home one day, he accidentally shot and killed himself while playing with a handgun. Anna mentioned the Million Mom March in her column, quoted Judy, and then made the point that it is usually the widows and wounded who try to remedy America's lax gun laws.

> *"Perhaps it will take one more school shooting to move the majority of Americans into a position more powerful than that of the NRA. Perhaps it will take one more school shooting to move us from people who support gun control to people who vote it. But as we continue to let the widows and the wounded do the work, be warned. That next school may be the one your children attend; the next accident could be close to home."*
> —ANNA QUINDLEN, *Newsweek*, November 1, 1999

———

The same month Anna Quindlen's column appeared, there were back-to-back high-profile shootings: one at a Xerox office building in Hawaii and the other at a shipyard in Seattle. Between these two incidents, a total of nine people were shot dead. We realized that we could create a place for people to gather and vent, find solace, and voice their anger at this madness. Those clever, innovative young men at Abstract Edge, our Web boys, as we called them, created a Tapestry Page for our Web site. It was a blog (Web log) page, where people could share their frustration, their poetry, or the reasons why they wanted to join us in our Million Mom March crusade.

There are horrible shootings every day in America. In fact, not many people know that 80—yes, 80—people are shot in this country each day. Part of the reason we created our Tapestry Page was so that the countless citizens who are affected by gun violence would have a place to gather. However, there were days when the gun nuts would try to dominate the page and try to wreak havoc on our system, but the clear, sane voices would always find their way through to us, and we would reach back out to them.

Spring Venoma, our Michigan state coordinator and one of the hardest working of the working marchers, rarely called with problems or to ask for anything other than an occasional supply of T-shirts. But one day, she e-mailed to say how upset she was that her congressman, Bart Stupak, was being targeted by the NRA because he had voted for child safety locks and closing the gun-show loophole. Up until these votes, Stupak—who, like Spring, is from the Upper Peninsula of Michigan, a hunter's paradise—had voted with the NRA. But now that he had taken a pro-children stand on guns, the NRA was trying to unseat him.

Spring asked that we give the congressman an Apple Pie Award, and we did, through our Web site. For weeks afterward, our site was hit with vicious and venomous attacks by the gun nuts who all decried Congressman Stupak as a traitor to the Second Amendment. "What a pansy. He should read the Second Amendment," they'd write. "It doesn't call for childproofing guns!" But it does call for regulating them, I'd write back. After a while, I realized I was wasting my time trying to communicate with the other side of gun control. One day, I asked Rene if she wouldn't mind taking on filing the gun-nut mail for me. As it turned out, Rene relished this role. Instead of getting upset by the often rude, explicative-riddled messages, Rene found them amusing. Just because we were waist deep in a serous issue, she reasoned, didn't mean we shouldn't have a few laughs.

We were now reaching and recruiting women from states as far away as Hawaii, Alaska, and Idaho. But I was having trouble getting my own JCC in northern New Jersey, the one my own children attended, involved. (So much for thinking globally and acting locally.) Unbeknownst to me, some people there were upset over the name, Million Mom March, feeling that it might in some way echo or condone the alleged anti-Semitic stance of Louis Farrakhan, the founder of the Million Man March. I personally felt that adopting this name was akin to "turning the other cheek" and that our goal was to unite, never divide. After I explained this, the JCC invited me to one of their executive meetings. At last I was making progress! It had taken 10 weeks to get this meeting, but the timing of it couldn't have been worse, as the meeting fell on Jeff's birthday. Jeff, payer of the Visa bill, was beginning to lose patience. I tried to explain how crucial the meeting was, so we compromised by agreeing to officially celebrate his birthday that weekend at Sammy's Restaurant. We would have birthday cake at home when I got back from the meeting.

The meeting was at a sister JCC in East Hanover, New Jersey. When I arrived, the meeting was already running late, so I sat there worried about picking up Jeff's birthday cake on my way home. By the time it was my turn to make my presentation, I was a mess. I stammered along, barely able to put a subject and verb together. I was doing a terrible job of winning over the board. One of the women there interrupted me and asked why we didn't just write a bunch of letters to Congress. Letters were good, I tried to explain, but we needed to make a bigger impression on Congress. We needed them to see our faces and hear our voices. I didn't want to discourage them, because letters are important, particularly on close votes, when every letter is counted to gauge the constituent feeling on the issue. I thought back to my days on Capitol Hill when I shared an office with an automatic signing machine. I don't remember my boss ever reading and signing his own name, unless the correspondence had been flagged by the mailroom as being from a donor or the head of a major organization that could influence voters. Those letters would be read and signed by the senator himself, and maybe he'd even scribble a little note on the top, "Hi, Fred. How are Gladys and the twins?"

I tried to persuade this group that the best way to get through to

Congress, in addition to writing letters and donating money, was to physically put ourselves in front of them. As I spoke, the people around me just stared at me blankly. It was not their fault. I could hear that damn birthday cake calling to me, begging me to pick it up and go home. I was doing a terrible job. I was saved by a woman named Estelle, the grandmother of one of Lili's friends, who stood up and not only came to my defense, but eloquently addressed the group on why we needed to march for the future of our grandchildren.

This was not about gun ownership, Estelle declared. This was about reclaiming our country from a lobby that had no regard for human life. A gun lobby that felt AK-47s and Uzis had a place in American society! She then went on to talk about the march for the freedom of Soviet Jews. "That was a turning point!" she exclaimed. "We are at a turning point in this country over guns. Do we take a stand, or do we run away?"

Whew. Estelle blew me—and everyone else—away. We walked out together, and I thanked her for saving me, and she confessed that she was, in fact, a legal gun owner. Now I was even more impressed. We hugged as we said good-bye.

I left that meeting bone tired, and as I drove off to pick up Jeff's cake, I almost jumped a curb and nearly blew out a tire. Afraid I would fall asleep at the wheel, I skipped the cake and went straight home. The girls were already in bed, and Jeff had fallen asleep. As I went to kiss the girls good night, Lili looked up at me through a gauze of sleep and whispered, "Mom, you blew it." She was talking about the cake. She was right. I blew it. As in a marriage, or a grassroots movement, sometimes it's the little things that count most. I should have gotten that damn cake.

My only consolation for bungling Jeff's birthday was that the JCC meeting spurred a flurry of invitations to address Jewish organizations across the country. The Catholic girl who married into a religious Jewish family was now practically one of the tribe. And from these meetings, more local Million Mom March meetings sprouted up around the country. One of the invitations came from Rabbi Marc Israel from the Religious Action Center in Washington, D.C. He was a little lukewarm about us, being weary of watching so many marches fail. But he was willing to meet me, and we scheduled a meeting for January, right after the holidays.

For us moms, our Million Mom March meetings became as addictive as a cup of Starbucks coffee. Or perhaps we were just addicted to the coffee. (Someone suggested maybe we needed to start holding our meetings someplace else).

Hilary Wendel, our chief New York City mom, suggested that we meet early one morning at Rockefeller Center, the home of NBC Studios, so we could be seen on the *Today* show. Clearly the moms were getting media savvy fast.

I called a few friends, trying to book ourselves on the show, but it wasn't as easy as I thought, despite my connections. Going back to Hilary's original idea, I asked the booker if we couldn't be inside, could we at least get some time with Al Roker outside? With the tone of someone used to saying no, she dangled an "I'll see" at me, and added, offhandedly, "You know, we had a stagehand who was shot. I'll see what I can do."

What stagehand? Shot when? Slowly, it came back to me. A stagehand who had worked for the *Today* show was shot and killed outside of Rockefeller Center in 1994. This would have been another random act of violence and would not have gotten any media coverage if it weren't for the fact that the shooting took place at the heart of the media industry in midtown Manhattan.

And what was even more bizarre was the fact that the killer, William Tager, later allegedly confessed to having mugged Dan Rather in 1986. When he made this confession, he apparently did say that he heard things, what he called "frequencies," and that he had, indeed, infamously asked Dan, "Kenneth, what is the frequency?" It seemed that he blamed Dan and Katie and the entire media industry for beaming those "frequencies" into his head. I kind of felt guilty that I (like the rest of the world) didn't originally believe Dan's story.

What is so tragic and troubling about Dan's mugger and the stagehand's killer is that the records of people with mental health problems are not routinely entered into law-enforcement databases. Congress could provide funding to do this, but some protest that these records violate the privacy of the patient and that the job of actually recording these records would be too costly and time consuming. But ask any mother of a mentally ill shooter if the family's privacy is protected after the rampage. It isn't. But this doesn't make sense to me. It shouldn't be easier for people like John Hinckley, Buford Furrow, and William Tager to buy a gun than to get Prozac.

I got a call back from the *Today* show producer with good news: We would get a few minutes with Al Roker outside the studio! So at 7 A.M.

on a chilly, rainy November morning, two dozen moms (plus a few dads) boldly stood holding signs—big signs—with our Web site and toll-free number emblazoned on them. The signs were so enormous that it took three of us to hold each one. We were determined to get our message out, and that message was "Here we are! And here's how to reach us!" We honored a special request from Anna in Texas and publicized her Dallas meeting that night, and we also mentioned a meeting that Greta, Elizabeth, and Dania (our working marchers in Boston) were holding at Harvard University.

Al Roker didn't know what had hit him. In the 3 minutes we were allotted, we used the airtime to recruit the next wave of volunteers. Julie heard us in Ohio, and she signed up. Amanda in Tennessee heard us, and she signed up. Ona in Pennsylvania signed up, too. All of these people either e-mailed us or called our toll-free number, and we had two volunteer grandmas, Andrea and her friend Norma, sitting in Short Hills to transcribe the voice mail each day and help us triage it out to the troops.

Andrea Douglas, Voice Mail Grandma, never missed a day of work—nor did she miss a beat. Because of the volume of calls we received, it was inevitable that some would be from gun nuts trying to scare us away. Andrea once took this message after such a call: "A man called. He wouldn't leave his name. But he says he wants to do something to us. And it sounds kinda dirty!"

For us, the *Today* show was a home run. But popping champagne to celebrate would have been in poor taste, because just about the time we were shouting out our Web address to 6 million viewers, a seventh-grader in Fort Gibson, Oklahoma, was pumping 9mm bullets into the bodies of his classmates.

The news of another senseless tragedy was never how we wanted to recruit people, but these tragedies kept on coming, and the e-mails kept on coming, and the calls to our toll-free number kept on coming. We were building momentum. We were getting stronger every day. We were moving well past the embryonic stage into a newer phase. And the bigger we got, the bigger our list of enemies got. And I'm not just talking about the gun nuts who wanted to shut us down. There were people on our side of the issue who were working against us in ways I was too naive to see.

PATERNITY SUITS

4

"You just can't waltz in here and organize a march without my approval first!"

—MR. BIG FISH,
THE EXECUTIVE DIRECTOR
OF A SMALL STATE GUN-CONTROL
ORGANIZATION

The more visible we got, the more we seemed to rattle the men in the movement. Of course we didn't mean to. But as we grew, many of our male counterparts in gun control began to act like soon-to-be teenage fathers who didn't want to acknowledge what was inevitably coming their way. I think they just didn't know what to make of us moms, since they were mostly white professional men in suits who took a rather corporate approach to gun control.

All of this talk from the Million Mom March about giving birth to a movement made them nervous. How could they support us? There was too little money for the entire gun-control movement as it was. In contrast, the veteran female activists among them had a different reaction to us. Most of them were supportive, knowing we worked for cheap—as in free. And they were happy to have us on board. But a few did act like they were the long-suffering wives of the movement and treated us as though we were the new, younger trophy wives ready to make off with their husbands' fortunes.

The fortune in this case was the $10-million fund created by the billionaire financier, George Soros, and philanthropist Irene Diamond, which was specifically earmarked to fund gun-control efforts in this country. Aside from this fund, a $4-million grant from the Richard and Rhoda Goldman Foundation had just been awarded to the newly created Bell Campaign.

For a movement that was supported for the past 30 years by nickels and dimes, this infusion of serious cash was like manna from heaven. Particularly because the gun-control movement was up against such well-funded adversaries as the NRA.

I was told that we needed at least $1 million—minimum—to pull off an event that would get Congress's attention. I'm not sure why I was crazy enough to believe I was capable of raising that much cash. Perhaps it was simply that I felt the way other parents must feel when they have to raise money to provide lifesaving medical care for their critically ill children. In that situation, "no" or "I can't" simply wouldn't be an option. I felt exactly this way about the MMM.

To raise money, I first needed a Federal ID number to apply for nonprofit status—and the Million Mom March was as nonprofit as it got. I was nervous about entering this world of bureaucratic red tape, but Elise Richman, Westchester mom, recommended an attorney to help guide us. (Coincidentally, the lawyer she recommended, Richard Taffet, had done some work for my husband and was the brother-in-law of our Corporate Sponsor Mom, Debbie Taffet.) Richard Taffet did mostly intellectual property work, but he offered to do all of the Million Mom March copyright work pro bono. He, in turn, found a lawyer in his firm to do our tax work, and Jeff Berger became a knight in shining armor for us. Jeff had clearly paid attention in tax school (or wherever these people learn the ins and outs of our country's frighteningly complex tax laws). He showed us how the Million Mom March needed to be structured to raise money and be in compliance with IRS rules. Jeff felt we should be structured like Mothers Against Drunk Driving (MADD), a 501(c)(3) nonprofit organization. This type of organization could spend no more than 20 percent of its funding on actual lobbying—none on electioneering—and the rest of their resources had to be spent on the actual issue.

Back in September, I had stumbled across a *Time* magazine article about a new victim-led grassroots organization called the Bell Campaign (the ringing of a bell is symbolic of remembering a victim). I recalled that the Bell Campaign had nonprofit status and knowing that the organization had just been awarded a start-up grant of $4 million from the Richard and Rhoda Goldman Foundation, I had an epiphany. If we were to ally ourselves with the Bell Campaign, perhaps we could share resources, and we would not have to establish ourselves as a stand-alone organization.

I didn't quite know what I was up against (in terms of the competitiveness of the other gun-control groups), so I told Jeff Berger to forget about applying for a separate 501(c)(3) for a new organization. Instead, I told him, I would approach the Bell Campaign and see if they would take us on, perhaps even become our fiscal sponsor. I had already tried to interest HCI's sister organization, The Center to Prevent Handgun Violence (CPHV), an educational outreach group dedicated to reducing gun violence. CPHV also had 501c3 status (unlike Handgun Control Inc., which was primarily a lobbying group). A very nice man called me back after my fifth call and politely declined to help us.

Like the other organizations, the Bell Campaign was initially hard to reach. I finally connected with a man named Eric Gorovitz in the Bell Campaign San Francisco office, and he referred me to a woman named Tina Johnstone, who was their New York representative. I proceeded to hound Tina until she agreed to meet with me.

Tina had lost her husband, David, the father of her two kids, when he went to San Francisco on business and was shot by a 16-year-old with a handgun. The bullet didn't kill David right away; it paralyzed him. When David's minister went to visit him in the hospital, David expressed his concern over what would happen to his shooter, because the boy was nearly the same age as one of his own children. It looked as though David would recover, although he would spend the rest of his life in a wheelchair, when a blood clot in his leg traveled to his brain and killed him.

Tina became a champion for putting laws into place so that guns like the one that led to her husband's death could be traced. Tina made headlines during the Brady Bill debate the following year when she and a friend named Ellen Freudenheim placed hundreds of pairs of shoes, to symbolize those killed by guns in New York State, in front of then-Senator Alfonse D'Amato's office. In this way, she created the first of many "Silent Marches" that have had such a profound effect on our understanding of the gun-violence epidemic in this country. A 1996 Silent March in Washington displayed 40,000 pairs of shoes, which represented all the gun deaths in the United States that year, and in 1998, Tina even placed empty shoes on the doorstep of the Smith & Wesson factory in Springfield, Massachusetts.

It was Tina who led me to our fairy godmother when she introduced me to Rebecca Peters, who controlled the $10 million of the Soros-Diamond Fund that was set aside for supporting gun-violence prevention. Tina literally marched me into Rebecca's office—with no appointment—and insisted that Rebecca listen to me. Rebecca was amused by our Web site and was particularly impressed that our legislative agenda was solid, especially our endorsement of licensing and registration. She was interested but noncommittal, and then she asked me what I later learned was something of a trick question: How had I been funding the MMM up until now? I realized I didn't have any choice but to be honest. "Visa," I said.

Apparently that was the right answer, since Rebecca was more an activist at heart than an administrator. Immediately, she knew we were serious about the march. She herself had successfully worked to get a licensing and registration system instituted in Australia shortly after the 1996 Port Arthur massacre, in which 35 innocent people were slaughtered by a lone gunman. She and her fellow activists managed to do this on a shoestring budget. Rebecca believed that all activists needed to dig into their own pockets before looking for financial aid. And it was only when there was no money left that outside help would be appropriate. We were getting close to that point, I assured her.

With conservative optimism, Rebecca said she would consider a grant proposal from us. Even just a promise to look at our application felt like money in the bank to me. In order to begin the process, Rebecca would need proof that we were in fact a viable organization and that we had reach throughout the country. So I shared my Tulsa, Oklahoma, story to give her just one example of how we had truly become a national movement.

Rebecca was trying to unite the gun-control movement around a single piece of legislation, a bill that would require the licensing of handgun owners and the registration of all handguns.

To hear Rebecca explain it, without licensing and registration, all of the other laws proposed or already on the books were difficult to enforce. Licensing would help curb impulse buys and reduce overall gun sales, and registration would make it possible to track down those trafficking in illegal guns.

"YOU THINK CRIMINALS ARE GOING TO REGISTER THEIR GUNS?" the gun nuts would write to our Web site.

No, but if registration becomes law, all guns will be registered before they leave the manufacturers, and they would be more easily traceable as a result. Without the licensing of drivers or the registration of cars, police would not be able to enforce traffic laws or track down reckless drivers or stolen cars. Rebecca clearly articulated why it is the same for guns.

Not everyone in the movement saw the wisdom in this completely sensible thinking, however.

A *New York Times* opinion piece authored by the Violence Policy Center (VPC) sent the entire movement into a tailspin by criticizing all the other groups for being "enablers." That's because the VPC called for the banning of all handguns. The piece also dismissed the smart-gun technology that was central to Ceasefire New Jersey's Childproof Handgun Bill, calling it a "doodad" that wouldn't save many lives. (A research team at Johns Hopkins University disagreed, suggesting that if a gun could only be fired by its owner, there would be far fewer gun deaths in this country each year.)

It wasn't just the fact that well-respected groups like the Violence Policy Center had agendas that clashed with Rebecca's desire to create a unified legislative goal; it was, quite simply, the fact that there were so many groups in the first place. And new groups were sprouting up all the time. In the fall of 1999, the same month the VPC op-ed piece appeared, two new national gun-control groups popped up: Common Sense about Kids and Guns, which was started by Victoria Reggie Kennedy, a member of Handgun Control Inc.'s board of directors and wife of U.S. Senator Ted Kennedy. (This was not the first time an HCI board member decided to start a competing group.) Then HCI announced the formation of Mothers Against Senseless Shootings (MASS), an organization that seemed to have a post office box but no Web site and no phone number. Once I called HCI anonymously and asked the receptionist to please connect me with the person who founded MASS. But even the receptionist had no clue who that person was. Instead, she gave me the phone number of a woman in New Jersey who was organizing a march on D.C. As I jotted down the number, I realized it was mine.

The oldest gun-control organization in the country is the Coalition to Stop Gun Violence, currently run by Michael Beard. Mike used to be a legislative aide to Congressman Bobby Kennedy. After Kennedy's assassination, Beard dedicated his life to stopping gun violence through advocacy and education. In 1974, the year Michael founded the Coalition to Stop Gun Violence, a man by the name of Dr. Mark Borinsky, a victim of gun violence, started The National Council to Control Guns, which was eventually run by a former DuPont executive named Nelson "Pete" Shields, who left corporate life after the gun death of his son.

Another of the venerable older gun-control groups was Ceasefire, which had been founded by Jann Wenner, publisher of *Rolling Stone* magazine, after he lost his good friend John Lennon to a gun. Wenner's national organization, which creates superbly effective public service announcements, should not be confused with some of the state gun-control groups that go by the same name (i.e., Ceasefire New Jersey).

These national organizations represent some of the more established gun-control advocacy groups, but there are many others—too many to name here—especially on the state and local level.

At the request of Stephen Smith of the Civil Institute, I spoke at a kickoff conference of yet another new organization called States United that was started in response to the Bell Campaign and whose stated mission was to unite the myriad nonprofit gun organizations under one umbrella. Both the Bell Campaign and States United were onto something, because the redundancy—and waste—in the gun-control movement was outrageous. Every gun-control group had to have its own accountants, lawyers, policy directors, communications directors, outreach directors, political directors, development directors, Web designers, receptionists, etc. And each organization also had to cover the overhead of office space, phones, travel expenses, and so on.

The Funders Collaborative for Gun Violence Prevention, started by Irene Diamond and George Soros and headed by Rebecca Peters, came the closest to achieving a united movement by using their financial clout to encourage the different groups to rally around a single piece of legislation (licensing and registration), and, miraculously, they were finally able to get all but the Violence Policy Center on board.

And this explained Rebecca's initial hesitation in funding us. She would do so only if the MMM were willing to work with the other groups. I was willing. We were willing, but most of the other groups just wanted us moms to go away.

———

It came as something of a shock to me to find out that not everyone in the gun-control movement welcomed the mommy lobby with open arms. I'm not sure why I was so naive about this. After working in television, I should have been used to the occasional vicious sniping among competitors. And I should have known that an organization is an organization, whether it is nonprofit or not, and that because of this, the clash of egos, money, power, and control are inevitable.

There were certain people in the nonprofit gun-control world who thought that they—and only they—"owned" the movement. And just about everyone takes credit for fathering the movement. But there are only a handful of people who can truly be given this credit, and at the risk of naming names, I would have to say the movement had two fathers—Mike Beard, currently president of the Coalition to Stop Gun Violence, and the late Pete Shields, who founded Handgun Control Inc. The rest of us have simply jumped on the bandwagon, or at least tried to. Little did I know room was scarce for us moms on that bandwagon where the majority of seats, curiously, were occupied by men.

My first lessons on how to navigate the male politics of the gun-control world came from an unlikely source—the Reverend Jack Johnson, founder of Ceasefire, New Jersey, a highly successful state group that got assault weapons banned in New Jersey, which was one of the first states to do so.

Reverend Johnson invited me to speak to his group in South Jersey in January 2000. He thought that speaking about our Mother's Day march would help recruit new activists in his area. Afterward, I had to go to Washington for another meeting, and the Reverend graciously offered to drive me to the Philadelphia train station to catch my train. As we drove along, he gently, yet clearly, sermonized on what happens to male gun-control activists who spend too much time basking in the red glare of the TV camera.

"A few of the men in the movement never had any media attention in their lives until they became activists," he said thoughtfully. "Suddenly, they become big fishes in their little ponds." Reverend Johnson was right: I even heard about one male activist who tried to use that media spotlight to pick up women.

I don't think I would have been able to navigate the mostly male waters of the gun-control movement successfully if we had not found the Bell Campaign, which, much to my delight and that of Jeff Berger, our tax lawyer, agreed to be our fiscal sponsor. This meant that the Bell Campaign would oversee all the funding that came into our organization, and in this way, we would be free to focus our energy on planning and executing our event. Now we didn't have to worry about financial oversight. And we had access to some terrific mentors in the Bell Campaign, particularly Beckie Brown, who was a former national president of MADD. Beckie had lost one son to a drunk driver, and, unbelievably, another to a gun.

Beckie felt that we in the gun-control movement should follow MADD's model and make it our goal to work toward reducing gun violence by 10 percent every 2 years. Having such a clear goal would help us all stay focused on the lifesaving mission—rather than get distracted by fundraising, the secondary goal that consumes so many nonprofits.

As our fiscal sponsor, the Bell Campaign would not give us 1 cent of their $4 million grant. But they would open the doors to their own benefactors for us, and they would then oversee any gifts, donations, or other transactions that occurred on our behalf.

We were off to the races. Or so I thought.

———

The Million Mom March had only been alive for 8 weeks when we were taken on by the Bell Campaign. With this fiscal sponsor on our side,

Rebecca Peters at the Soros-Diamond Fund was ready to give us a grant. And she did so, offering us $100,000 to begin to pull together our event.

The Violence Policy Center was the first group to flip out when they heard this news. Someone there called Irene Diamond directly to stop this "foolish" proposal of mine. Mrs. Diamond called me and urged me to modify our stance and adopt the VPC's goal of outright banning of guns. She dangled the grant money over my head like a carrot. I said I couldn't do it. The Southern moms already made it abundantly clear: They would bolt faster than a bullet if we changed our stance from regulating to banning handguns. One Southern mom had even told me that she'd have to start shopping at her Piggly Wiggly in disguise if our mission became to ban guns entirely. Banning guns, like banning abortions, is a hot-button issue in many communities, even among people who would never touch a gun and who support strict gun control.

———

If money is the root of all evil, then in the nonprofit world, it is the grassroot of all evil. The Bell Campaign, started and led by victims, also started getting the cold shoulder from other gun-control organizations that were jealous of their $4 million grant, even though the money was to be used solely to educate and train gun victims to be advocates for gun control.

Since I was so new to the movement, and still, frankly, a bystander in terms of actually running an organization, I was horrified by all the infighting. The fact that the gun-control movement was so fractured seemed to feed right into the gun-toting hand of the NRA.

To be fair, the NRA also suffers from serious infighting. I learned this firsthand when I somehow found myself on a gun-nut Listserv (a private Internet mailing list). I'm not sure why these guys thought I was one of "them," but I was privy to a flurry of e-mails where they were plotting to overthrow NRA executive vice president and CEO Wayne LaPierre. Why? Because during a closed-door NRA session, LaPierre allegedly made the remark that perhaps guns "don't really belong in schools." The response to this on the Listserv was pretty eye-opening: "Off with LaPierre's head!" one gun nut demanded. "Traitor!" another blasted back. I almost felt sorry for LaPierre, and for a split second, I thought about reaching out to him, to warn him to watch his back. But LaPierre didn't need me: I'm sure he had his own mother watching out for him.

Sadly, with an annual budget of $200 million, the NRA can afford to engage in a bit of infighting. In the gun-control world, where we had a combined annual budget of only $20 million, we couldn't afford a minor tiff.

———

Right after Thanksgiving, in an e-mail from Rebecca, I got the news that our grant had come through, and the news couldn't have come at a better time. Andrew McGuire flew in from San Francisco to meet me in Irene Diamond's office on Park Avenue where we personally, and profusely, thanked her. She didn't want thanks. She wanted results! She promised us an additional $200,000 by January if we could show her that our event was going to be as big as we promised.

Mrs. Diamond, like Carolyn McCarthy and so many other dynamic, powerful women, became what we called a working marcher, as these were the women who were the most focused on action and results. Mrs. Diamond made me promise to get on the phone right away and start calling the other foundations. She in turn promised to write her friends and find us some more funding. Like Rebecca, she was hoping to rally the gun-control movement around the idea of a piece of legislation that specifically addressed the issues of licensing and registration. And word on the street was that an actual bill was about to be introduced in the U.S. Senate by Dianne Feinstein of California and in the house by Congressman Marty Meehans of Massachusetts.

We had our start-up grant of $100,000, our fiscal sponsor in the Bell Campaign, and we even had our moment in the rain with Al Roker. But just when you think nothing can go wrong, inevitably it will.

Yet again, a man tried to rain on our parade. But this time, it was someone within our world. Bob Walker, the highly respected president of Handgun Control Inc., called a meeting in New York at Rebecca Peters' office. I was looking forward to it. I arrived, still bathed in the afterglow of the *Today* show home run of December 6. I was surprised to see Andrew McGuire of the Bell Campaign there, in from San

Francisco, and as Rebecca herded us into a small conference room, she said that the meeting wouldn't start until Bob Walker arrived. Bob had come up from Washington, D.C., and was meeting with Rosie O'Donnell first.

Almost every day, I would get an e-mail from a mom in the field asking when we would be on *The Rosie O'Donnell Show*, which in 1999 was probably the top-rated daytime show among moms. I was working on it, I kept saying. But I couldn't seem to make any headway. David Letterman, who was renowned for not giving interviews, also refused to do her show. I was one of the people who kept having to tell her people that he was not going to be a guest on *The Rosie O'Donnell Show*, despite the fact that she appeared on his show many, many times. Could this little comedy-drama really be what kept her from taking my calls? I wasn't sure. Because we all knew she was (and is) a huge supporter of the cause.

When I heard that Bob was meeting with her, I got very excited. I immediately assumed it had something to do with recruiting her for the Million Mom March and that this was the reason he had called the meeting in the first place. While we waited for him, I happily chatted with Rebecca and Andrew McGuire, telling them proudly about all of the local successes of the Million Mom March. I regaled them with stories that highlighted the creativity and chutzpah of the women in the grassroots, who were busy giving out Apple Pie Awards, calling news conferences, and announcing Time-Out candidates. Despite the grim reason they were doing all of this, the Million Mom Marchers were having fun.

Rebecca and Andrew said very little in response. I thought that was odd. Something wasn't right. But I wasn't sure. Then Bob Walker walked in.

"Hi, Bob. How's Rosie? Can she emcee our event?" I blurted out with enthusiasm. At that point, the room went positively cold. Apparently, Bob Walker did not sing our praises to Rosie. In fact, just the opposite. HCI, apparently, had been telling Rosie for weeks that an event like ours would most likely fail and that it would set the movement back. I was astounded. In the world of television, I knew that bookers sometimes got very protective of their celebrity lists and contacts, but for a cause like gun control, I could not fathom people being so petty.

But was this just pettiness? Or were organizations like HCI—despite its victories in the early nineties with the Brady Bill and the 10-year assault weapons ban—just so doggone tired of the constant uphill battle against a rich gun lobby that they were simply losing faith? Or did Bob Walker know something I didn't?

Even though I kept admonishing a few of the volunteers that a million was just a metaphor for "a whole lot of people," the moms really believed it was possible. I got so swept up in their enthusiasm and faith that I failed to see that the seasoned gun-control advocates had become used to looking at the glass as half-empty rather than half-full.

And now, here I was in this meeting on December 8, where, it seemed, HCI had come to kill our grant! Why? Because Bob said the media was going to hate the Million Mom March. Hate what? A bunch of moms standing up to the gun lobby? Which media? The McLaughlin Group? I had no idea what he was talking about. Perhaps Bob needed to spend a little less time watching C-Span and more time watching Lifetime TV. Clearly he didn't have his finger on the pulse of the kind of media attention we moms were generating. Worst of all, Andrew McGuire and Rebecca Peters were buying in to this foolishness. Andrew told me that the Bell Campaign—because of HCI's strong objection to the march—would now only agree to support regional marches. Without the Bell Campaign's full blessing, Rebecca said she was forced to pull our funding for the Washington, D.C., event.

I admit, I didn't know a whole lot about putting together a national event, never mind a bunch of regional events. Despite their arguments to the contrary, my gut told me that, without a national event to drive people to the regional events, the regional events would flounder. But there was one thing I knew, and that was the media. And I knew that Bob Walker was dead wrong. The Million Mom March was something the media would love. In fact, they were already loving it.

Then Bob warned, suppose it rains? It *always* rains on Mother's Day in Washington, D.C., he said. At least that's what he—and everyone else with an opinion—kept saying. And it seemed like *everyone* had an opinion. I guess I figured that we'd just march with bright pink umbrellas, which was Julie (T-Shirt Mom) Levi's idea. To me, it was not enough of a reason not to try. It seemed that there were too many excuses being offered for why this would fail and not enough solutions being offered to help us succeed.

I was devastated by Andrew's and Rebecca's sudden lack of faith. Before the meeting adjourned, Bob proposed that, instead of marching on Washington, why didn't we send a giant Mother's Day card to Congress? A Mother's Day card?! That will get Congress shaking in their boots, I thought to myself sarcastically.

I left the meeting completely deflated. I honestly felt that, with the loss of our funding, we had nowhere else to turn. Maybe it was time to pack it in. Maybe Bob was right. "Nobody shows up at these things, Donna," I'd heard so many times, but until now, I had ignored it.

If I hadn't already committed to dinner that night with our Georgia state coordinator, Judy Harper, I would have gone straight back to New Jersey and put out the bad news. Judy was in New York to tape the *Queen Latifah Show* (our pro-bono accountant, Jeff Lieberman, was Queen Latifah's neighbor, and his wife had taped a flier onto her mailbox. As a result, Judy got booked on the show!)

Judy and I had e-mailed each other many times over the past few weeks, but as with so many of the moms, we hadn't actually met in person. I scanned the hotel lobby where we had planned to meet, and I watched a country western–type beauty with long, curly red hair glide across the floor toward me. "Donna?" she asked, "Is that you?" Then we hugged like old friends. At dinner, I asked her, "If you had a choice of protesting at a regional march in Atlanta or going to Washington, D.C., which would it be?" Washington, she said. No contest.

To be honest, I was hoping Judy would say Atlanta. I didn't know how much longer I could take the pressure of planning a Washington event without funding and without a professional event planner. It was simply becoming too much for me.

I decided to tell Judy that perhaps it would be best if she didn't mention the Million Mom March on Queen Latifah's show the next day. Judy was invited on to tell the story of her son Jason, who accidentally shot and killed himself while playing with his stepmother's gun.

After dinner and saying goodbye and good luck to Judy, I stopped by Hilary Wendel's apartment to feel her out, before picking up my car at the garage for the drive back to Jersey. Hilary, without a moment's hesitation, said she, too, would rather march on Washington than march in New York City. I decided to come clean with Hilary, and I told her that we'd just lost our funding, and I didn't know if we could pull off any kind of march, let alone one in Washington, D.C. Her answer was classic

PROFILE | Joe Jaskolka

Some unenlightened gun owners like to ring in the New Year by firing a gun into the air. This doesn't just happen in rural areas. It even happens in big cities, like Philadelphia and Los Angeles and New Orleans.

But what goes up must come down. Especially bullets.

Joe Jaskolka was the youngest state coordinator for the Million Mom March. When he was just 12, he e-mailed me and asked if he could be our Delaware state coordinator. If Joe were an ordinary kid, I might have hesitated. But Joe was a kid with a bullet lodged in his brain, a result of a New Year's Eve celebration on the streets of South Philly in 1998. While visiting his grandmother on New Year's Eve in 1998, Joe and his cousin went for a walk up South Second Street in downtown Philadelphia, looking for a string band that had its clubhouse on that street. The neighborhood was vivid and noisy, with fireworks and guns ringing in the air. Just 15 minutes before midnight, Joe fell to the ground with blood spurting out of the top of his head. Then he lost consciousness. He was in a coma for nearly 2 weeks, and then spent 6 months in the hospital. He also endured 10 surgeries.

Brenda, Joe's mother, refused to believe that Joe might not live. She is a petite woman who weighs less than her young son. But she has a strength that belies her size. As Joe's primary caregiver, she must pick him up to dress him, feed him, and put him in his wheelchair. Although he never lost brain function, Joe lost his motor skills and his ability to speak for a time, and one vocal chord remains paralyzed. With Brenda's help, Joe has spent some of his boundless energy creating a life for himself that is as close to normal as possible.

grassroots: "What do we need? A megaphone and a soapbox to stand on? Screw the funding." I wanted to kiss her—and I wanted to cry.

I drove home despondent. And exhausted. In some strange way, I felt relieved that it was all over. All of the running around I had been doing was making me brittle and shrill around Jeff and the girls. And I could feel their resentment about how little of my time they had gotten over the past several months. The irony here was that I had begun this for my family, but now the Million Mom March was pulling me away from them. As I drove home, I mentally composed the letter I would send to the troops. It would be simple. One line, in fact:

The march has been canceled due to lack of faith. Donna

"The bullet went off and came straight down through the top of my head," he says, somewhat matter-of-factly. That bullet is still lodged in his head. That's good news to the lunatic who shot him, because without a bullet to match to a gun, the police have no way to even begin to track down the shooter.

Joe was an honor student, a black belt in karate, starting quarterback for the football team, and a star basketball player. He can no longer play sports, and he is confined to a wheelchair. Getting out of bed and brushing his teeth are now his daily challenges. "Courtesy of whoever shot me," he says.

Brenda works the overnight shift at UPS in Philadelphia so she can spend her days taking care of Joe. His dad, Gregory, a Vietnam vet, former police officer, and ex-NRA member who now works at Sunco, has nothing but admiration for his brave son. "I was in combat in Vietnam, and I have yet to run across someone with more courage than Joe," Greg says.

With nearly $12 million in medical bills stacked up already, the Jaskolkas are living out a perverse version of the American Dream, where the rights of gun owners are valued over the rights of citizens to live free from gun trauma.

Despite Joe's brain injury, he remains one of the smartest people I know. He was asked by a documentary filmmaker what he thought about the law George W. Bush passed in Texas that allows guns to be carried and concealed in churches. Joe thought about it for only a moment, then replied, "If you feel you need to carry a concealed weapon into a church, then maybe it's time to find a new church."

When I got home, I stopped in the kitchen to pick up a stack of mail on my way into my office. The first envelope held a letter from Carole Ann Taylor in Inglewood, California, who wrote: "I've been waiting for this march ever since my only son was gunned down. If I have to walk from California, I will be there on Mother's Day." I could almost feel her determination as I held that letter in my hand, and it prompted me to think about Joe Jaskolka, a 12-year-old boy who was also determined to walk at our march.

Joe had been paralyzed by a bullet the year before and was confined to a wheelchair. But Joe was determined to come to Washington. And he had made me a challenge I couldn't refuse. He told me that if I could pull the march off, he would come to Washington, rise up out of his wheelchair, and take a step for gun control. As cynical as I thought I was, this was one challenge I couldn't ignore.

How could I let people like Carole Ann and Joe down? I knew that I couldn't. They were counting on me to provide the forum where they could express their outrage, their passion, and their commitment to a safer world. Thinking about all this, I knew that I would not send that terse e-mail. Though I was bone tired and my heart was broken, I knew I couldn't give up. Tomorrow, I would figure out how to get us back on track. "Please, Lord, give me a sign; give me a reason to keep at this," I thought as I went to bed.

In the morning, the sign came. It was in the form of an e-mail from the National PTA that said, "We are pleased to announce that we will endorse the Million Mom March." Lisa Laursen-Thirkill, Oregon mom, had worked on getting this endorsement for us, and here it was, like an eleventh-hour reprieve from an execution.

I knew this single endorsement from the PTA was worth more than all the money in the Soros-Diamond Fund—and then some! The Million Mom March was back in business!

Then a funny thing happened. When the news of this endorsement hit the streets, our grant money came back to us, along with the endorsement from some of the other national gun-control groups who had previously been quite ambivalent about our plans. They all said that they were there to help keep us from running off track and possibly damaging the movement. But I knew the truth: I knew they had come back because they knew that we—the moms—had power. We had the juice. And we were just beginning to learn how to use it.

Handgun Control Inc. did make one last attempt to pull the plug on us. I was summoned to Washington a week later, and Bob Walker sat me down in a harshly lit conference room. One by one, Bob called in every white male in a suit he could round up. To be fair, these men were some of the smartest people in the movement, who spent most of their time suing those in the gun industry who recklessly sold arms to bad-apple dealers. They were doing fine work. But I'm not sure why they all thought having a law degree made them experts on how women think.

"Nobody's gonna show up!" was their hue and cry. "It's Mother's Day, for Chrissake! Women want to get cards and get breakfast in bed!" they each said in their own way. But by then, it was too late to convince me to abort. Before I left that day, most of these guys made it clear to me that they would distance themselves from us, so certain were they that the Million Mom March was going to be a colossal, embarrassing, expensive failure. I'm sure they would have submitted to DNA testing just to prove they had nothing to do with this Million Mom March. They made it clear that if we were going to give birth on Mother's Day, we would have to do it without them.

I left feeling like a mother who has just been abandoned by the father of her kids. Now I would have to somehow find the courage to go it alone. I couldn't quite put my finger on it, but this feeling was beginning to feel familiar—even in my own home.

"You think asking your neighbor if there's a gun in the home is hard? Trust me. Picking out your child's coffin is worse."

—CAROLE PRICE

WINTER 1999–2000

The second trimester is usually the time in a pregnancy when reality sets in. You are over the euphoria of the "news," and now you start to worry about how you'll feed and clothe the little person you're going to be taking care of for the next 18 years. This is also true when trying to plan a march on Washington. In late 1999, I still had raised only $300,000 of the estimated million-plus we would need to make this march happen. On top of that, we still didn't have a permit, and therefore we had no place to march to. I felt like my cover was going to be blown as I had to bluff my way to an answer every time somebody asked me exactly where it was we were marching.

"In Washington," I'd answer the legions of volunteers, "don't worry about the specifics yet."

They did not need to worry. I was worrying enough for everybody. The permit snafu was keeping me awake at night until James Day, a Washington, D.C.–based event producer, approached us about using his company as our event planner. James heard about the march through the D.C. grapevine and believed this was a march whose time had come. (I was always taken a bit aback whenever someone in Washington took us seriously.) Over a beer at an Arlington bar, I explained our permit situation to him, and within a few days, he had not only connected with the National Park Police, but had finagled a piece of the famous National Mall for the Million Mom March. Most of it was already booked up by the Smithsonian, which would present a Spring Arts and Crafts fair. The section of the mall around the Washington monument was already reserved for a counterdemonstration that was going to be held by the Second Amendment Sisters. The SAS was a new group that sprouted up right after we did. Though they were clearly on the wrong side of the issue, I had to admit that their name was clever.

The only drawback to our securing a piece of National Mall real estate was that it was a much bigger space than the Capitol steps, where we had originally hoped to hold the event. As James pointed out, 50,000 marchers on the Capitol steps looked like half a million. Fifty thousand on the mall looked like a backyard barbecue on a rainy afternoon. Now we had a venue, but we would also have to put our money where our mouths were and deliver the marchers.

Until this point, I never actually worried about getting a million people there. Give or take 200,000, I thought, and we'd be a huge success. But now that I knew where we'd gather, I became paralyzed by the number. Even the great marches of the Civil Rights era maxed out at around 250,000 people, and this was the watermark number by which the media would measure our success. If we did attract only 50,000 or fewer, our march would be branded a failure. But even among our ardent supporters in the gun-control movement, the common wisdom held that we'd be hard-pressed to reach 250,000. "It's like pushing a boulder up a mountain," one gun-control activist explained to me, and he was right. In order to push that boulder up the mountain, we needed bodies—and lots of them.

So I began to make lists. I made lists of those people who I believed would be interested in marching with us and who could be counted on to bring large numbers of people. Knowing that we had the PTA, I figured that the next logical source for marchers would be teachers. If what the Department of Education estimates is true—that 3,523 students were expelled for bringing guns into school during the 1998–1999 school year (and that just counts those kids who were caught), then I was sure teachers would want to be part of this crusade.

When I called the National Education Association in Washington, D.C., to talk with the president, Bob Chase, I was told to schedule a conversation with him through a woman named Isabelle Rodriguez. Ms. Rodriguez was very enthusiastic with me, and she mentioned to me that she had planned and organized several events on the mall, including one for the Children's Defense Fund and the other for Cancer Research. (This was before she took the job with the National Education Association.)

A light when off in my head, and I asked her if she happened to know a woman named Isabelle Tapia, who was well-known for organizing similar events, but who was impossible to find. "I am Isabelle Tapia," she replied, explaining that she'd begun using her maiden name after a divorce. I couldn't believe my luck; here I had been searching high and low for Isabelle Tapia for months! And now I had her on the phone!

Though she was utterly sympathetic to our cause, Isabelle told me that she was unable to help us, even as a consultant. And her reasons were very sound: Both the "Stand for Children" and cancer-research marches had budgets of several million dollars, and even then they had each attracted fewer than 150,000 people. She pointed out that the stress and difficulties of producing even a well-funded event were enormous, and that she just couldn't imagine pulling it off with little funding. Of course, I completely understood her reasons for declining to help us, but I would be lying if I didn't say I was disappointed. We hung up, and I consoled myself with the fact that I had at least finally found Isabelle Tapia. But that wouldn't be the last I'd hear from her. After she had checked out our Web site, Isabelle Tapia—now Isabelle Rodriguez—called me back. "It's very earthy," she said. "Let me give it some thought." Ultimately, she liked what she saw, and she wanted in.

Slowly, my confidence was beginning to build, and I felt like the boulder had inched up the mountain some. We had our permit and our place to gather, and now we had our event organizer on board. I took the time to send out an e-mail to the grassroots, thanking all of the volunteers for their hard work so far. I also asked them to *please* rest and take some time off for the holidays. At that point, we had hundreds of marchers signed up, and about 25 of those were working full-time as volunteers. They were working at such a feverish pitch that I feared they'd burn themselves out, and we still had 6 months to go. And I, myself, needed the break. The holidays were on top of me, and I hadn't shopped. Family life filled up most of my December: first Hanukkah and then the midterm graduation of my youngest stepson, Greg, from the University of Wisconsin. Jeff, the girls, and I flew to Madison for the ceremony. I was tempted to call Stephanie Spicer, our Wisconsin state coordinator, while I was there but then thought better of it. This was family time, so the only MMM work I did was to leave a stack of "Save the Date" postcards in every ladies' room from Newark International Airport in New Jersey to Madison, Wisconsin. I wondered, like someone putting a note in a bottle and sending it off to sea, would anybody find them and pick one up?

After Greg's graduation, we celebrated Christmas like we always do with a party at our house for our Jewish friends and family. Even work was easy. The Monday after Christmas, December 26, the *Late Show* was in repeats. I drove into the city for work anyway to catch up on some odds and ends.

Jeff called that morning and asked me to meet him for lunch, which was odd because we rarely met for meals when we were both in the city. There was something he needed to tell me, he said. Couldn't it wait until we got home? No, he wanted to meet me in a public place. He had just had some cardio tests done, and I remember asking him, "Are you alright? Is it your heart?" He was fine, he said. I had no idea that, over lunch at an Applebee's diner in midtown, it would be my heart that would stop.

Cutting straight through any small talk, Jeff looked me in the eye and told me he wanted to end our marriage. I was stunned. Like all married couples, we had had our rough times, but things had never gotten so bad that I thought divorce would ever be an option, at least not for me, as I was madly in love with my handsome husband. While I tried to absorb what he had just said, he explained that he had made this decision back in September, just when the Million Mom March was beginning to jell and right around the time I pulled the plug on our moving back into the city.

But I didn't want to live near the World Trade Center, I tried to explain. Then he said it was the birthday cake. That stupid cake! I'll do better, I promised. Then he said it was because I hadn't shown enough concern when he had been sick a few months back. Maybe I had been neglectful.

I remember excusing myself at one point to go to the ladies' room, where I piled some MMM postcards on the vanity by the sink after washing up. I was acting on autopilot, or maybe I was in shock. Or maybe this was a sign that the march had taken over too much of my life and was the cause of this. As soon as I got back to the table, Jeff told me he was ready to leave. I left that diner shaken and numb. I went back to the quiet of the tiny office I had at the Ed Sullivan Theatre and tried to take all of this in.

I can't explain why, but for some reason, I did not immediately share this bombshell with my oldest friends or anyone in my family. The only people I confided in were my new Million Mom March friends, the people I'd become so close to, the women I felt really understood what I was trying to do, or more accurately, what we were trying to do together. Gail Powers was the most supportive: She and her husband, John, separated briefly after the JCC shooting, she told me. They got some counseling, and now she felt their marriage was stronger than ever. Her words made me feel hopeful that Jeff and I might be able to weather this, too.

I got through the rest of the holidays, alternating between states of shock and denial. The other three stages of grief—anger, sadness, and acceptance—were not far behind. Jeff, on the other hand, had the demeanor of someone who couldn't wait to register with www.matchmaker.com. He was whistling. He was smiling. This was not encouraging.

There is never an ideal time to go through a divorce, but I felt that this ranked right up there with being dumped after finding out you were pregnant, and in a sense I was experiencing some of the same roller-coaster emotions that come with pregnancy. The march was growing, and I was undeniably the woman carrying it to term. Now, more than ever, I needed to be nurtured and loved, too.

I don't know if it is the same phenomenon that happens when you buy a car and then you see the same model and color on the road everywhere, but at this time, I started to notice that many of the shootings I read about in the newspapers had something to do with divorce: "Estranged Husband Shoots Wife, Then Himself." There's nothing worse than the threat of divorce to make one feel out of control, I thought. And when some people feel out of control, they reach for their guns. Thank God we didn't have a gun in our house. I may have used it on myself.

Divorced people are three times as likely to commit suicide as people who are married, a study by the National Institute for Healthcare Research in Rockville, Maryland, indicated. The study further showed that divorce ranks as the number one factor linked with suicide rates in major U.S. cities, ranking above all other physical, financial, and psychological factors. I wondered why the surgeon general did not put a warning label on guns. This product may be hazardous to your health. I thought maybe he should also be making public service announcements warning people to lock up their guns during the holidays and other times when depression may strike.

——————

Aside from divorce, the other trigger for many suicides is clinical depression. Columbine—and all of the other recent school shootings—were linked to depression, according to a study conducted by the Secret Service after the Littleton massacre. Instead of just being a self-contained suicide—enough of a tragedy—these school shootings added homicide to the mix, becoming an outrageous sin. Rarely is a single suicide publicized, unless the suicide is in a public place, and even more rarely does it make the national news—unless it involves a public figure. Such was the case for one Columbine mother. Anne Marie Hochhalter was shot by the Columbine killers and was left paralyzed and in chronic, excruciating pain. Six months after her daughter's shooting, 48-year-old Carla June Hochhalter walked into a suburban Denver pawnshop, asked to see a revolver, loaded it with bullets, then killed herself right there in the store—in front of half a dozen people. Sadly, this great tragedy probably would not have even made the news if it weren't linked to the Columbine massacre in such a horrendously intimate way.

Suicide is rarely spoken about, and I knew this to be true, as I never would have learned of my aunt's suicide if I hadn't overheard the whispers of her sisters—including my mother—when they thought we kids were out of earshot. The theory was that my aunt, who was suffering from a severe postpartum depression after the birth of her fourth child, sent her three oldest children, ages 3, 4, and 6, outside to wait for the ice-cream truck. With her 6-week-old tucked away in the bassinet, my aunt took a loaded revolver out of the top dresser drawer, wrapped a baby's blanket around her head, lay down on her bed, put the gun to her temple, and pulled the trigger. Her 6-year-old daughter found her dead. She left four children under the age of 6 motherless and many other people grief-stricken for years. Everyone tried to find something to blame my aunt Margaret's death on, but nobody ever blamed the presence of a gun.

I spent the rest of the holidays walking on eggshells in my own home, with my own husband, not sure what the next steps were. He apparently had already talked to the attorney who had handled his previous two divorces. I, on the other hand, didn't know what to do. I once heard that the pain one feels during the death of a marriage is similar to that of losing a child. Until divorce hit me, I could not imagine the correlation. But as a friend who had been through both explained, when a child dies, the friends and family surround the mother to comfort her on her loss. When a husband leaves a wife, the friends and family—never imagining the magnitude of her pain—dial up their single women friends to set the bastard up.

If I could have gotten away with it, I would have spent the next few months in bed with the covers over my head. The depression that followed the shock and denial of my pending divorce started to kick in right after the first of the year, and I was barely able to function.

My husband and I went through the motions of celebrating New Year's Eve with family. I had to beg him not to break the news to his sons until a few days after. This was the celebration of the new millennium, and I didn't want them to always remember it as the day their dad left yet another wife. This was also the New Year's Eve when the gun nuts were predicting all hell would break loose and Armageddon would arrive. If I could have gotten away with it, I would have handed over the march to someone in more stable emotional shape than I was feeling. But the demands of the kids and the demands of the march required that I somehow pull myself up by my bootstraps, and, despite the terrible pain, keep going. I finally broke down and told my sister-in-law Susan about Jeff's decision. It seems funny now, but she told me to get a good lawyer and a good accountant—the same advice she gave me when I called her about the March.

Rene, our mom in Kentucky and keeper of the gun-nut mail, helped me through the rough days by sending me what she referred to as the "love letters" we were getting from the gun nuts. One such letter blamed school shootings on "them lesbian shows like *Mad About You.*" I don't know why that one made me laugh so hard. Another favorite was the one from the guy who wrote directly to Annie, my database assistant. Annie was trying to sell some antique shoes on eBay. She included a link to the Million Mom March Web site with her shoes. She then received a note that said, "We never should have let you silly bitches wear shoes, much less vote!"

James Day confirmed our space on the National Mall, but I was expected to meet with the National Park Police at their office in Washington, D.C., on January 6. This was a day when I would exchange the surreal world of an impending divorce for the equally strange world of planning the physical, logistical, and organizational aspects of a national march. In truth, I appreciated the chance to take my mind off my marriage for a while.

I took the 5:53 A.M. train from Metropark, New Jersey, to Union Station in Washington, D.C.

I had a full day planned, as I tried to pack in as much as possible so I wouldn't have to leave the kids again soon. The first stop was the National Conference of Mayors, a group, it turns out, that was absolutely giddy with support for the Million Mom March. The mayors had been waiting for this kind of movement, this kind of groundswell of support for gun control, because their cities were bearing the brunt of the costs of so much gun violence.

Gun violence costs the United States approximately $100 billion annually, according to a Packard Foundation estimate, and America's cities and America's taxpayers bear most of this burden. The Conference of Mayors offered to lend us their Wall of Death banner to use as a backdrop, which was, I'm sorry to say, as depressing as it sounds. Like the Vietnam Memorial, it lists all of the people murdered in U.S. cities in 1 year due to gun violence. The Wall of Death for 1999 included 4,001 names of the approximately 30,000 people killed by a gun (never mind the legions injured or maimed) that year. I was honored to accept the Wall of Death banner on behalf of our group, and I assured the mayors that we would display it on Mother's Day.

My next meeting was with the National Park Police. This was a critical meeting, because they would lay down the rules for what we could and could not do on Mother's Day. The detail I remember most was that the National Park Police informed me that we would need to provide one portable toilet for every 300 expected attendees. I made a mental note to be sure that we would not only meet the permit requirements, but we would exceed them, since most of our marchers would be women, many with children in tow. The National Park Police were polite and patient with my many questions, such as "Where will we park our buses?" This question was particularly crucial to those in the grassroots who were in charge of hiring and filling buses across the country. The police understood that this was a top-priority concern, and they promised to let us know as soon as possible where we would be able to park.

A reputable trigger-lock company had been asking if we would hand out trigger locks at the march. I asked the National Park Police if this was something we could do. Absolutely not, was the reply; this was a free-speech event and not a product-promotion event.

I looked around the conference table at all these serious yet kind faces. These guys had managed so many marches over the years. Who in this room, I wondered, had met Martin Luther King Jr.? Did Dr. King have to worry about such trivial details as where we could sell our T-shirts? I had a cheap camera in my pocket, and I wanted to take a picture, but I was too shy to ask these guys (and the EMS woman who was there) to pose for me. I was afraid it would make me look like an amateur. I was uplifted by my meeting with the Park Police because I knew that we were in good hands and that they would keep the MMM safe.

After another couple of meetings, I got on the train to head back to New Jersey. It had been a good day—the first in many.

The following Monday, my workday, would turn out to be absolutely nuts. First Lady Hillary Rodham Clinton was due to appear on the *Late Show.* This was a big coup for Dave because he had spent months browbeating the first lady on air, saying that she'd never be elected to the U.S. Senate from New York without first appearing on his show. Rudy Giuliani, who was assumed to be running for the seat at the time, was a frequent guest, but Mrs. Clinton kept refusing all of Dave's overtures, and her rejection became an ongoing gag.

That day, the greenroom was packed with Secret Service, and our conference room was packed with traveling press. While I was ordering pizza for them, a production assistant came and surprised me by saying Mrs. Clinton wanted to see me after the show. The Granada Hills moms had tried to recruit her a few weeks before when she went to the North Valley Jewish Community Center to read a book to the children still traumatized by the Buford Furrow shooting. But, according to the moms, she was initially cool to the idea. Maybe she had changed her mind. Maybe she had seen one of the MMM postcards I had Michele, the *Late Show* makeup artist, tape on all of the mirrors in the dressing rooms, and this had piqued her interest in us. After the show, she came up to me, took my hand, and whispered, "I spoke with Susan this morning. I'm so sorry." She didn't add it, but I knew she was referring to my husband and me. Then she gave me one of those knowing "been there" looks. I had been in a state of shock and denial for weeks about the state of my marriage, and now here was the first lady of the United States feeling my pain. And she was sincere. She was also funny and turned out to be a big hit on the show.

I had to run back upstairs to my office to go do what I do, which was publicize her appearance to the media for that night's local news and the day's newspapers. She had really knocked the audience over during a bit where Dave, to see if she was really qualified to be a U.S. Senator from the State of New York or if she was just a carpetbagger, gave her a pop quiz.

Dave: What is the New York State bird?

First Lady: Uh, the bluebird?

Dave: What is the New York State tree?

First Lady: Uh, the sugar maple?

Dave: How many counties are in New York State?

First Lady: 62!

Dave: New York State borders which of the Great Lakes?

First Lady: Ontario and Erie!!

And although she answered correctly to all of the above, the real trick question was about to come (drumbeat, please) . . .

Dave: In New York City, who is thought of, with equal measures of fear and reverence, as "The Big Man"?

If the first lady seemed a little shaky on the other questions, she answered this one with complete confidence. She looked at the audience and delivered the punch line without missing a beat.

First Lady: Dave Letterman!

The audience roared. They loved her. Whoever didn't like Mrs. Clinton before was now in love—including David Letterman. But back in the conference room, the traveling press corps was not amused. I was barraged with questions, including whether or not Mrs. Clinton had been prepped before Dave's pop quiz. This was a comedy show, I said, trying to calm them down. But they wouldn't take a nonanswer for an answer, so I went to Rob Burnett, the executive producer, and asked him. No, Rob answered, she wasn't exactly given the answers. I must have glossed over the word, *exactly.* I just needed a straight yes or no. No, he said more firmly, she was not given the answers. She in fact knew the answer to every question about New York State on her own. And that is what I told the *New York Times.*

What he failed to tell me, unfortunately, was that she may have received a hint or two back in her dressing room before the show.

The next day, Bluebird-Gate broke. I was quizzed by an outraged press as though I'd been involved in a cover-up. What Did the First Lady Know about the State Bird and When Did She Know It? I kept pleading with them: This is a comedy show! But the press was relentless. I feel bad saying this, but when Dave went in for open-heart surgery the next day, he swept the bluebird controversy from the headlines. I was relieved. I was too busy with the Million Mom March to worry about such trivia.

Ironically, prior to Bluebird-Gate, I was one of the publicists who pumped out press releases on the Clintons' missteps during the 1992 presidential campaign because some of those gaffes were reported first or "exclusively" on *CBS News*. I am ashamed to admit that now—how gutter level even network news publicity can get.

I was one of the publicists on duty the night the president and Mrs. Clinton gave the explosive Gennifer Flowers interview on *60 Minutes*, a CBS show; ditto the day he admitted smoking—but not inhaling—marijuana. Other than these nonencounters, I had no relationship at all with the Clintons. I didn't even vote for the man in 1992. And despite their relationship to my sister-in-law, I wasn't sure if the Clintons would ever support us publicly. In hindsight, I should have put out a one-page press release outlining this, just to get the NRA off my back.

The NRA's absurdity didn't stop me from trying to get the Clintons to notice us, however. I once managed to get in the president's line of sight at an event at a Times Square theatre in 1999, where I waved a letter from 4-year-old Nathan Powers, a camper from the JCC in Granada Hills, asking the president for his help in keeping guns out of the hands of bad guys. From the president's brief reaction, I understood that he got the issue—especially since he had signed the Brady law and the 10-year Assault Weapons Ban in 1994.

I remembered the shooting that spurred the debate that assault weapons should be banned. I was at *CBS News* at the time. It was January 17, 1989—when Patrick Purdy bought an AK-47 assault rifle over the counter of a local store. He then went to Cleveland Elementary in Stock, California, and began randomly shooting at kids while they sat at their desks. He killed five students (all of them between 6 and 9 years of age) and then calmly walked back outside and let loose with the AK-47. Survivors say he was firing the weapon in wide swoops, in all directions, which would cause maximum carnage. After firing more than 130 shots from the automatic rifle, Purdy pulled a handgun from his waistband and blew his own head off.

This entire incident lasted only 2 minutes, but in that time, Purdy killed five kids and injured 29 others. By the time Congress passed the bills that this shooting prompted, it was 5 years later, and I was the preoccupied mother of a newborn.

But I had little recollection of President Clinton's brave and important stance on gun control when I took on the Million Mom March. At my first gun-control conference, after listening to presidential aide

Deanne Benos list the president's past accomplishments, I demanded—rather loudly—to know what he was going to do now to keep guns out of our children's hands. After the conference was over, a few of the seasoned gun-control advocates gave me a tongue-lashing and educated me to the fact that President Clinton was one of the few U.S. presidents to stand up to the gun lobby in a meaningful way.

I wrote Deanne Benos and apologized profusely for my rudeness. But not knowing when to leave well enough alone, I then asked again: What more is the president going to do for us moms? Telling us what the president did in 1994 was a bit like telling my hungry kids at dinnertime to go away because I fed them at breakfast. We moms were scared. Kids were killing kids. What was he going to do? What about licensing? What about registration? What about childproofing guns?

Two weeks after Bluebird-Gate, I turned on the State of the Union address not really expecting much in the way of new announcements on gun policy. But I had my fingers crossed. When Clinton began to speak about gun control, I almost fell off the sofa.

President Clinton: Soon after the Columbine tragedy, Congress considered commonsense gun legislation, to require Brady background checks at the gun shows, child-safety locks for new handguns, and a ban on the importation of large-capacity ammunition clips. With courage—and a tie-breaking vote by the vice president—(*applause*)—the Senate faced down the gun lobby, stood up for the American people, and passed this legislation. But the House failed to follow suit.

Now we have all seen what happens when guns fall into the wrong hands. Daniel Mauser was only 15 years old when he was gunned down at Columbine. He was an amazing kid—a straight-A student, a good skier. Like all parents who lose their children, his father, Tom, has borne unimaginable grief. Somehow he has found the strength to honor his son by transforming his grief into action. Earlier this month, he took a leave of absence from his job to fight for tougher gun-safety laws. I pray that his courage and wisdom will at long last move this Congress to make commonsense gun legislation the very next order of business. (*applause*)

Tom Mauser, stand up. We thank you for being here tonight. (*applause*)

I had never heard of Tom Mauser and made a note to track him down.

President Clinton: We must strengthen our gun laws and enforce those already on the books better. (*applause*) Federal gun-crime prosecutions are up 16 percent since I took office. But we must do more. I propose to hire more federal and local gun prosecutors and more ATF agents to crack down on illegal gun traffickers and bad-apple dealers. And we must give them the enforcement tools that they need, tools to trace every gun and every bullet used in every gun crime in the United States. I ask you to help us do that. (*applause*)

Okay. How about licensing and registration?

President Clinton: Every state in this country already requires hunters and automobile drivers to have a license. I think they ought to do the same thing for handgun purchases. (*applause*) Now, specifically, I propose a plan to ensure that all new handgun buyers must first have a photo license from their state showing they passed the Brady background check and a gun-safety course before they get the gun. I hope you'll help me pass that in this Congress. (*applause*)

This was big. Although the president failed to mention registration, the noir dire of gun control, licensing for handgun owners is a major policy proposal in a country where guns are easier to buy than Big Macs.

President Clinton: Listen to this—listen to this.

I'm listening!

President Clinton: The accidental gun rate—the accidental gun-death rate of children under 15 in the United States is nine times higher than in the other 25 industrialized countries combined. Now, technologies exist that could lead to guns that can only be fired by the adults who own them. I ask Congress to fund research into smart-gun technology to save these children's lives. (*applause*) I ask responsible leaders in the gun industry to work with us on smart guns and other steps to keep guns out of the wrong hands, to keep our children safe.

This was a home run. The smart-gun legislation was exactly what Ceasefire New Jersey was proposing for childproofing guns. I wanted to kiss the TV.

Despite my state of marital depression, I was uplifted by the president's speech and energized to march on. I was sure the rest of the world of gun-control advocates felt the same way. WRONG! The next day, those cranky folks over at the Violence Policy Center criticized the president's speech, saying that licensing would not reduce gun violence (the theory being that people still get killed in automobile accidents despite drivers having to be licensed). Sure, but can you imagine how crazy the roads would be if we didn't require licensing?

To make matters worse, the extremist view of banning and nothing short of that even began to gain some favor within our own group—especially among the always-helpful 151s. No wonder it has been so difficult to get commonsense gun legislation passed, I thought, when even gun-control advocates lose sight of achievable goals.

———

Somewhere in the middle of this Million Mom March trimester, Jeff changed his mind and decided not to move out. He decided instead to stay in the house—indefinitely—for the sake of the girls. And I was grateful. To make life easier for both of us, I would find any excuse to travel so that we wouldn't bump into each other—or worse. I was hurting badly, and I didn't want to lash out at him. I wanted him to stay, but I knew I had to give him as much space as possible at the same time.

First chance I got, I hopped on a plane to California to meet with some potential donors, and when Gail Powers heard I was coming, she insisted on picking me up at LAX at 11:00 P.M. She also insisted that I stay with her. We'd become so close, Gail and I, it was hard to believe this was our first face-to-face encounter, and we embraced like old, dear friends.

We had never discussed the day at the JCC. And I never asked. But now Gail gave me a tour of the JCC and a blow-by-blow account of the worst day of her life.

"I'd just gotten my hair cut. I was driving down Devonshire and had to pull over three times for fire trucks," she began. "And I thought, 'that must be one helluva fire.' When I got home, my ex-brother-in-law telephoned me, saying, 'Did you hear about the shooting?' And I said, 'Where'?"

Gail drove me down Devonshire Boulevard. "It was right here that I saw the helicopters. I'm not sure when I stopped stopping for red lights and began running them. I kept praying, 'Oh please, God. Don't let anybody be dead.'"

Gail pointed to where she thinks she parked the car and got out to run. We pulled up to the JCC, and she showed me where the police tape blocked the entrance. "Moms and dads were hysterical, talking on cell phones, arguing with the police. 'Ma'am, you're just going to have to wait behind the line like everyone else, they told us.'"

Her heart was pounding, she said. She was frantic, not knowing if her son was one of the children hurt. Hysterical, Gail was led to a stranger's house where she watched her son, Nathan, on television as he was led away to safety by the police.

Gail then brought me inside the JCC to show me around. She showed me the room where Nathan sat listening to his teacher read a book on dinosaurs, until the sound of gunshots and smoke seeping into their classroom interrupted them. "Run! Run! Run!" his teacher had yelled to her class.

Gail introduced me to the school receptionist, Isabelle, who was one of the five people shot that day. Isabelle seemed still in shock almost 5 months after the shooting. It was just more evidence that living with the posttraumatic stress of a shooting incident is just one more burden that survivors of gun violence must bear.

That evening, I met other women whose children were victims of the Granada Hills shooting. I met Loren Leib, whose 6-year-old son, Joshua, was struck in the leg by a bullet. And I met Loren's new best friend, Donna Finkelstein, the mother of Mindy Finkelstein, the camp counselor who had been shot while leading her campers back into the JCC.

Donna told me her daughter's story. It was a warm August day, and 16-year-old Mindy, a camp counselor at the North Valley Jewish Community Center, was bringing one of her campers, 6-year-old James Zidell, back into the building after playing outdoors. Just as they were entering the building, Mindy was shot. As two bullets pierced her legs, Mindy managed to shield young James from harm. Mindy, the first to be shot, lay in agony as she heard more than 70 more shots ring out. She never saw her shooter's face.

Mindy's physical recovery was quick, but she does have permanent nerve damage in part of her leg. But the emotional toll was heavy. She would wake in the middle of the night sometimes, crying out in pain, her legs afire.

Then Loren talked a little about her son, Joshua, who was injured, too.

These women had taken on the task of raising money to help get financially challenged families to Washington, D.C. They had become activists when they found themselves part of a special community, the community no one ever wants to belong to—that made up of gun-violence survivors.

The rest of my trip to California included a very "Hollywood" agenda, as the support we were beginning to build in the entertainment industry was growing by leaps and bounds. I had the chance to meet with Marta Kaufman, producer of the hit sitcom *Friends*. Marta had heard of the march from her friend Daena, wife of actor Jason Alexander. Daena had heard of the march from a friend in Montclair, New Jersey. We were truly expanding by word of e-mail and by word of mouth. I also had lunch at Melissa Manchester's house, where she sang the song she wanted to perform on stage on Mother's Day. Isabelle would not let me make a commitment to anyone about stage time, but I did a naughty thing and asked Melissa to perform anyway. These experiences were wonderful—and encouraging—but I left California a changed person after having met Gail, Donna, and Loren—three of the most pulled-together women I would know.

A couple of months later, I would meet another Granada Hills mom, who's son Ben Kadish was the most seriously wounded among the children shot. Ben was only five at the time, and the fact of his young age touched a group of parents an ocean away. I hadn't heard of the Dunblane, Scotland, massacre until I received an e-mail from Emily Crozier's dad soon after my California trip. Emily was a 5-year-old kindergartener when a man armed with four handguns and 743 rounds of ammunition walked into a school gymnasium in Dunblane on March 13, 1996. Without warning, he opened fire on Emily's kindergarten class, and in a few short minutes, the teacher and 16 of Emily's classmates were dead and another 17 were wounded.

Rebecca Peters gave me a CD by a Dunblane musician named Ted Christopher who had convinced Bob Dylan to let him record a new version of the classic, "Knockin' on Heaven's Door," in memory of the

Dunblane school children. I would pop the CD into the CD player in my minivan every time I felt frustrated by either the gun nuts or the 151s. And that version of "Knockin' on Heaven's Door," as well as Christopher's song, "Throw These Guns Away"—a tribute to the slain kids—became anthems of sorts, for me and, I think, many in our movement. Ted Christopher offered to come to the states to play on the National Mall, and I thought it would be powerful to have him there with us, along with some of the Dunblane families. We did not have the funds to fly these people in, so I asked Alison, in Montclair, New Jersey, to see if she could somehow wangle free airfare for us. I wasn't terribly hopeful, but it was worth a try.

By now, we were seriously beginning to outgrow the national office of the MMM, which was in my New Jersey basement. I made the trek to Washington, D.C., in search of more suitable temporary office space, while Isabelle, our event-planning consultant, began searching for a management team to oversee the event. When I was in Washington, Isabelle interviewed three teams, but we both knew there was really only one choice, so we hired Jasculca/Terman, a Chicago-based firm. (The other two companies were D.C.-based and seemed too jaded to believe this kind of event would attract a decent crowd.) Rick Jasculca flew in from Chicago, and we were immediately won over by his bright Midwestern sensibilities. At last, we had a crack team in Isabelle Rodriguez, James Day, and Jasculca/Terman working to make this thing happen.

For every angel like Rick, Isabelle, and James, there seemed to be a dozen gun nuts stalking us. I remember one "love note" in particular, and it was the most disgusting thing I'd seen yet. The sender had actually pleasured himself into the letter. I didn't know what to do with it: It didn't qualify for the FBI pile, and it sure wasn't something I was going to hold onto. So I tossed it. But it seemed like every time I threw away one of these letters, another would come in the mail. Between the gun nuts and the 151s, I wasn't sure who I dreaded hearing from more.

In February, 2000, the 151s tried to stage a coup and get me thrown out of the role as chief coordinator of the MMM. They complained that I was not representing the best interest of the moms when I used our grant money to hire professional event planners. I kept trying to explain that it wasn't my money to spend. They didn't seem to understand that

PROFILE | Carole Price

f you think it's hard to ask people if they keep a gun in their home, consider this: It's much more difficult to select a casket for your child." Carole Price learned this lesson in the most devastating way when her oldest son, 13-year-old John, was shot and killed by a next-door neighbor.

More than 40 percent of American homes with children have guns, and too many of those guns are unlocked, loaded, and within easy reach of a child's hand. Every year, thousands of children are injured or die from weapons found in the home.

When I met Carole Price in Bethesda, I was immediately struck by her poise and passion. Carole has a beautiful, heart-shaped face and body piercings and tattoos. She has a down-to-earth nature and a natural charisma that draws people to her. By the time I met her, I thought I'd heard just about every kind of tragic story there was, but Carole's ordeal shook me to my core. On August 20, 1998, Carole's son John went next door to play with his friend. But before he did, he playfully ruffled his mother's hair and told her that he loved her. They were very close, Carole and John. Carole recalls watching him through the window, admiring her strong, lovable boy, and she remembers that he turned and blew her a kiss. That was the last time Carole saw her son alive.

Twenty minutes later, the police knocked on her door. While John was watching television, his friend's 9-year-old brother took a 9mm handgun from an upstairs bedroom, and in the process of showing it off, he pulled the trigger. The bullet struck John in the face and killed him instantly.

Carole and her husband, John, are raising their two surviving children while they grapple with their grief over losing their son in such a senseless way. "Every day of your life you wake up and feel the grief." John says. "And the sad part is that, as a parent, you normally can fix things, but there's nothing in the world we can do to fix this." Despite her initial reluctance, Carole took over the helm of the Maryland chapter of the Million Mom March and has worked tirelessly since, helping the group Marylanders Against Handgun Abuse pass the toughest childproof handgun bill in the nation. She also served as honorary chairperson for the ASK Campaign (Asking Saves Kids) through the organization PAX—Real Solutions to Gun Violence.

"My home was safe," Carole says. "So I assumed this was the case in the neighbor's house where John went to play. Since this tragic day, I have dedicated myself to encouraging parents to ask the question: 'Is there a gun in the home where my child plays?'"

our money came from a foundation and that the allocation of every dollar we got was overseen by the Bell Campaign, our fiscal sponsor. But the moms should have first crack at these highly specialized jobs, they ranted. But no moms within our ranks had ever put together an event of this size. To appease the 151s, I found them some temporary office space in the offices of the Coalition to Stop Gun Violence. Mike Beard, one of the kindest people in the movement and head of that group, even gave us a desk and a phone. I even offered to buy them a computer and asked that they just let me know what kind they wanted. I watched, bemused, as e-mails went back and forth furiously for 3 weeks as they argued among themselves about whether they should go with an Apple or a PC. In the end, they never did make a decision.

While the 151s were busy arguing over what kind of computer to buy, I was able to provide some solid answers for the grassroots volunteers. But there were many questions that I still couldn't answer, and they came at me like a barrage of friendly fire: When was the march to start? I didn't know. Where would we march? I wasn't sure. Would there be entertainment? Yes, but since we didn't have a budget to bring entertainment to Washington, it was still unclear who would appear.

The one question that continued to plague me—and the one that was asked literally every day—was "What about Rosie?" Her daytime talk show was hugely popular, and her influence was widespread among our moms. Rosie would be a natural, but, as we knew, nothing worthwhile ever came easily. Back in December, Elise Richman had caught Rosie's attention with the tragic story of her father's murder, but in the eleventh hour, Elise had to cancel her appearance on the show because her bosses thought it was too controversial. The producers of the show were not happy. And they vowed that we would not get another shot at the show until we "got our acts together." I wasn't sure if that day would ever come.

I was still doing most of the media interviews, sharing as much of this work as possible with Gail Powers, Dana Quist, the Bell Campaign's president, Mary Leigh Blek, and a few others. I had long given up on the possibility of a celebrity spokesmom, realizing that the press really liked talking to moms who were not overly coached and who were clearly sincere. But we still did not have a "real voice" of the Million Mom March, and I felt we needed one.

During one of my many treks to Washington, I would attend a local

Million Mom March meeting. They were popping up all over the Beltway. Jane Vandenburgh, one of the D.C. local coordinators, convinced me to attend a meeting in nearby Bethesda, Maryland, and it was there that I found the voice of the Million Mom March, at least for the next few months.

I was introduced to John and Carole Price at an MMM meeting, a loving couple and the parents of three who'd lost their oldest boy to a gun that was left unlocked and loaded in a neighbor's house. Carole, a beautiful, brilliant bartender with a quick wit, didn't say much at this meeting and seemed reluctant to join us, but we bonded in the ladies' room after lunch that day. I was taping MMM postcards to the bathroom mirrors, and Carol saw my zeal and agreed to jump in—with both feet. Post fliers? She could do that, she said. Within a few months, she became our highest-profile spokesmom.

> "As bad as it hurts,
> you have to keep pushing,
> and remember that the
> end result is worth all
> of the pain."
>
> —CONNIE RUCKER,
> VOLUNTEER COORDINATOR,
> HANDGUN CONTROL INC.

Movements, like babies, are rarely born without any help. And the bigger the baby, the more help is needed to guide it through the birth canal. The Civil Rights movement didn't just happen because Rosa Parks refused to give up her seat on the bus: The NAACP, religious and political leaders, and other African-American organizations helped set the stage. But it takes a Rosa Parks to ignite the fire of passion that only flickers within most of us and to marshal the forces to bring an issue to life.

Because there are so many external—and sinister—forces that wish to strangle the gun-control movement with its own umbilical cord, many midwives are needed to keep it alive. To me, Sarah Brady is the mother of the movement, but a woman by the name of Dorothy McGann is one of the more notable midwives.

Dorothy, now 76 years old, was outraged in the 1980s by the increase in the epidemic of bloody gun massacres that seemed to be raging across the country. One day she decided she simply couldn't—and wouldn't—stand for it any longer. Dorothy convinced her husband, John, to help her set up a card table outside a Montclair supermarket, and 5 hours later, they had collected 725 signatures of outraged citizens who sought to ban assault weapons. Dorothy didn't stop there. She joined a small group of ministers, including the Reverend Jack Johnson, founder of New Jersey Citizens to Stop Gun Violence (now called Ceasefire, New Jersey), and as a team, they succeeded in making New Jersey one of the first states to ban assault weapons when Governor Jim Florio signed the ban into law in 1991.

In the early 1990s, Governor Florio was among the few brave elected officials in this country who took a stand against gun violence. The NRA allegedly retaliated by financing a soft-money campaign that generated anger and resentment over the Governor's unpopular property-tax hike. Governor Florio may have been defeated because of his courageous act, but the state of New Jersey is now one of the safest in the country, thanks to his courage. New Jersey's and California's stance against assault weapons were instrumental in bringing about the federal ban on assault weapons that President Clinton enacted in 1994. But that ban automatically expires in September 2004—unless Congress renews it.

Dorothy did not rest on her laurels. When a tragic postal shooting in Montclair rocked not only her community but the entire country in March 1995, she rolled up her sleeves and went back to work to help her grieving community. People were numb and in shock after a man by the name of Christopher Green, a former postal worker who was allegedly behind in his rent, killed four people and wounded another during a holdup at a Montclair post office. (The phrase "going postal" had already been coined at this time following what seemed to be an epidemic of shootings by postal workers in the 1980s and 1990s.)

While others may hear about these things and do nothing, Dorothy organized a community coalition to address gun violence at the most local level, including sponsoring essay-writing contests for local high-school students as a way to educate young people about the dangers of guns. Three years after the shooting, Dorothy was still chairing this coalition, which was the Montclair Chapter of Ceasefire, New Jersey.

I heard about Dorothy McGann right after our September launch from my friend Ann Brunett who lived in Montclair. Ann described Dorothy as one of those high-energy, can-do women. That was an understatement. I wanted to recruit Dorothy for the Million Mom March, so I invited her to attend my first Short Hills meeting at a local Starbucks. Instead of me recruiting Dorothy, she recruited us to work on Ceasefire, New Jersey's next initiative—passing the Childproof Handgun Bill, which would require so-called smart technology on all guns. As sensible as this legislation was, it was going nowhere fast. Many of the state legislators feared reprisal from the NRA and wouldn't touch the bill. New Jersey State Representative Loretta Weinstein and New Jersey Senators Dick Cody and Donald DiFrancesco were trying valiantly to finesse the bill through the New Jersey Statehouse, but the gun lobby successfully blocked it each step of the way.

Being in the trenches of a movement, particularly one as controversial as gun control, is hardly glamorous, and it can even at times be pretty ugly. But our midwives rolled up their sleeves and got to work—usually starting this "third shift" after their first two jobs (family and paying jobs) ended for the day. These moms would cook dinner, get their kids into bed, then log on to their computers and work on behalf of the MMM until long past midnight.

Dorothy was a model Million Mom midwife; she worked tirelessly to rally her community around the issue of gun control. She and my friend Ann—despite a 30-year age difference—became fast friends, and together they worked to organize a dozen buses and a train to Washington, D.C., for Mother's Day.

Isabelle Rodriguez, our event consultant, served as our event midwife, and she was clear with us that this would be no picnic. She had organized a huge event for Cancer Research that was underwritten by a $5 million grant from Michael Milken, the former financier who is himself a cancer survivor. What shocked even Isabelle, a seasoned pro, was the amount of in-fighting among the various cancer groups. The prostate-cancer folks feuded with the breast-cancer delegation, and the breast-cancer delegation duked it out with the colon-cancer contingent—mostly over who got what placement and publicity from the event. No matter how good the cause, Isabelle warned us, there will always be tension within the ranks. You can count on it, she said. Part of Isabelle's unofficial job description was to serve as referee among the various egos, including mine.

Getting everyone to play nice is more caregiver than midwife; however, our MMM fairy godmother, Rebecca Peters, deftly juggled her role as financial savior with that of babysitter by trying to encourage all of us kids to share our toys. This was no easy task, particularly because there were so many male egos (and a few females ones too) involved. Rebecca spoke a language that these men also spoke, and that was the language of money. She artfully dangled the notion that everybody would share in the wealth of the Million Mom March—not that we had any money. But if each group shared their resources with the Million Mom March, there would be a nice Soros-Diamond treat for everybody at the end of the day, in the form of a grant.

The promise of these grants gave birth to a steering committee that was made up of representatives from each of the major gun-control organizations involved. What turned these organizations around wasn't so much that they were finally taking us seriously; they took Rebecca and the Soros-Diamond money she sat on seriously.

Even Bob Walker from Handgun Control Inc. suddenly perked up about us. The first time all of the national gun-control groups gathered at the first steering committee meeting (all except the VPC, who didn't show), Andrew McGuire snapped a photo for posterity. He said this was the first time in years that he could remember the top person from every organization sitting down at the same table.

This was all because of Rebecca. It was Rebecca's vision to get each group to take ownership of the Million Mom March in order to ensure its success. Each group had something to bring to the table, particularly the Bell Campaign and PAX, the hippest group and one that would focus on getting celebrity involvement.

Together, these groups would pool their resources to produce the Million Mom March. The challenge for Rebecca was to get them all to focus on moving one piece of legislation. That was quite a challenge. I had already spoken to and polled these national organizations on what their long-term legislative priorities were. There wasn't a whole lot of consensus. So the founding moms narrowed 20 legislative proposals down to five.

1. Licensing of gun owners
2. Registration of guns
3. Childproofing handguns

4. A minimum 5-day cooling off period and background check on every gun sold
5. Limiting the sales of guns to one a month per buyer

That last one used to stump us moms. Wasn't one handgun a lifetime enough? But as it was explained to us by Eric Gorovitz of the Bell Campaign, this proposal would curb bulk sales by straw purchasers, thereby significantly cutting into the black market trade of guns.

The moms seemed comfortable with the easy five-point legislative agenda. But in one of the first meetings of the MMM steering committee, the group voted, somewhat reluctantly, to narrow this agenda even further to include only licensing and registration. Senator Dianne Feinstein was expected to introduce a bill addressing licensing and registration in the Senate, and the Million Mom March on Mother's Day 2000 would be the public muscle behind the bill. Even Senator Jack Reed of Rhode Island saw the moms as the troops preparing to land. Senator Reed is one of the unsung heroes of the movement, and he immediately glommed on to the Million Mom March. He introduced a bill to register guns, and set up a Web site exclusively for the bill. He even used our MMM logo on the site, as if it were the Good Housekeeping Seal of Approval. The moms loved that!

In the beginning, the Million Mom March steering committee worked beautifully together, with the Million Moms, the Bell Campaign, and PAX doing the lion's share of the work. Still smarting from Handgun Control Inc.'s initial aloofness and its blatant attempt to kill off our grant, I didn't ask them for much, except for use of their mailing list (which they declined) and to borrow staffer Connie Rucker full-time. Little did they know it then, but I really wanted Connie more than I wanted their mailing list—she was a master at motivating volunteers. Her worth reminded me of that MasterCard commercial: The HCI mailing list: Value, $12 million. Connie Rucker, volunteer motivator: Value, priceless.

The Coalition to Stop Gun Violence offered us office space in their already cramped quarters off K Street until we could find some space of our own. And we were already using a Coalition board member, the Reverend Jim Atwood, full-time. Reverend Atwood is a retired minister from Springfield, Virginia, who has worked with the Coalition since 1975, when one of his parishioners was shot and killed by a teen with a gun. His undying devotion to the cause and, subsequently, to the Million Mom March made him our first spiritual midwife.

I first met Reverend Atwood at the Coalition to Stop Gun Violence's Annual Citizens' Conference (the same conference where I made a fool of myself with President Clinton's aide Deanne Benos). When I wasn't busy embarrassing myself, I guess I was making a good impression on Reverend Jim, who came up to me during a coffee break and introduced himself. "This is one of the most exciting things I have ever heard of," he said of the Million Mom March. And then he did a dangerous thing—he volunteered to help in any way he could, not knowing the trap he'd just stepped into. I innocently asked him, "What would you like to do?" He replied, "I'd like to try to get the interfaith community involved." I immediately anointed him as the Million Mom March interfaith coordinator. I didn't know Jim from Adam, and he was quite surprised to be given this much trust.

The Reverend Jim is an avid hunter with a big booming voice. He proved that real men are true Million Mom Marchers, and he embraced the movement wholeheartedly. From his kitchen table, he stuffed 700 envelopes asking churches across America to endorse the Million Mom March.

There is so obvious a connection between spiritual faith and protecting our children's lives that, taking a cue from Reverend Jim, I made a strong effort to recruit representatives from all religions. I had gotten a call from Rabbi Marc Israel of the Religious Action Center, who was curious to know what we were up to. When we finally met, he was a tad reluctant to get involved—trying to rally the religious community can be an uphill, thankless job, he said, and I could believe it.

"And Saturday events always pose a problem for us," Rabbi Marc said, referring to the Orthodox Jewish communities that do not drive on the Sabbath. "This is on Mother's Day, a Sunday," I reminded him.

He finally agreed to put out a fax and e-mail alert to several dozen religious contacts of his in the D.C. area, including the representatives of other religious organizations. Once he'd heard back from nearly everyone—and they'd all agreed to attend a Million Mom March meeting—Rabbi Marc became energized. "We usually only get five or six people to show up for any given meeting," he explained. "For the record," he joked, "I was always on board with this idea."

Rabbi Marc's meeting was packed. From Episcopalians to the Islamic Communities, they were all there to hear about the Million Mom March, Mother's Day 2000. And, other than the date, I still had no details to give them except the fact that I needed their help in generating a crowd to prove that we were, in fact, stronger than the gun lobby. I handed out some materials hastily prepared for us by Physicians for Social Responsibility and by Elizabeth Miles of the Massachusetts state group, Stop Handgun Violence. I didn't have enough money in our budget to produce our own materials beyond our hot pink "Looking for a Few Good Moms" postcards. And I was amazed and eternally grateful when Elizabeth and this group of doctors dug into their own budgets and did this for us.

Many of those present at the Religious Action Center were there because of Columbine or because of the shootings at the Jewish Community Center in Granada Hills, California. A few came because of the shooting at the Fort Worth Baptist Church. And in just a few weeks, Sikhs would join the interfaith effort following a shooting at a temple in El Sobrante, California, just north of Berkeley in the East Bay area of San Francisco. A man walked into a service at a Sikh temple there and opened fire with an assault weapon, killing one person and wounding another after he had been denied the opportunity to address the worshipers. (He was told by temple officials there simply wasn't time during the service.)

Church shootings in America were not as uncommon as one would think—or hope. Just a few weeks before Columbine, four people were killed at a Baptist Church in Gonzales, Louisiana, a shooting I'd only learned about at the meeting at the Religious Action Center. But I was familiar with Gonzales, a town I'd driven through many times on my way from New Orleans to LSU in Baton Rouge.

The pastor that day had just started reading a Bible lesson about being born again when the gunman kicked open the doors, fired twice into the ceiling, and ordered everybody to hit the floor. He then marched down the aisle, shooting between the benches as screaming parishioners scattered in horror. The shooter paused once to calmly reload. Among the crowd, police said, were the man's own wife and child.

According to news reports, his little son turned and said, "Daddy?" Then his father shot the boy and his mother before turning to shoot another parishioner in the back of the head. He killed all three. Four others were injured during the rampage, two critically. Apparently the shooter also killed his mother-in-law at home before traveling the few blocks to the one-story stucco church 20 miles southeast of Baton Rouge.

The most highly publicized (but since forgotten) church shooting occurred on June 22, 1980, in Daingerfield, Texas, when a man armed with two handguns, two assault rifles, and several hundred rounds of ammunition burst in through the back doors of a Baptist church and killed five people, including a 7-year-old. He wounded 10 others. The gunman was Alvin King III, a former math teacher at the local high school, who, according to witnesses, burst into the church declaring, "This is war!"

Although I hadn't yet heard of a Catholic church in America becoming a war zone, I did want to reach out to the Catholic faith, and I kept stopping by St. Rosa of Lima in Short Hills, New Jersey, trying and failing to get an appointment with the parish priest. I wasn't a parishioner and figured the priest had too few hours in the day to administer to his own parishioners, much less a mom on a mission. But I did remember when the pope was shot in Rome back in 1981, while he was riding in an open car in St. Peter's Square. Perhaps this fact alone would be enough to get the Catholic Church on board.

Through the efforts of Reverend Jim and Rabbi Marc, the church community was in! I went to my temporary office at the Coalition and borrowed a computer to type up the monthly newsletter. For the first time in weeks, I really had something to share with the grassroots. I had the interfaith effort to tell them about as well as the news that we had joined forces with other gun-control groups and that there was a formal steering committee in place that would act as midwife for our event. And, of all the good news, I was giddiest about my meeting with the National Park Police. I loved those men in uniforms—they were so professional, so polite, so helpful! I shot the newsletter off by e-mail, but a computer glitch sent many of the newsletters into some kind of cyber-never-never-land, and a few of the working marchers in the field never got it. All hell broke loose, and those pesky 151s began acting up again.

In the vacuum created by my technical glitch, the troublemakers began floating rumors that we were being co-opted by "the suits," namely the male-dominated established gun-control groups who were now backing us. This also gave the 151s another opportunity to demand

tervention. Every time I stumbled, somebody, some angel somewhere, would take the time to pick me up, brush me off, and get me back on track.

Even though the march was on track, time seemed to be running in short supply; there just weren't enough hours in the day to take care of everything that needed to be done, and as march day drew near, I was stretched even further with more and more requests to do interviews and make speeches. I would usually just write up some thoughts and hope for the best. But I was slated to speak at the Conference of Mayors, and this gave me a terrible case of public-speaking panic. I was also—on the same day—slated to appear on *Good Morning America*, and this would be the MMM's debut on this show. Even though I dreaded live TV, there wasn't much I had to prepare for. I had my four or five key bullet points down cold, and I was getting pretty adept at getting these points out, no matter how little time I had. It was a trick I had learned from watching my old boss, Senator Long, in action. The GMA interview would be over in 4 minutes, tops. But the Conference of Mayors was expecting a lot more from me than a few minutes and a handful of sound bites.

It was now 2 A.M. I was supposed to be up and out by 6 A.M. to get to the ABC studios. From there I'd have to get to Atlantic City by 9 A.M. for the conference. So much for getting some sleep, let alone having a speech prepared. It wasn't looking good.

I sat at my computer trying—but failing—to put together a coherent speech.

I was exhausted from the kids, depressed about the state of my marriage, and overwhelmed by the details of the Million Mom March. I couldn't think of anything remotely inspirational to say.

I stared at the computer for about an hour, thinking that maybe if I just looked at it hard enough, the words would suddenly appear. When that didn't work, I procrastinated by praying and saying, "Please, please, somebody help me," while I pulled out my hair. It must have worked, because an e-mail popped up from a man from Virginia named Bill Jenkins, who is the author of a book called *What to Do When the Police Leave: A Guide to the First Days of Traumatic Loss*.

Once I read Bill's letter, I knew what I would say at the Conference of Mayors. I printed his letter, put it in my bag, and went to bed that night with a sense of peace and readiness. I don't remember much about the GMA interview, but I do remember the mayors. I read Bill's letter to them. It was the first time in my life I was given a standing ovation.

Dear Donna:

I am a college professor and an unwilling expert on the effects of firearms on our society. Two and a half years ago, I benignly believed the gun lobby's lines, and why not? I grew up in a house with hunting guns and learned how to shoot. My rural family members hunt regularly, and my brother is a competition shooter in his spare time. I naively thought that was the extent of the interaction with guns in my life.

Then, my 16-year-old son was murdered—while he was working at his new job at a fast-food restaurant—by a man with a handgun, during a robbery. I began researching the instrument of his destruction and tore back the cardboard facades and specious claims of the gun industry. I looked closely at the economics and marketing practices of an industry that has enjoyed enormous protection throughout its history. My conclusions shocked and sickened me.

With 250 million guns in society today, more than 1 million handguns alone are placed in circulation every year for a legitimate market of merely 60 to 65 million private gun owners. Hundreds of gun laws have been cobbled together by various localities in a desperate effort to protect themselves, yet these are often trumped by state laws where lobbying efforts are more focused and well-financed. Indeed, no concerted legislative action has ever been allowed to adversely affect the industry's bottom line directly. Instead, attention is diverted to postsale issues of possession and use. I see a silent and insidious third party to the issue, the one who built the fence between the vocal factions and those whose primary goal is to keep the argument raging for their own economic benefit. I see an industry that has allowed itself to be seduced by the easy money of a burgeoning illegitimate market. It resists voluntarily marketing products ethically and responsibly, incorporating sensible safety measures, establishing specific training requirements for buyers, and even guaranteeing that the purchaser of these products will be the end user.

A brief history is in order. In the 1970s and 1980s, facing a rapidly saturating market and foreign competition, the gun industry seems to have reinvented itself. It doesn't require much effort to observe the following unethical, yet profitable practices: It began marketing military and police-style weapons to private citizens, firearms which are not for defense, nor sport, but are for attack and urban warfare. It began following the market trends of the illegitimate market, incorporating features that appeal to the criminal user. It began capitalizing on a growing attitude of uneasiness and paranoia in society, supplying a false and dangerous hope for protection from people using their products, effectively profiting from both sides at once. And it began manufacturing product far beyond any reasonable ability to sell it to the limited legitimate market. Make no mistake, this small group of people has benefited greatly and has blatantly used their profits to perpetuate their commercial and legal protection.

Who has suffered? The sportsmen and sportswomen have suffered as the reputation of something they have dearly loved and enjoyed has been ruined by irresponsible marketing, sales, and use. The police have suffered, having been shot at and ambushed by those with more firepower than any officer has ever carried. Families have suffered as children find a gun and kill unwittingly, or guns bought ostensibly for protection are turned on another family member or self. Society has suffered as ready access to a limitless supply of disposable guns enables and emboldens criminals. Our state legislatures have suffered as rural interests are pitted against urban interests by manipulating lobbyists. The gun industry has truly soiled its own nest. Sadly, it is our nest also.

Despite claims to the contrary, our children are not being sacrificed on the altar of personal freedom and protection. Our children are not being sacrificed on the altar of constitutional rights. Our children are not being sacrificed on the altar of patriotic, democratic, and lifestyle values. Our children are not being sacrificed on the altar of any ideology whatsoever. No, our children are being sacrificed on an altar dedicated to nothing more than base profit and commerce. And that I will not excuse.

In 1997, my son was one of more than 20 homicide victims in our county in Virginia. He was one of 115 Virginia children and teens who died from firearm use and misuse. He was one of 902 Virginians of all ages who met their end at the barrel of a gun. And one of the 32,436 Americans who died with a bullet in them that year.

From 1990 to today, more than 9,700 people in Virginia and more than 343,000 people nationwide have been killed with firearms. And for every firearm-related mortality, the Centers for Disease Control and Prevention estimates another three people have received nonfatal injuries.

Want to have some more fun with numbers? Let's say that each of those fatalities in the past 10 years has between five and six close family members or intimate friends in their lives, and that is a low estimate. That is nearly 2 million grieving parents, siblings, grandparents, children, spouses, and best friends, and I am one of them, and perhaps some of you are, too.

There are two ways to hunt. In one, the hunter takes time to learn of the quarry and its habits and life. The hunter enters the forest alone and tracks the quarry for hours or even days, hoping for a clear shot. This is how the gun industry has been fought in the past. Dedicated lawyers and lobbyists who have learned its every move have been fighting one-on-one. Sometimes they have gotten clear shots and scored minor victories.

But there is another way to hunt, and while less elegant, it is far more effective. The entire village enters the forest. Not highly trained, just willing participants. They beat the brush, driving the quarry to open ground, and surround it, and the hunt is over.

On Mother's Day, the village enters the forest.

The Million Mom March will succeed through honest education of the facts, unflagging determination, and a sincere desire to bring about change. I believe and lay my hopes on this. And if the Million Mom March is not successful this year, next year perhaps the 2 Million Mom March will be, and the next year, perhaps the 3 Million Mom March will be. For this is an effort that will not easily be turned aside.

We have the right to demand action. We have a right to demand safety. And above all, we have a right to demand peace. I am in awe of the success of your determined efforts to make these demands known. I appreciate it more than you could ever know. Thank you.

Sincerely,
Bill Jenkins,
The Million Mom March—Virginia

Thank me? No. Thank you, Bill. Bill Jenkins went on to enlist other Virginians to charge into "the forest" of Washington, D.C., on Mother's Day 2000. He later married a Million Mom Marcher from Illinois, and they both live there now.

> "Hi, I'm calling from
> the Michigan office of the
> Million Mom March."
>
> —ORGANIZER LORI SPILLANE,
> USING A PAY PHONE OUTSIDE
> OF A LADIES' ROOM IN
> A MUNITIONS PLANT

MID-FEBRUARY TO
MID-MAY 2000

Six months after our Labor Day conception, as we entered our third trimester, the Million Mom March was alive and kicking up a storm. There was no hiding it; we were in the muumuu phase, and it seemed like every media maven (both good and bad) wanted to touch us or glom on to us in some way.

While I never thought of myself as "the mother of the Million Mom March," I was now being sought after by competing magazines and media outlets for exclusives on me. Like the publicist I was trained to be, I managed to deflect most of the attention and redirect it to the mothers who had more poignant stories to tell, like Carole Price and Mary Leigh Blek—one a bartender, the other an Orange County

Republican—two different women, alike only in that they had both lost their firstborn sons to guns. But in every mother's life, there is a time to be selfless and a time to be Queen for a Day. My day to be queen came in mid-February. It came while I was being chewed out by the mother of one of Lili's classmates because she thought her daughter had caught head lice from mine. "You really should consider checking her head *before* sending her to school," she lectured me while completely ignoring the fact that maybe her daughter gave lice to mine. She went on and on about how this was the greatest tragedy she could or would experience. Having heard so many real tragic stories, I didn't have much patience for her. Before I could say something I would later regret, call waiting chimed in. It was an editor from *Parents* magazine calling to tell me that I had been selected to be the May Mother of the Month. I clicked back to the lice-police mom and said "I must run! That's *Parents* magazine on the other line," and in that bragging tone that I would chastise my own children for using, I boasted, "I'm Parent of the Month!" Then I hung up. A few days later, we all posed—me, my girls, and a couple of head nits—for *Parents*. I felt it was good for promoting the march, to say nothing about preserving my pride as a mom. So much for being the poster mom for good parenting!

———

Probably the best article ever written about us appeared in the *Detroit Free Press*. A reporter by the name of Tamara Audi wrote about how unique and "by the seat of our pants" we really were. The article described the resourcefulness of the Michigan moms, especially Lori Spillane, who, on her lunch hour, would recruit people to the Million Mom March on the pay phone next to the ladies' bathroom inside an army munitions plant where she worked. With the sound of the toilet flushing in the background, she would call top politicians in the state, like U.S. Senator Spencer Abraham, an NRA ally. Lori would identify herself as being from the Million Mom March, then either convince them to join us in our crusade or tell them that their career would go down the drain. It was one thing to read about these women. It was something else to hear them. Once the Michigan moms conquered the print media, they moved on to talk radio.

The last day of February 2000 was the 29th—the first leap year of the new millennium. As I walked Lili to the corner to catch the bus for school, I tried to explain to her exactly what leap year was, but in truth, I really wasn't sure. So I sent her off to school with some vague explanation, hoping I would in no way contradict her kindergarten teacher, Mrs. Wolfe, who would undoubtedly have the real answer.

On my way back to the house, I waved to Kelly, my new neighborhood friend who had never stopped by for so much as a cup of coffee before the Million Mom March, but who now stopped by often, mostly to pick up MMM fliers. I got home and went down to my basement office (also known as the War Room) which was once wallpapered in Ralph Lauren but was now covered in Post-it notes listing the millions of mundane things I had to do, like order the groceries, ship a box of T-shirts to Spring in Michigan, or call Mr. Second Amendment over at Kinko's.

As I got settled in at my desk, feeling cozy in my denim Gap overalls (which were now taped together because I had no time to shop for a new pair), Connie Rucker of Handgun Control Inc. called. "Turn on CNN," she said. A 6-year-old shot and killed another 6-year-old with a handgun in Flint, Michigan, and Connie was calling on behalf of Sarah Brady to see if I could help her with a few radio interviews. I didn't know it at the time, but Sarah had been diagnosed with lung cancer.

Since the launch of the MMM, I heard from one or two mothers and fathers of gun victims every day. And every story was sadder and more senseless than the last, from the father whose kid was killed on his first day on the job at Burger King to the mother whose son was killed his first week on the job at Starbucks. There was even a day when I heard from three mothers and an aunt about their respective 13-year-old boys. All but one of the boys had been shot and killed accidentally, and the fourth boy had shot a 12-year-old girl. His aunt had called to tell me what it was like for the family, living with that kind of guilt. I hadn't really thought about it that way until her call, and it was clear that she wasn't looking for sympathy. Instead, it seemed as though she called to apologize in some heartbreaking way. Most of these shootings were 1-day stories. Sad, yes, but the media always moves on. With the death of Kayla Rolland, this was about to change.

Kayla Rolland was shot and killed at school by one of her classmates. Both were 6 years old.

Connie Rucker gave me the name and number of the producer for *The Mitch Albom Show* in Michigan, because they were interested in doing a piece on Kayla and gun violence and children. (Mitch is the author of the bestseller *Tuesdays with Morrie.*) When I called, I was floored to hear that the producer had already been contacted by the Million Mom March organizers in Michigan. In fact, every media outlet I called had already spoken to and was quoting a Michigan mom regarding this terrible, senseless tragedy.

Kayla's killing even made the front page of the *New York Post*. There was the face of this precious 6-year-old victim, who reminded me so much of my own 6-year-old daughter. She had the same color hair, the same little knotty, "I want to comb it myself" style. The Michigan moms forced America to feel what Kayla's mom must have felt. They forced us to feel the shame that the shooter's mother must have felt. These were two mothers, who could have been any of us, neither of whom would now have anything to celebrate this Mother's Day—or perhaps any other Mother's Day.

Of course, on the Internet and on talk radio, the gun nuts were blaming everybody and everything except, of course, the gun. This was an illegal gun, they would argue, so no law could have prevented this kid from shooting another kid.

No? Well, I heard one of the Michigan moms point out that if our grandmothers had marched for gun-industry reform way back when this country was putting a man on the moon, then guns—legal or otherwise—could have been designed so that no child would be able to pull the trigger. Another mother said if we can clone a sheep, surely we can childproof a gun.

Later that week, when things began to settle down a bit, I called Spring Venoma in Michigan to thank her for all of her hard work during the Flint tragedy. Rather than letting the story of little Kayla just die, Spring and the Michigan moms decided that if they refused to stop talking about it, maybe some *good* might come from it.

I hadn't spoken with Spring since she'd nominated Congressman Bart Stupak for an Apple Pie Award. (Stupak was the congressman attacked by the NRA, all because he voted for a bill requiring child-safety locks and another to close the loophole that allowed the Columbine kids to get guns so easily.) I was shocked when she hit me with some terrible news of her own: Her husband had been diagnosed with leukemia. She would have to drop out of the Million Mom March entirely, because he was so ill. She wouldn't even be able to join us on Mother's Day. I was devastated. It was selfish, I know, but Spring—who came from a family of deer hunters—had been crucial to our establishing credibility and getting off the ground in Michigan, the state in which the NRA claims the most members next to Pennsylvania. Spring would be impossible to replace and terribly missed. But she taught me something invaluable about good leadership: She had groomed so many so well in Michigan that the Michigan moms would not fall apart. This is what great leaders do, and Spring was right up there with the best.

We had lost several organizers over the course of the march, mostly because of pressing family matters, and we shared these intimate issues with each other as if we were, in fact, family. Regina Kaut, whose niece was killed at Jonesboro, had to drop out when her husband became sick. There were a few divorces and other less-severe cases of marital upheaval. Kathy in Maryland called me to cry about her husband leaving her over some chocolate chip cookies: She'd baked them for her Million Mom March meeting, and when she caught him trying to sneak one, she demanded he put the cookie back. He did, and then he packed his bags and left. (Fortunately, he came home a week later, and they were able to laugh over the cookie affair.) But between stolen cookies and missed birthday cakes, we wives were getting so consumed by the Million Mom March that we sometimes didn't have much time for our husbands. Not every husband was being neglected, of course, and in fact, there were quite a few Million Mom March pregnancies. Some women called with the happy news that, come Mother's Day, they would be marching for two.

Not every Million mom had to scale back her involvement when her life changed. Dana Quist called to tell me that she was pregnant with her second child. Nauseous but not deterred, she vowed that she'd continue to work for us right up until the big day. (She meant our big day of course, because her baby was not due until October.)

Rene, the keeper of gun-nut mail in Kentucky, called me out of the blue with her great news. She proudly informed me that there was going to be a bus or two out of Kentucky. Rene got a whiff of courage and started conducting her own media interviews. And once word got around in Kentucky that she was our contact, her phone began to ring!

She even heard from several of the families of the West Paducah, Kentucky, school shooting of December 1997. Rene heard from Sabrina Steiger, a pediatric nurse whose 15-year-old daughter, Kayce, was one of the three kids killed by a fellow student while attending a prayer service. Five more kids were injured in that shooting, and one of them, Missy Jenkins, was determined to attend the march in Washington. Missy was left paralyzed and in a wheelchair from a bullet, but that would not stop her, she told us, from leading a caravan from Kentucky.

As media interest increased in the Million Mom March, I needed help. I was used to job-sharing with Rosemary Keenan at the *Late Show*, and so I looked for a job-sharing partner for my Million Mom March work, too. Carole Price, a mother of three who had lost her oldest son to a gun, became my media partner. She juggled her jobs as a bartender, a wife, and mother of Carley and Michael, and was the Maryland state coordinator for the Million Mom March. Carole has the kind of face and voice the media loves. But more important, she is focused, sincere, and nonplussed by the gun nuts who love to nag her. I was still as shaky as Jell-O when it came to debating with the gun nuts on radio, so I would always beg Carole to join by phone. Occasionally, we'd team up in person in New York or Washington, D.C., and on more than one occasion, she'd save me from myself. One time I referred to the Million Mom March as the largest grass (as in marijuana) movement in the country. At first I didn't catch my mistake. With an arched eyebrow, Carole mischievously pretended to smoke a joint, and then I realized—a little too late—what I had said on air to a national audience. Together, we burst into uncontrollable laughter. And, of course, having had a few babies (and therefore weak bladders), we peed in our pants.

The laughter, the camaraderie, and ultimately pulling a success from the jaws of defeat—this was the fun part of the Million Mom March. The not-so-fun part was the constant drama involving those rascally rabbits from the gun lobby who were now hopping all over the place trying to cause trouble. And, I'm afraid to say, sometimes succeeding. The first real sign of trouble came from Oregon mom Lisa Laursen-Thirkill who, in a carefully worded e-mail, asked "Are you sure we have the endorsement of the National PTA?"

Of course I was sure. It was the PTA endorsement that helped us get back our startup grant, and it was Lisa who got us this endorsement. What did she know that she wasn't telling me? I had to dig up the e-mail from the PTA that I had filed away with the mountain of en-dorsements we'd received from churches, synagogues, and other major organizations. I forwarded the endorsement to Lisa, who remained vague about why she needed it. When I did not hear back from her for days, I began to worry. Was there a problem? Lisa told me not to worry, that she'd take care of it. It seemed that one of the members of the National PTA board of directors was closely tied with the NRA and was trying to strong-arm the organization into retracting its endorsement. Lisa strong-armed back. Normally as gentle as a lamb, Lisa threatened to pull the entire state of Oregon out of the PTA if they didn't honor their commitment to us. I suppose I should've known this had something to do with the NRA, but it shocked me to find out how fragile our sup-port could be. The gun lobby, I learned, kept a kind of "blacklist" of companies and organizations that supported sensible gun laws. A men's magazine that had taken pity on us by running an ad for free got slammed by a couple of gun nuts, and by a couple, I mean they got all of two letters. But those two letters had the effect of prompting the magazine's editor to apologize to its readership for running the Million Mom March ad. Fortunately, most of our endorsers ignored the gun nuts, but the few that almost caved could have brought us down fast. The loss of the PTA would have been devastating. But like the Soros-Diamond grant, lost and then returned, we eventually got our PTA en-dorsement back. Lisa and her Oregon PTA moms prevailed.

In 1999, the American gun industry produced 4 million guns, which added a staggering arsenal to the millions of guns already in circulation. There were also an added 1.3 million guns imported into the United States that year. This meant that just about every lawful American who wanted to buy a gun already owned one. The only untouched market left—besides criminals—were kids and women.

This made us Million Mom Marchers a gun-marketer's dream. We were sitting on a potential e-mail list of a million people who most likely did not own guns. Lusting after our list was a group called the Women's Shooting Sports Foundation. The WSSF glommed on to one of my favorite working marchers, a feisty Colorado character I'll call "K." K was an Annie Oakley type of gun owner, but she, too, had been pushed over the edge by Columbine. K thought it would be a good idea to meet with the WSSF—at least hear them out and see how we could "work together." But like a drug pusher hanging out on a schoolyard gate looking for new kids to get hooked on crack cocaine, the WSSF (the marketing arm of Colt Manufacturers) looked at the Million Mom Marchers (the vast majority of whom had never laid a hand on a gun) as lucrative virgin territory.

When K asked me to meet with Shari LeGate, head of the WSSF, I agreed—provided our meeting would be off the record. This would have allowed us to talk honestly and openly without worrying that our conversation would ever be made public. This was crucial to me, as my main priority was to protect the MMM.

The day of the meeting, Carole Price happened to be in New York City for some media interviews and to promote the Maryland Childproof Handgun Bill, a bill she'd been actively seeking to pass for quite some time and which, if passed, would be the strictest child-proofing law in the nation. I convinced her to join me for dinner with Shari, who'd flown in from Colorado.

Carole and I walked into the Grand Hyatt restaurant—both of us drained after a hard day of interviews. I had slipped into something more comfortable—my taped-up Gap overalls—and we found Shari, a 40-something aging beauty queen, who was elegantly dressed in de-signer duds, waiting for us. Shari looked every bit the part of a corpo-rate network weasel that I used to mock, but she seemed sincere, even volunteering that she locked up her guns. Most of the rest of the con-versation with Shari was pleasant, until I tried to turn the conversation to legislation, particularly to the bill Carole was working on to child-proof guns. Shari dismissed me, saying she'd rather focus on "common ground" by promoting her Project Home Safe, a trigger-lock giveaway program. The WSSF wanted to share our day in the sun on Mother's Day, she said, and be there right on the mall with us.

On the face of it, trigger-lock giveaways sound great. But Eric Gorovitz, the policy director at the Bell Campaign, had already warned me about the danger of promoting trigger locks as "the" panacea for gun violence. Trigger-lock giveaways, he explained, are like giving people seat belts and expecting them to install them properly—if at all. Since guns are banned in the District of Columbia, we couldn't exactly en-courage gun owners to bring their guns to the mall to get a proper demonstration on how to install a trigger lock. Plus, Safe-T-Lock, a reputable trigger-lock company, had already asked us to display their product on Mother's Day, and we had had to say no to them because the National Park Police prohibited this kind of product marketing during a free-speech event like ours.

Shari mentioned that they were working with some sheriffs' and police departments, and to me, this seemed like a better match. A trained police officer could show a responsible and legal gun owner the proper way to install a trigger lock. And this would happen in a more proper setting, too. (As she spoke, I had a terrible vision of gun owners showing up on the mall that would be packed with moms and kids, in order to get their trigger locks installed.)

Shari wouldn't take no for an answer—she was clearly a woman used to getting her way. I was tired and wanted to get some sleep. Carole was tired, too, so we politely excused ourselves after dinner. Before we could make a clean getaway, Shari pulled out propaganda about the immorality of suing gun manufacturers for the alleged reckless distribution of their products. Ah, so this was the real reason for our meeting. I wish I had known this beforehand, or I wouldn't have let her waste my time.

Just as the tobacco industry has been sued by local and federal governments, dozens of cities and counties, as well as some states, like New York, have filed lawsuits against the gun industry for "willful negligence" in allowing gun sales wherein legitimate buyers act as front men for criminals and kids. The lawsuits want the gun industry to compensate those who have suffered damages because of these bogus sales. In response, the gun lobby has fought tooth-and-nail to strip victims of their rights by seeking immunity for the gun industry in such lawsuits.

I said goodnight to Shari, thanked her for picking up the bill, and checked into the Grand Hyatt because I too tired to drive home. I went to bed relieved that I'd had the sense to extract a promise from her that our meeting was entirely off the record.

A few days later, Jeff and I, in one of many attempts to reconcile, took our girls and my stepson Greg to Vail for a ski vacation. I didn't know how many more family vacations we would have, so I hoped to savor this one. But my bag was barely unpacked when the fireworks began. This time, it was the Colorado moms who were up in arms. Lucky me. It seems that Shari, the lovely representative of the Women's

Sports Shooting Foundation, had called the press and publicly accused me—and the Million Mom March—of lying about who and what we were! If we were really about safety, she implied to newspapers, we would give away trigger locks at our events. She created quite a stir within our network, particularly with our fiscal sponsor and partner, the Bell Campaign. (With support marches sprouting up across the country, Bell was in charge of promoting the regional events and providing insurance and guidance to local organizers while I concentrated on the D.C. event.)

The Denver chapter of the Bell Campaign was furious with K about her relationship with Shari LeGate, mainly because it did not want its membership list to fall into the wrong hands. And now here was a public indictment of the Million Mom March by a cozy contact of our Colorado state coordinator. I could not cope with this. I was on vacation with my family. The phone in our hotel room rang so much that the desk manager jokingly asked if my name was a code name for Madonna; surely, there must be a pop star staying with us, given how much our phone rang!

I returned home to New Jersey without any rest, and Jeff—rightfully so—resented that our family vacation had been ruined by a woman who couldn't keep her word.

I found myself back in Colorado in early March. The Bell Campaign dispatched me there to do some damage control as well as drum up support for the national march. I went straight from the airport to a beautiful church in Denver. A bit jetlagged and tired, I stumbled along, trying to give a coherent 10-minute chat on how I got involved and why. I tried to talk about the horror of watching on TV while little kids, who should have been playing duck-duck-goose, fled a madman who was shooting up their Jewish Community Center in California. As I looked around the room, I noticed that most of the people were listening to me with a frozen look on their faces. They sat there, unmoved, like zombies. Then it hit me: Many of the people there that night were from Littleton, the home of Columbine. They had come all the way into Denver just for this meeting, and here I was rambling on about something that had happened clear across the country. It dawned on me that though the Columbine tragedy had happened almost a year earlier, most of the people, like many victims of gun violence, were in some stage of posttraumatic stress disorder. A sweet woman, who must have sensed my discomfort, came over to me and hugged me, making me feel better despite my poor presentation. Her name was Anne Coakley, and she was from nearby Boulder. Anne's daughter, Tara, was killed by a bullet that had pierced the wall of her condo. Tara's neighbor claimed he was just cleaning his gun, and it went off accidentally. Just when I thought I'd heard it all, I would hear a story like this.

There were a few men and women in that church that night who had somehow managed to move beyond the Columbine massacre by starting an organization called SAFE Colorado, whose mission was to garner public support for a referendum that would close the gun-show loophole in Colorado. If the U.S. Congress was too cowardly to do it, then damn it, these Coloradoans would do it themselves, at least in their own state. The NRA was vowing to defeat this referendum. A member of SAFE used this meeting to plead for funds to fight back. One of the leaders of this group and one of the kindest people I met that night was Tom Mauser. Tom's son Daniel was killed in the Columbine massacre, and it was Tom who was honored in President Clinton's State of the Union Address in January 2000. As if he somehow knew what his fate would be, Daniel, in one of his last but prescient conversations, asked his dad if he knew about the legal loopholes in the Brady Law that made it easy for kids and criminals to buy guns at gun shows.

I asked Tom if he'd be interested in speaking at the march in Washington, D.C., to explain how it was that it was illegal for kids or criminals to buy guns, but that it wasn't illegal for unlicensed dealers to sell them without first performing a background check. I wanted him to tell Daniel's story. But Tom declined, saying he was already committed to speaking at the local Million Mom March rally in Denver the same day. Just as I was about to leave the church, a woman came up to me and introduced herself. Had I heard of the California 101 shooting? Of course, I said, not quite lying, and not wanting to sound shallow and uncaring. Her name was Reajean Stotler, and she told me about her daughter who was killed in that 1993 shooting in San Francisco. A madman with an assault weapon pumped bullets into a law office, killing nine people, injuring five, and devastating scores of others. In the summer of 1993, I was preparing to get married and was knee-deep in bridal magazines. Somehow, my only memory of this shooting was that of a man testifying before Congress about losing his wife in the shooting. He testified with his baby daughter strapped to his back in a baby carrier. It looked just like the kind I had been given during my baby shower, which was around the same time. That was my son-in-law, Raejean told me. That baby is my granddaughter. I got chills. I left quickly after my conversation with her, feeling drained and humbled by the heart-wrenching stories I heard that night.

By the time I got home, I was back on that teeter-totter, that constant up and down of the Million Mom March. Denver was an emotional low. The up was a call from Rob Dauber, the senior producer of *The Rosie O'Donnell Show.*

After what seemed like an eternity of back-and-forth phone calling, Rob gave us a firm date of March 8. His only request was that we make sure a "real" mom was available for the segment. Well, moms don't get much more real than Brenda Jaskolka, mother of young Joe, the boy who had been paralyzed when he was hit by a bullet on New Year's Eve.

In our typical nick-of-time way, we got our Washington, D.C., national office up and running the day before the Rosie broadcast. Brenda was scheduled to do the Rosie "announce," meaning announce that day's guests, then walk down the aisle to the set and have a chat with Rosie. Rosie would ask her about the march, Brenda would tell her story about her son, Joe, and then she would give the date of the march and make the plea that we needed every mom available to make her way to Washington to show Congress we were stronger and more formidable than the gun lobby.

At least that was the plan. But we found out there is such a thing as being overprepared. The day before the interview, Brenda was put through an intense "media training" session. Our consultants, believing *The Rosie O'Donnell Show* was too important to leave to amateurs, sent a media expert in to work with Brenda. Well, it "worked," alright: It made Brenda think the success of the march rested on her tiny shoulders. After she did the "announce," Brenda joined Rosie on stage. After the first question, Brenda broke down on stage and cried. And then I started to cry—I couldn't believe we had made Brenda so anxious that she could barely speak. But Rosie, being the pro she is, pulled a victory from the jaws of defeat: She gave out our Web site address, gave the date of the march, and I think I remember her saying she would be there. I made a mental note to ask Rob Dauber: Did Rosie, in fact, plan on attending the march in Washington, D.C.?

Right after the appearance, I called our new national office to ask if or what the response to Brenda's appearance on Rosie had been. But I couldn't get through. Brenda's appearance opened a floodgate of calls. It didn't matter that she froze. She stood there next to Rosie looking vulnerable—just like Sally Field in *Places in the Heart*—and I think moms everywhere could only imagine how hard Brenda's life has become because of some reckless jerk with a gun. America saw her, loved her, and wanted to help her. All 25 phones were ringing off the hook. (Eventually we added another 50 phones, and as the march drew closer, most days even that wasn't enough.)

We couldn't even log the number of Web site hits we had that day. Our server kept crashing under the weight of so many Americans trying to reach us!

Rosie had come through for us. But would she again? Would we be able to get her, the most popular mother in the country, to attend our march? Her handlers told us that she would be in Florida taping her show around Mother's Day and that a trip to D.C. would be impossible. Impossible? That was no longer a word in our vocabulary. I decided to do something about this. I got on a train, went to Washington, and met with Congresswoman McCarthy. During that meeting, she asked me if there was one thing—and one thing only—she could do to help, what would it be? I told her it would be to get us a commitment from Rosie O'Donnell. She got on the phone that day, and not only did she get Rosie to agree to appear, she got her to sign on as our emcee.

While our success with television was gratifying, we also needed to get attention from the serious print media, specifically the *New York Times* and the *Washington Post*, mainly because that was the way to reach deep-pocket donors. We had raised about $500,000 at this point, but we still needed at least another $500,000 to pull the event off. Our two first attempts at the national editions of these newspapers were near disastrous. I didn't have a secretary, so reaching me was hit-or-miss. Phoebe would sometimes convince callers that she was taking down their name and number, but she was still in nursery school, and while skilled as a joker, she could neither read nor write. My little "helper" almost cost us the national edition of the *New York Times*. A phone call came to my house from a friend of a neighbor who saw our flier. Not knowing who the caller was, I listened as I heard Phoebe say, "No, my mommy's not available right now," then, not knowing I was within earshot, she started jabbering away about intimate family stuff. When she started to tell whoever was on the other end of the line that I was lactose intolerant, I grabbed the phone from her, only to hear a Times reporter laughing hysterically. Eventually—sans Phoebe's quote—an article about the MMM did appear. And not buried, but on the front page of the Sunday edition, with a bright, eye-catching photo of an anonymous volunteer wearing the MMM T-shirt.

And our time finally came with the *Washington Post*, for us a critical newspaper because it was read by every politician we were hoping to influence. A reporter named Meg Rosenfeld reached me on my cell phone one day as I was sitting in the carpool line at Phoebe's nursery school. First she asked where I was. "Sitting in the carpool line at Phoebe's nursery school," I answered, as if this response was validation that I was in fact a mother. She seemed happy with that answer. Then she dropped a bomb: She had already interviewed volunteer 151 who had complained about the staff of our management team, Jasculca/Terman. "What kind of complaints?" I asked, clearly taken off guard. "My source said they were taking over and pushing the moms out," she replied. I couldn't believe what I was hearing! Our first shot at a mention in the *Washington Post* was already tainted by the 151s! I assured Ms. Rosenfeld that we were more than happy with our management team, who were, incidentally, working for us on a shoestring budget.

Let me say right off the bat that in every organization and in every company there are good people and bad, and our management team was great—they certainly did not deserve any bad press in the *Washington Post*, and any hint of internal discord—fictional or not—would make us look like a bunch of amateurs. I blew off the criticism and attributed it to those annoying, cranky souls who haunt every organization. Meg said she figured that was the case but she felt she had to ask. She then went on to ask me if I was related to Susan Thomases. "Yes," I replied, "she's my sister-in-law." "What is she doing to help you?" Meg asked. "Nothing, except she did advise me to get a good accountant and a good lawyer," I said, now knowing that that was Susan's boilerplate great advice, whether it's for organizing a march, weathering Whitewater, or surviving a divorce. The article turned out to be fabulous. In fact, too fabulous. The article gave me undeserved credit for the line calling gun shows "Tupperware parties" for the criminally insane. That line came from the Violence Policy Center Web site, and I used it often. But instead of looking at this as a form of flattery, or at the article as being good for the movement, I got a call from the VPC public-relations person who insisted that I call Meg Rosenfeld and demand a correction. The VPC is considered to be one of the best nonprofits for its studies and research, but when it came to winning friends and influencing people, the VPC stumped me. They just didn't get us. In fact, they didn't seem to want us around at all. They even ridiculed us in *USA Today*, saying that instead of a march, we should all just be writing letters to Capitol Hill. But I knew, from my days of sharing an office with the signature machine, that letters alone weren't enough.

While others in the movement shot themselves in the foot by wasting time trying to discredit us, guns continued to go off every day. And we Million moms were hearing from victims of gun violence almost by the minute. Just when I thought I had heard it all, I learned that somebody in the GOP of Carroll County, Maryland, thought it would be a nifty fundraising idea to raffle off a 9mm semiautomatic gun. This was beyond bad taste. This raffle idea prompted the resignation of Betty Smith, vice-chairwoman of the Carroll County Central GOP Committee. "As a mother of five, I cannot tell my children that I have had a part in raffling a gun," she said, after quitting the post. Carole Price nominated Betty for an Apple Pie Award. And for everyone else on the Carroll County GOP Committee, there was the Time-Out Chair.

Even in the state of New York, stupidity was at a premium. The State Legislature had passed an NRA-sponsored bill that would have made Eddie Eagle—the Joe Camel of the gun industry (another great line by the VPC)—the mascot for gun safety. Most New Yorkers probably would never have heard of this until it was too late. Thankfully, a group called New Yorkers against Gun Violence alerted Hilary Wendel, our New York City mom, just as the NRA bill was on the desk of Governor George Pataki, awaiting his signature. Hilary sent out an e-mail imploring all New York Million moms to call the Governor and demand that he veto Eddie Eagle. The word on the street was that the top NRA lobbyist in New York State was a close friend of the governor's, and he was certain to sign the bill into law, basically institutionalizing the NRA in New York State public schools.

The Governor suddenly did a moonwalk and not only vetoed the bill, but he also introduced a series of sweeping gun-law reforms in New York State. Tom Brokaw broke the news as the lead story on *NBC Nightly News*.

"Good evening. Guns and their place in America. This is quickly taking shape as one of the major issues for election year 2000, and tonight there are several developments. President Clinton stepped up his campaign against the NRA and for gun control. He wants it this year, and . . . in New York, that sweeping gun-control legislation from Republican Governor George Pataki surprised almost everyone, especially since he's been frequently mentioned as a possible vice presidential candidate on a George W. Bush ticket. Today, I was with the Governor when he made his announcement."

Brokaw: As you know, the NRA is opposed to the ballistic testing because they say that it will lead to registration, that you'll know where every gun is in America, and when you know where every gun is, it means you can take them all away.

Pataki: If you look at it from the standpoint of a gun owner, is this going to be an undue burden? Is it going to in any way take away my right to own a gun, to use it in sporting activity or to defend my family? The answer is no, it will not.

Brokaw: Let me ask you about raising the minimum age from 18 to 21. We ask 18-year-olds to serve their country in the military. We give them the right to vote.

Pataki: We tell someone who's 19 or 20 that they have to be 21 to drink, because drinking can lead to dangerous activities. I think the most dangerous risk that a young person faces, in addition to car violence, is handgun violence.

Brokaw: In any discussion of George W. Bush's vice-presidential prospects, the name Governor Pataki ends up on the list. If your name comes before the convention, can't you hear those conservative Republicans saying, 'No way; he's a gun-control guy'?

Pataki: Oh sure, Tom. You know, there are always those who are going to oppose you for whatever reason. But my obligation as an elected official is to advance what I think is right for the public, and that's what I'm doing here.

Hilary Wendel called on us to give the governor an Apple Pie Award! For the first time, the pie seemed an amateurish and inadequate way to acknowledge the governor's good deeds.

I was now taking the Metroliner back and forth to D.C. every Monday for steering committee meetings. Initially, I was miffed that the men on the steering committee scheduled the meeting for the only day I earned a living. But I reluctantly took a leave of absence from the *Late Show* in order to be there. And since my daughters were already used to having me gone on Mondays, it worked out in its own way. I would really miss my paycheck, but what I got in return was the help and resources to mount this event, and that is not something I could have ever achieved on my own. Dan Gross and Talmadge Cooley of PAX were on the steering committee, and they had successfully packaged large events before. They would act as our executive producers until we hired one person full-time. The very first day, Dan, a hip former ad executive, announced that he didn't want this to be a weepy women's event. We politely told him that this was exactly what it was going to be. And after we set him on the right track, he and Talmadge—an equally hip thirty-something—worked hard to pull a rabbit out of our tattered, financially depleted hat. Although it sounds glamorous to plan a huge, potentially star-studded event, it is, in fact, fraught with ego clashes at every turn. It's like putting on a colossal wedding, where you have to think of everyone, otherwise Aunt Martha or your mother's second cousin is going to be upset over some imaginary slight. And our event was no different. We had more offers of theme songs than volunteers, and by this time, we had thousands of volunteers. "More gifts," Dan and Talmadge would say whenever some songs came in.

But I understood everyone wanting their due. I had a vision of my own. For example, I got kind of pushy when I wanted the Dunblane, Scotland, mums to speak. They were shining examples of what we were trying to do here in the United States. Following the gruesome mass shooting at the Scottish school their children attended, the Dunblane mums marched right to Parliament and got the laws changed. They, like so many of us, were baffled about what was taking America so long to do the same. I wanted Ted Christopher and his Dunblane band to attend, too, and perform their song, "Throw These Guns Away," which had become our anthem. (And I got my way: Alison, the New Jersey volunteer I'd assigned to wangle airfare, came through with flying colors by convincing Virgin Airways to donate both airfare and hotel accommodations for the party from Dunblane!)

I also found myself fighting Dan and Talmadge and the rest of the committee over whether a "real" mom or a high-profile celebrity mom should sing the national anthem. Also, many elected officials were reading about the Million Mom March in their local papers, and many of them began to request some face time on our stage.

This led me to realize that the one serious staffing mistake we'd made as a steering committee was not to hire a political director to handle these requests. Bob Walker, who resigned from Handgun Control Inc., was replaced by former-Congressman Mike Barnes. Mike offered his staff to take on this job, but there was some sort of rivalry brewing among members of the steering committee. It was like they were all playing a version of *Survivor.* It was becoming apparent that the Million Mom March might be a bigger deal than first thought. And now all of the men on the steering committee were trying to vote each other off the island of the Million Mom March. Mike, being the newest member of the committee, was told by a few other members regarding his generous offer, thanks, but no thanks. This was one big mistake.

Politicians buzz around media events like flies at a picnic. The bigger it looked like our picnic would be, the more flies we drew. And we needed to make these flies happy. Since our goal was to influence politicians to pass sensible gun laws to save kids, we needed to find a way to keep the political friends we already had content, while we recruited those politicians who were still on the fence. This is a highly sensitive diplomatic assignment. And we needed some help.

I did agree with the rest of the steering committee that we did not want to turn our event into a boring political convention. And we, as a steering committee, made the tough decision that only those members of Congress who had lost a loved one would be invited to speak on stage. This included members of the Kennedy family and Carolyn McCarthy. But there was also Representative Bobby Rush, whose son was killed by a gun in Chicago, and Senator Feinstein of California, who was a champion of the 1994 assault weapons ban bill. Senator Feinstein, while president of the San Francisco Board of Supervisors in 1978, found her colleague, Harvey Milk, shot dead in his office. Down the hall, the mayor, George Mascone, also lay dead. The kill was himself a former member of the board of supervisors.

In the end, we determined that even Senator Feinstein's story seemed too removed, and she was not invited to speak. She was, however, a good sport and threw us a party the day before the march. More important, she announced at a news conference that she was introducing a bill that would require the licensing of handgun owners and the registration of their guns. As hard as it is to believe, this simple concept was considered cutting edge, at least here in America where it is so tough to regulate guns.

At this time, some national gun-control groups, many with their own bills and agendas to push, started to swipe at us in the press. The MMM had quickly surpassed many of the other gun-control organizations as one of the most identifiable names in the movement, and like when there's a new baby in the house, our siblings were feeling somewhat jealous. This became particularly apparent when Senator Feinstein put us in contact with Andy McKelvey, the CEO of Monster.com. McKelvey had deep pockets and a passion for gun safety, and he eventually became an extremely generous supporter of the march. He had been trying to give money to the movement for some time, but he had always been politely turned away. Handgun Control Inc., not willing to share its toys, never told us that McKelvey was on their board of directors and that we could have approached him for funding all along. Anyway, Andy came on board not a moment too soon: Until he came along, the moms and the steering committee had been scraping together nickels and dimes.

While I was in Washington to attend a lunch in our honor at the National Education Association, I was told I would finally have the chance to meet Andy McKelvey in person. He and his team turned out to be the "dream team" for the MMM, and I immediately fell in love with the entire gang during that initial Washington meeting. "What do you need?" he had asked. By this time, we were desperate for cash, since we had to pay for so much: a stage, a sound system, a Jumbotron screen or two. Andy would ultimately front about a third of the costs of the march—a huge contribution. The rest of our funding came from corporate donors, family foundations, small Internet contributions, and our T-shirt sales.

By our third trimester, our T-shirt business was really booming. Julie, T-Shirt Mom, was always on the brink of pulling her hair out, as the orders were coming in fast and furiously. I am sure that when she signed up for this task in September, she had no idea it would become a full-time job. I remember one day noticing a sudden spike in T-shirt orders on our Web site, and I remember thinking how strange this was, as we usually only saw a spike like this after an appearance on a national television show. Incredibly, it was Rush Limbaugh who boosted our sales that day. A caller had apparently asked Rush why he wasn't going after us on his show. He took the cue and immediately started in on the "500 Mom March."

I didn't hear his broadcast, but I sent him an e-mail, and he did confirm that he'd mentioned us on air that day. He also wrote that his mother had passed away earlier that month. Death hits people differently, and although I didn't know Millie Limbaugh very well, I remembered her chipper voice when we spoke back in August, when I asked her if she'd be our spokesmom. I couldn't believe that was only 7 months ago. With all that had happened between then and now, it might have been 7 years.

I remembered Millie's last words to me which were: "I wish you gals luck."

Luck was something we always needed. Though we were certainly gaining momentum, here we were, just a few months from "the day," and we only had 30,000 people officially signed up for the march. Despite the lack of physical evidence, I knew in my bones that the numbers would come. I just wasn't sure how or when. Again, I needed some kind of sign that my instinct was right, and it came from a most unlikely place.

On a cold March morning, I was in D.C. for another steering committee meeting. It was so cold that I decided to take the Metro from Union Station to our office on 17th Street NW. As I hurried toward the train station, I paused long enough to glance at the goods laid out by one of the many street vendors. There, among the knock-off designer sunglasses, watches, and the fake Gucci bags was a rip-off of one of our MMM T-shirts. I had to buy it. "How much?" I asked eagerly. "Twenty bucks," he said. If he had taken credit cards, I would have bought 100. There was something so flattering—and so affirming—about our T-shirt being bootlegged! I wanted to believe this vendor was some kind of mystic with a sixth sense about events like ours, and I wondered if he could feel the thousands of feet that would be coming to town on Mother's Day. Whether he knew something we didn't or not, I took his having our shirt as a sign that we were on course.

One of my next trips to D.C. was far less affirming. I came to town the Monday after Easter 2000, which happened to be the day that seven children were wounded by gunfire that erupted between groups of teenagers at the National Zoo. On the train back to New Jersey later that day, I got a call from a *Fox News* producer, who wanted me to come into Manhattan and tape a piece on this latest tragedy. I was bone-tired, hungry, and wearing rumpled clothes. I didn't have time to wash my hair that morning, so it was pulled back in a tight ponytail. It definitely wasn't my day to appear on TV. But the producer seduced me by promising a car service to pick me up from Newark's Penn Station, take me to the studio, and deliver me back home after the taping. I was running up so many charges on my Visa that anything free sounded good. And it was important. So I said yes. It wasn't until I was in the makeup chair that I learned that I wouldn't exactly be "taping a segment." I would be a guest on *The O'Reilly Factor.*

I felt sick. Bill O'Reilly tends to pounce on his guests' weaknesses and make perfectly intelligent people sound like blathering idiots. But there was no turning back. The producer told me not to be afraid, that all I had to do was keep the show lively. That wouldn't be a problem, I thought, as long as the viewers were bloodsport fans. O'Reilly grilled me on how I thought gun laws would have saved those kids at the zoo from being shot. I said licensing and registration would absolutely have prevented this senseless tragedy if the laws had been passed 20 years ago when they should have been. I kept my voice steady, but I was clearly indignant. Did we have to wait another 20 years before something would happen in Congress? Let's act now, and pray that we're creating a safer world for our grandchildren, I said. Bam. Home run. I even managed to achieve my ultimate goal for all national media appearances: I gave out the address of the MMM Web site.

I went home that night completely drained and somewhat embarrassed, knowing that I had looked a bit like the dishrag I felt on a national TV show. But my first review, from Rene in Kentucky, was a rave: "It was better than *Cats*," she wrote. Well, it just doesn't get much better than that.

Not all reviews were good, of course. As the now-familiar face of the MMM, I was getting used to being a target for every gun nut out there, and my experience with the gun lobby at this time can only be likened to a case of hemorrhoids . . . and a bad case at that. I was suddenly the poster child for the leftist, liberal, feminist, "commie mommies," as one irate gun lover described us. The bulldog members of the NRA attacked me relentlessly, accusing me variously of being a liar, a bitch, or a lying bitch. If the rhetoric hadn't been so patently ridiculous and potentially damaging to the MMM and our goals, it would have been laughable. But I was a tiny target compared with the Clinton administration, and in mid-March the gloves came off and things really began to get ugly. On an *ABC News* program, NRA executive vice president and CEO Wayne LaPierre blamed President Clinton personally for the death of former Northwestern basketball coach Ricky Byrdsong.

He stated, and I quote: "The question here is, has the president looked into the eyes of Ricky Byrdsong's family? Because that death is on his hands. Ben Smith walked into a gun store on June 23, was flagged under the instant check system, committing a brand new federal felony right under the president's nose. The president's policy did nothing to him except let him walk out the door and go home . . . His policies of not enforcing existing federal gun laws are getting people killed."

LaPierre argued that Byrdsong's killer, Benjamin Smith, had a history of violence—he had been arrested for battery and drug use—that should have led authorities to prosecute him after he failed the background check.

But the Clinton administration responded that the charge was absurd, and it is simply not feasible to make an on-the-spot arrest of every individual who fails a gun-store check. Clinton called the NRA's assertion that he "has blood on his hands" ironic. "If it were up to the NRA, we wouldn't even be doing background checks" the president charged back.

The Brady Law had actually worked as it was written in this instance: It stopped Smith from buying a gun in a licensed gun shop. But 3 days later, Smith bought two guns, a Bryco .38 caliber handgun and a Ruger .22 caliber handgun, from a private seller from Pekin, Illinois, who had taken out a classified ad in the *Peoria Journal Star* newspaper. The seller broke no laws because as a private seller, he was not required to perform a background check. Over the 2-year period of 1997 to 1999 that same private seller had purchased 65 inexpensive handguns—often referred to as Saturday Night Specials—from a single gun store, the Old Prairie Trading Post in Pekin. He then resold the guns through classified ads at double the price.

Under the Brady Law, federally licensed gun dealers are required to conduct criminal background checks on all buyers and maintain records of their transactions. However, unlicensed individuals selling firearms from a "personal collection" through classified ads are not required to conduct background checks or keep any records. This is another one of the terrible catch-22s that are built into our current gun laws. Like the Columbine gun-show loophole, this one is known as the newspaper loophole.

While the NRA was taking potshots at Clinton, the House of Representatives took a small but significant step toward passing sensible gun legislation, handing gun-control advocates a rare, though symbolic, victory in Congress. The House, in a nonbinding 218–205 vote, urged House and Senate negotiators to meet within 2 weeks to work out a compromise on long-stalled gun legislation.

Reiterating his call for tougher gun laws, the president also released the FBI's first annual report on the National Instant Criminal Background Check System (NICS), the computerized background-check system created under the Brady Law and in place nationwide since December of 1998. The new report showed that in its first year of operation, 10 million checks were run, and these checks stopped 179,000 felons, fugitives, domestic abusers, and other prohibited persons from buying guns.

Through NICS, the FBI and its state and local law-enforcement partners performed instant searches of more than 35 million records to help prevent the sale of guns to prohibited buyers. Here are some of the key findings of the report.

Most checks are completed within seconds. During the first year of NICS, 72 percent of checks were completed within 30 seconds, and 95 percent were completed within 2 hours. In the remaining cases, there is a good reason for additional time: An individual whose check takes more than 24 hours is almost 20 times more likely than the average gun buyer to be a felon or other prohibited purchaser.

PROFILE | Shikha Hamilton

I t's been reported that homicide is the leading cause of death among children in Detroit. Among 15- to 18-year-olds there, most of these murders are committed with guns.

In the summer of 1999, the nation was reeling from the high-profile shootings in Columbine and Granada Hills. But in Detroit, Shikha Hamilton was reeling from what was going on in her own neighborhood. Shikha was coping with her own misery, sitting at her daughter's hospital bedside, where she remained for more than 2 weeks as her baby girl struggled through a vicious bout with whooping cough. Little Avani was close to death, Shikha was told, but night after night, she held her child's hand and prayed. She also watched the news, and night after night she saw the children of Detroit being gunned down. This infuriated her. Here were children dying on the streets from something that was completely preventable while her own child lay dying from something over which she had no control.

Then, 6-year-old Kayla Rolland was shot and killed by a 6-year-old classmate right there in her schoolroom. The shooting took place in Flint, which, like Detroit, was an urban battleground with one of the highest rates of poverty and violence in the country. When Shikha heard this story, she decided then and there that she would not only fight for her daughter's life—but she would fight for the young victims of gun violence, too.

Shikha saw a news piece about the MMM, and she immediately knew what she had to do. She called a friend who works for Congresswoman Carolyn Cheeks Kilpatrick and asked him to solicit the congresswoman's support (which was immediately forthcoming). And then she traveled to Grosse Pointe, an affluent Detroit suburb, to attend her first Million Mom March meeting. Although Grosse Pointe abuts Detroit, the two communities couldn't be more different—Detroit is 90 percent African-American, whereas Grosse Pointe is almost exclusively Caucasian, and recognizing this, the Michigan state coordinator asked Shikha to help mobilize Detroit.

The majority of sales blocked were to felons and other criminals. Of sales denied by the FBI, 71 percent were to felons, 15 percent to individuals with domestic violence misdemeanors or who were under restraining orders, and 4 percent to persons with histories of drug abuse.

NICS checks help law enforcement apprehend fugitives. The report shows that 2,400 of those prevented from buying guns were also identified to federal, state, and local law-enforcement agencies—leading to the apprehension of dangerous fugitives from justice.

She hit the streets with zeal, flooding her community with fliers, attending community events, visiting police precincts. A complete novice on gun issues, Shikha, a lawyer, was a quick study. She downloaded fliers and passed them out wherever she went, and she recruited people from every corner of town. Lucky for us, Shikha isn't shy; she even went into the Detroit mayor's office in her MMM T-shirt, and after just one look, the mayor vowed his endorsement and offered her his help with the press. The press became a part of Shikha's campaign—a big part, in fact, because she knew if the media made it news, everyone from politicians to parents would pay attention.

Now that she had her congresswoman's and mayor's support, she set her sights on another prominent politician: the president of the United States.

As a member of the NAACP, Shikha knew the annual Freedom Fund dinner in Detroit was the organization's largest. She also knew President Clinton was scheduled to speak at the upcoming event. Once again, she put on her MMM uniform—our T-shirt—and Shikha and a teenager she mentors, Shannon, stood outside the dinner handing out MMM information to the elegantly dressed guests as they arrived. But Shikha wanted more. She turned to Shannon and said, "I cannot leave here without meeting the president." With that, the two of them casually walked into the dinner. President Clinton was speaking then, and no one seemed to notice the uninvited guests.

After his speech, the president moved around the room to shake hands with the guests. But Shikha couldn't get close to him. So she stood up on a chair and called out, "Hey, President Clinton!" and then she pointed to her T-shirt. He looked up and smiled when he saw her and shouted back, "I love you guys!"

That was it. Shikha decided she wasn't going to leave without having her picture taken with the president. The next day, the front page of the newspaper featured two photos from the big event: one of the president with the NAACP president and the other of President Clinton with Shikha and Shannon in their MMM T-shirts. The Detroit MMM was on the map.

Clearly, allowing time for the FBI and other law-enforcement outfits to run these checks is crucial to keeping guns out of the wrong hands. But Congress got held up on this one point. The NICS report shows that if the time allotted to conduct a check is cut to only 24 hours instead of the 3 business days currently allowed by law, nearly 34,000 prohibited purchasers—more than 38 percent of the FBI denials—would have received guns since the NICS first took effect. The NRA and their lobby keep pushing for Congress to shave 2 days off the current mandated waiting period. The gun-control lobby insists that 3 days be the minimum. This one point still has Congress stalled to this day.

I know all of this sounds complicated, but a few congressmen were doing their best to educate their constituents to the fact that closing these simple loopholes would save them grief as well. And despite the rhetoric to the contrary, this kind of legislation would not interfere with anyone's perceived right to own a gun.

Bart Stupak was one of these congressmen. He was busy holding town-hall meetings trying to explain his vote to his constituents. He did not run away from the problem, but instead tried to tackle it head on.

During the last few weeks, I would get on planes, trains, and subways to push for more buses. To beg for more people. To beg our volunteers not to give up. Nancy Gordon, our Pennsylvania state coordinator, had been worried that she was not going to fill many buses, so I started going back and forth to Philadelphia to do some media interviews, hoping to help out. In the end, Nancy didn't need me: Because of a recent spate of shootings in the state, the buses started to fill on their own. In one tragedy, five people were killed and one critically injured in a shooting spree near Pittsburgh that included a residential area, an Indian grocery store, a karate studio, and two synagogues. In early March, another incident took place in which two people were killed and several others critically wounded during a shooting rampage in the Pittsburgh area at a Burger King and a McDonald's.

This wasn't the worst shooting ever to happen at a fast-food restaurant, however. In July 1984, in San Ysidro, California, 22 people were shot dead at a McDonald's, and 19 others were injured. An unemployed security guard, James Oliver Huberty, 41, walked into the McDonald's that was within sight of his San Ysidro–area apartment and opened fire with three weapons. It was the worst single-day mass slaying in U.S. history.

The weapons Huberty used were banned in 1994 by President Bill Clinton when he signed the Assault Weapons Ban. Unfortunately, this ban is set to expire in September 2004, meaning that unless Congress *renews* the ban, Uzis and AK-47s will be legally back on our streets.

The NRA sometimes likes to boast that its highest membership is in the state of Pennsylvania. But by the spring of 2000, the people of Pennsylvania were paying attention to gun violence, and Nancy began filling buses faster than any other volunteer.

But buses weren't the only vehicles being put into service for the

MMM. In March, I got the news that the Jewish Community Center in my New Jersey town, which had been initially so indifferent to the Million Mom March, was now organizing an entire Amtrak train to Washington, D.C., for Mother's Day! Many of the seats hadn't been filled yet, but with the news of so many shootings, the Jewish leadership in New Jersey felt this was a spiritual mission and a social obligation.

As the march date approached, I started to get late-night phone calls from the grassroots, and the calls were usually bad news. But one night, Carole Price called me late with some fantastic news. The Maryland State Assembly had that night passed the toughest childproof handgun bill in the nation, something she and her husband, John, had been working tirelessly on with Marylanders against Handgun Abuse for a long time. The Governor was expected to sign the bill, and President Clinton was expected to attend the signing.

By now we were all on President Clinton watch, trying to draw his attention to the moms and what we were doing. We were even trying to invite him to the march. For some reason, the gun lobby liked to portray me as someone with easy access to him, but the truth was, I couldn't get within shouting range of the White House. (Remember that little incident with a presidential aide back in October?) But within the ranks, we had had a couple of close presidential encounters: Lisa Laursen-Thirkill attended a White House press conference but couldn't get close enough to ask a question and invite him. Another mother, Shikha Hamilton of Detroit, shouted out to him at an NAACP dinner from the cheap seats in the back of the room. He yelled back, "I love you guys!" He loves us, but will he come to the march and bring the White House press corps with him?

Carole, emboldened after her legislative victory, made it her mission to snare the president for Mother's Day 2000. Many of the moms wanted him there. He was our president. He should be there, marching with us. I, on the other hand, wanted him because I thought he could not only boost our numbers, but ensure that we'd have the White House press corps there as well. Bob Walker had made it abundantly clear that the media is bored with these kinds of events, and he expressed some skepticism that we would get anything beyond a mention in *Roll Call*. So, I was willing to go along with Carole's fantasy of marching with President Clinton. And through the magic of live television, I got to watch her in action. It was an April afternoon, and I was in Secaucus, New Jersey, at MSNBC, where I was slated to do an interview. But as had happened so many times in those days, there was a chance that we would be bumped for the Elian Gonzales story. If it weren't for the MMM, I would have followed every detail of the Elian Gonzales story, especially because of his colorful cousins. But now I just wanted this kid to either go back to Cuba or settle down in Miami—but to do it quick! We were losing too much precious media time to his story.

In the waiting area, the MSNBC television monitor was showing the president making his way to the historic Maryland gun-bill signing, and I kept looking for Carole, knowing she must be in the crowd. But I had trouble finding her. The president spotted her right away and jumped out of his motorcade. I could see that Carole had asked him something. What? What did she ask him? Why wasn't there sound on this thing?

I looked at the monitor closely. Carole was whispering something to him, and then he nodded his head. YES!

A *Time* magazine reporter, who was standing next to Carole, over-heard the exchange and reported his commitment to the Million Mom March in the magazine. Everyone was thrilled—everyone except the president's Secret Service detail. It turns out that if the president pub-licly announces where he is going to be on any given day, security has to be beefed up beyond belief. This would create an impossible finan-cial strain on our march, I would learn from the bean counters, and even worse, his presence would require us to have metal detectors and Secret Service agents everywhere. I had visions—nightmares—of mothers and 4-year-olds booing him when they couldn't get to the portable toilets because of the ring of Secret Service surrounding the place.

Actually, it was the steering committee that made the decision. But when it came time to vote on who would be the one to uninvite the president, somehow I got elected. The sad irony of this was that we couldn't invite the president to our gun-safety rally because of the fear that a gunman might have easy access to him there. We simply could not guarantee his security in such a public place.

In the meantime, I was having chest pains and angina over being the one who had to deliver the bad news to President Clinton. How does one uninvite a U.S. president? Like the joke about the best way to kiss a porcupine: very, very carefully.

8

"The doctor said, 'Your son has lost a lot of blood.' I said, 'Take my blood.' He said, 'He's also lost half of his brain.' I said, 'Take my brain.'"

—JACQUEE ALGEE,
THE ATLANTA ORGANIZER
FOR THE MILLION MOM MARCH,
TO OPRAH

MAY 2000

As my good friend down in Louisiana, Daniel B., predicted back in the fall of 1999, the gun lobby was planning on derailing the Million Mom March by attacking my credibility as a New Jersey mother concerned about gun violence. I thought I was the queen of spin until I watched the gun lobby in action. They were good at what they did. They began a whispering campaign that I was not really the clueless New Jersey housewife I pretended to be. But instead, I was some sort of "secret Democratic party operative!" This was such a secret that even I didn't know about it, although it did sound terribly Charlie's Angel-ish and far more glamorous than who I was. I wondered if these secret operatives drove minivans. I thought secret operatives spent their time shredding documents, while here I was, copying our message like mad. I had the Kinko's bill to prove it.

The "Campaign to Discredit Donna" really started to escalate in late April 2000. In order to minimize any PR damage the gun lobby might do, I asked the steering committee to replace me with Mary Leigh Blek, the Bell Campaign president. Mary Leigh was an empty nester, so she would be available to work round-the-clock and hop on a plane at a moment's notice. Ever since meeting Mary Leigh at the Tulsa meeting back on Columbus Day, I knew she had the kind of work ethic this job demanded. I had learned, by Spring Venoma's example, that it was crucial that I find a replacement before I stepped aside. Mary Leigh, an Orange County Republican, dressed as elegantly as Nancy Reagan (as opposed to me in my taped Gap overalls). I needed Mary Leigh to be ready to replace me. I was already on shaky ground emotionally because of the tenuous condition of my marriage, and I wasn't sure I had the fortitude to defend myself from the gun lobby's assertion that I was a pawn of Bill Clinton's. I mean, I didn't even vote for the man in 1992 (yet here he was, in 1999, the only president ever to stand up to the gun lobby). I was in a terrible catch-22. Distancing myself from the Clinton administration would be the ultimate act of disloyalty to the cause. All of this ridiculousness came about because I was married to a man whose sister was one of Hillary Clinton's best friends. It was baggage that the march didn't need.

The members of the steering committee were not at all concerned about this, and they urged me to stay on through the march. They thought that my resigning would be far more disruptive to the march and that naming Mary Leigh as a successor would give the Bell Campaign more power than the other gun-violence prevention organizations. What a headache.

And as much as I tried to take two steps back, I found myself being thrust into an even higher stratosphere when it came to the limelight. On the last day of April, I would get a media call that was like getting a ticket to the moon. The call came from Oprah. Well, actually Oprah's people.

Oprah was the Holy Grail of television talk shows, and, as with Rosie O'Donnell's show, the grassroots was dying to know when we'd get our turn with Oprah. It's not like we hadn't been trying: We wrote, called, and begged the producers to give us some airtime. By March, I had pretty much given up hope that we'd ever land a spot. But then the call came. We're still not sure how we got the booking, and many people wanted to take credit for it, but I believe we finally got through to Oprah when a Michigan mom's uncle, who lived in her building, slid one of our fliers under her door.

No matter how we got it, we got it. It was a last-minute booking, and we would share the hour with Attorney General Janet Reno, who was coming on to explain the use of force in the Elian Gonzales case.

The Million Mom March interview on *Oprah* was slated for May 2, less than 2 weeks before the march on May 14, 2000. I would go to Chicago for the taping, along with Gail Powers from Granada Hills and Jaquee Algee from Atlanta. In just 2 days, the producers of the show pulled together two up close and personal–style pieces to accompany our appearance. The days before the taping flew by.

But still, as always, there was so little time, and so much more to do. On the Sunday before the taping, I packed the kids into the minivan and headed out to Staten Island for a MMM picnic. A couple dozen people were there, including U.S. Senator Charles Schumer, who would be receiving the Apple Pie Award for being lead sponsor of the 1993 Brady Law and the Assault Weapons Ban in 1994. Seated next to me was New York City Police Officer Catherine Murphy, our Million Mom Marcher from Staten Island. I had met Catherine a few weeks before at an MSNBC taping in Secaucus. She had dreadlocks and a moon-pie face. She looked more like a hip young rapper than a police officer who was also a mother and wife.

When Senator Schumer jumped up to receive his pie—a tad too eagerly, it seemed—I leaned over to Catherine and whispered, "These guys really like their pies." She giggled, knowing exactly what I meant. After a few speeches and more Pie Awards, I glanced over at Catherine and saw that she was weeping quietly. I awkwardly tried to comfort her, but there was no easing her pain. She was clearly thinking about her 11-year-old son, Christopher, who had been shot and killed by a 12-year-old friend. Pedro, Catherine's husband, was also a police officer, and every night they came home from work and unloaded and locked up their service revolvers. It probably never dawned on either of them that their civilian neighbors would be so careless with their guns. Her story was so similar to Carole Price's of Maryland. Two mothers, two boys, two lives ruined in so many ways. Simply childproofing guns may have saved their children.

The actress Lee Grant was at the rally filming a documentary for Lifetime Television. She had just returned from Delaware, where she interviewed Joe Jaskolka and, like all of us who had spent time with Joe, she remarked that he was one of the smartest kids she'd ever met. Grant told me she would be filming at Handgun Control Inc.'s fundraiser, which would be hosted by Rosie O'Donnell the following night, and she wanted to know if I would be there, at Cipriani's in midtown. I told her she should look for a woman named Elise Richman, our Westchester mom, who would be attending in my place. Between taking care of my girls and getting ready for Oprah, I simply couldn't fit in a fancy fundraiser. So I sent Elise to the dinner with one mission: Find Andy McKelvey of Monster.com. He was now our biggest sugar daddy, but he was hard to get hold of. And someone from the Million Mom March needed to say thank you to Andy on our behalf.

I flew to Chicago the next day, Monday, and that night, I had a working dinner with Gail and Jacquee at a restaurant overlooking Michigan Avenue. It was only the second time I had met Gail face-to-face, and it was the first time I met Jacquee. Though we wanted to get to know each other better, we knew we had to be focused and ready for tomorrow's taping, so we kept the small talk to a minimum. We ran through the checklist: We had the Web site address, the date of the event, and our mission statement. We also decided that we would take this opportunity to recruit like mad. We wrapped up our meeting, said good night, and went off to our respective rooms to rest up. But when I got to mine, the red message light was blinking on my telephone.

It was a frantic call from an *Oprah* producer, who said that a woman I'll call "S"—one of the 151s who was always trying to make trouble—was threatening to boycott not only the *Oprah* show but the Million Mom March because, according to her, we didn't properly represent the African-American community. I didn't understand this. I reminded the producer that Jacquee, our mom up from Atlanta for tomorrow's taping, is African-American. This seemed to calm her down some. Oprah, the producer told me, was very sensitive to any charges—founded or not—of being in any way unfair to African-Americans. The producer told me that they would have a powwow about this in the morning, and that she would call S and tell her they were reconsidering doing the show at all, so would she please call off the boycott. We said goodbye and hung up. I was exhausted, but I simply couldn't sleep that night. The next morning, we were picked up early and taken to the studios of Harpo Productions. As soon as I walked through the door, a very kind producer met me and assured me that the S crisis had passed.

The producers of the show had taped a piece about Jacquee's son, and it floored me when I saw it. Jacquee's college-age son had been gunned down while he was helping a friend move. On tape, she recounted the horrible truth of it. She said, "The doctor said, 'Your son's lost a lot of blood.' And I said, 'Take my blood.' He said, 'He's also lost half of his brain.' And I said, 'Take my brain.'" One would think that Oprah had heard it all, but she was also visibly shaken by Jacquee's story. She told her audience (which was tens of millions), "You've now heard it, and if you choose to do nothing, then you become part of the problem . . . everybody can do something." Then she opened the floor for questions and comments. The audience was filled with moms, but as always, I was concerned that there might be a plant from the NRA or the Second Amendment Sisters. Oprah called on a woman who identified herself as Sally, and I held my breath, thinking, okay, here comes a Second Amendment Sister.

Sally: Oprah, I think our values are a little bit skewed. We put safety caps on medicine and aspirin in our home, we put seat belts on our children in cars, but we have no consumer protection laws on guns. It makes absolutely no sense, and it's time to do something to help stop the senseless killing.

Oprah: Yea, it's harder to open a CD!

Sally: That's right.

Oprah: Now that is a safety precaution, those CDs, no question about it. Yes. So you're saying?

Sally: Well, I'm saying that it's time for commonsense laws. It's time for guns to stop being exempt from consumer protection laws and from some types of . . .

Oprah: What about that big old gun lobby out there? Aren't you all scared of them?

Sally: I don't like coming up to the big old gun lobby; I know there are more of us, and I know that what we say makes sense. We're not saying take the guns away from people. We're not saying stop hunting. We're saying let's use common sense and start saving people's lives by treating guns like we treat cars and other things that can harm people.

Whew. Sally was sure on our side. So was Oprah.

Did I say we were lucky when it came to publicity? It sure felt that way that day in Chicago, but as it turns out, our *Oprah* appearance ran on the one day that her show was blacked out in some key markets because of a cable dispute. In all, about 3.5 million households around the country were deprived of *Oprah* that day because of a quarrel between two cable giants over transmission rights. In retrospect, maybe this was a blessing, because I'm not sure if we could have handled the response to more coverage. As it was, our phones rang nonstop, and MMM volunteers heard phones ringing in their sleep for days afterward.

I went back to New Jersey that same day, and the next morning, I was no longer the mother who got in trouble for holding up the carpool line at Phoebe's nursery school—I was the mother on *Oprah*. At least they had seen it in New Jersey. My kids, however, were not impressed. On the same day as the Oprah taping, I was supposed to be "snack mom" at Lili's school. I forgot, and Lili was mortified. So there was no snack for the class that day, except for the emergency stash of animal crackers that were given out when mothers—bad mothers—forgot snack day.

After *Oprah*, it was clear that we were no longer just a bunch of moms frantically waving our arms for media attention. Andy McKelvey, founder of Monster.com and our millionaire mensch, launched an eye-opening ad campaign in the weeks before the march. Clearly, he had no nonprofit experience, for if he did, he would have realized that nothing can be done without first forming committees and holding meetings to debate the merits of the ads. Instead, Andy just assigned a creative advertising team to produce and place a series of advertisements for us in newspapers up and down the East Coast. One of the hardest-hitting was the ad that ran in the *Washington Post* with the caption, "Most People Don't Care about Gun Violence until It Hits Close to Home." Beneath it was a photo of the National Zoo as a crime scene, closed off with yellow police tape, with the caption, "Close Enough Yet?"

Even though it had taken us a while to get her attention, Rosie O'Donnell was now fully on board, right on the front lines giving us daily support. Working with Andy McKelvey, she took out a full-page ad in the *New York Times* touting the march.

Rosie also agreed to fund a series of promotions for Handgun Control Inc. This caused an outburst from a few members on the steering committee who felt it violated the spirit of the Million Mom March. I, however, felt this was not only shortsighted—a promo for sensible gun laws was a promo for sensible gun laws—but, more important, this was Rosie's money. She could damn well do with it whatever she pleased.

Through HCI, word got back to her that the MMM steering committee objected to her promos, and Rosie called me at home, rather peeved and very blunt: "If I hear there is infighting among the gun-control groups like there is in the breast-cancer organizations, I swear, I'll pull out!"

Calming her down, I assured Rosie that all was well and fine among the groups, and her promos were not only needed, but very much appreciated by the Million Mom March.

I also heard from Anna Quindlen, who had initially declined my invitation to speak at the march, saying that she felt the need to spend her precious weekend hours with her kids. She had to reconsider when her kids heard about the march at school and began to pressure her to march. Was the offer to speak still good, Anna wondered? Of course it was!

From Rosie and Anna to the folks in the grassroots, we were all getting ready for the big day. It seemed that a never-ending stream of volunteers knocked at my door, looking for information or fliers to pass out. A woman from North Caldwell, New Jersey, dropped by one day to pick up a stack of fliers, and like so many before her, she had a story to tell: Her daughter and her daughter's roommate had been shot in St. Louis while at college. Her daughter survived, but her roommate did not. I also heard from and met many people who had no story to tell, and they wanted to keep it that way.

I've never been a great housekeeper, and it's a good thing, because over 9 months, pink-flowered posters and fliers seemed to stack up all over my Short Hills, New Jersey, home. The war room had crept up and out of the basement and was now taking over our living space. The dining room table had become the Essex County, New Jersey, MMM command center. It was covered with the tools of revolution: T-shirts, buttons, and MMM organizing booklets. On the floor were crayons and pink markers to keep the kids busy during the countless MMM meetings with bus captains and New Jersey organizers. Now, with just 8 days to the march, I felt like cleaning it all up. This sudden urge to rid the house of every flier, every poster, every press release, became overwhelming, so on Saturday, May 6, I grabbed a couple of boxes of materials, loaded up the car, and drove around northern New Jersey dropping them off. I can see now that this was the "nesting instinct" taking over. I stopped by St. Barnabas Hospital Emergency Room in Livingston and dropped off a box of fliers; I stopped in Kelly Shuz in Millburn and dropped off another. I stopped at a pediatrician's office in Short Hills and finished the job by wallpapering their bulletin board with the last handful of fliers.

As Mother's Day approached, U.S. Airways made an incredible gesture, donating tickets to fly some of the more needy families to D.C. for the march, and the first person I thought of was Spring Venoma. I called her and asked if I could fly her in from Michigan and out of Washington on the same day. Would she be able to make it then? "No," she answered, sounding as sorry as I felt. She just couldn't swing that much time away from her sick husband. She called me back 2 hours later and said her husband was insisting that she go. But she wouldn't accept the airline tickets. Instead, she said she wanted to ride the bus from Michigan to D.C., just like everybody else. She would travel with her daughter, while her daughter's boyfriend would stay home and take care of Spring's husband.

SUNDAY, MAY 7

One week to go. I woke up to the kids singing "Happy Birthday" to me, but for the most part, this birthday was just one big inconvenience. I had two news conferences later that day in Manhattan and was expected at the White House the next day to discuss President Clinton's participation in the Million Mom March. This would be tricky, because the march's professional organizers had already decided it would be better for everybody if the president's participation was minimal because of the logistical and security nightmare his presence would create. As the founder of the MMM, I had the responsibility of telling the president of the United States he couldn't come to our party.

In the middle of the birthday song, Rebecca Peters called and asked me to attend a meeting with her and billionaire Andy McKelvey's CFO to talk about the future of the MMM, following the march itself. This was the one meeting I should have kept that day, but because my head was spinning, and I was being pulled in 50 different directions, I didn't make it happen. It wasn't until a few weeks later that I realized how badly I had blown it.

As I was ready to dash out of my house, Rene Thompson, Kentucky mom, called to inform me that one of the moms who lost a child in the Paducah school shooting in 1997 felt she had been threatened. She thought someone may have shot at her house, and although she couldn't be sure if it was Million Mom March–related, she—and many others, including Rene—was spooked. I called Eric Gorovitz from the Bell Campaign on his cell phone in a panic. I was completely over my head and had no idea what to do; the thought that anyone could get hurt by being involved with the MMM was too much.

Eric reminded me that James Day had already put a former Secret Service agent under contract to handle these kinds of emergencies, and he encouraged me to keep doing what I'd been doing. He assured me that he would follow up with Rene.

When I hung up with Eric, I drove into the city. I was still so rattled that I forgot to bring Rebecca Peters' cell phone number with me. I was to call her after the first news conference so we could plan when and where to meet. I was late for the first news conference, which was at the American Jewish Congress, uptown. That threw off my whole day, so I was even later for the second news conference, which was for 100 Blacks in Law Enforcement, and which was downtown. Both organizations were strong supporters of the MMM, and they were very forgiving. I don't remember much about the first news conference other than a very nice rabbi singing my praises and Joe Sudbay from Handgun Control Inc. showing an ad from the NRA that depicted the gun lobby bragging that "if George W. Bush is elected president, we'll work right out of the White House." Scary.

After the meeting downtown, I tried to reach Rebecca at her other numbers, the ones I knew off the top of my head, but she was expecting me to call her on her cell. Rebecca was frustrated with my scattershot schedule, and she was frustrated with our management team, too, for not providing me with a secretary to help me navigate the last, crazy days. As it turns out, I didn't have another opportunity to talk to her with a clear head before the march. For the few days before march day, I ran from one media appearance to the next. While we were optimistic that the march would be a success, we had no idea what would become of the MMM after Mother's Day, and this was a huge concern to Rebecca Peters and the Soros-Diamond Fund. And, as I would learn from Elise Richman, it was a concern of Andy McKelvey's too, since he had so heavily invested in us.

I made it home on my birthday at around 6 P.M., just in time for birthday cake and a huge hug from my girls. Jeff gave me a card that said, "Thank you for making the world a safer place for our kids." It was a sweet acknowledgment of the Million Mom March, and I took this as a good sign. I decided to skip the train that night and risk flying to Washington early the next morning for the 9 A.M. meeting at the White House. I had a week's worth of last-minute planning to take care of in Washington, and I would not come home again until after the march. For this birthday, more than any other, I needed to be home with Jeff and the girls.

At 5 A.M. the next morning, Monday, May 8, I handed the driver from the car service a suitcase stuffed with wrinkled, unmatched clothing. Almost as an afterthought, I ran back into the house and gathered up in my arms a huge stash of MMM fliers, the last batch. Like an expectant mother rushing to the hospital, I knew my life would change when I got home. I just didn't know how much.

As usual, I was cutting things too close, and 2½ hours later, I arrived at Baltimore-Washington International Airport. It was just about 8 A.M., rush hour. With the notorious Beltway traffic, I wasn't sure how long it would take to get to the White House, but the president would have to wait. With my suitcase dragging behind me, I stopped off at every ladies' room from the U.S. Airways gate to the front door of 1600 Pennsylvania Avenue, until all the fliers, every last one of them, were gone. It was totally insane—but in a good way.

I was warned prior to going into the White House that the president was expecting me to personally invite him to speak at the march. Little did he know that I was coming to do the opposite. We were ushered into a conference room—me, Mike Barnes from HCI, Andrew McGuire from the Bell Campaign, and Mike Beard from the Coalition to Stop Gun Violence. Attorney General Janet Reno was there, too, as were an assortment of Million Mom Marchers selected by the Bell Campaign.

Joe Podesta, the president's chief of staff, began the meeting: "So," he asked. "Is there something you'd like to ask the president?" Uh-oh, I thought, here it comes. The president was expecting his invitation. Joe Lockhart, the press secretary, had already slipped out to get the White House photographers and press ready for the announcement that the president would be the keynote speaker at the Million Mom March. All eyes were on me. "Is there something you would like from the president?" Podesta asked again, his look expectant.

"Uh, uh, uh, could the Dunblane moms get a tour of the White House?" I stuttered. It was lame, I admit. But it was the best I could do at the time. The president did not look happy, but he was nothing if not game. He kept trying to stay involved: Would we need Cabinet members to attend? How about Secretary of State Madeleine Albright? "Yeah, sure," I said, "as long as she doesn't need any Secret Service detail." We were asked to stay for a few photos, then we were all politely ushered out of the room. Just as we were leaving, President Clinton said, "Don't give up." I will always remember that—he knew we were in for an uphill battle, but those were his words: "Don't give up."

We went out to the White House pressroom, where Joe Lockhart had already announced that the president would be attending the Million Mom March. Now I stood before the press corps and nervously addressed the reporters, telling them the president wouldn't be speaking, that it was a matter of security—we simply didn't have adequate resources to provide for his security.

The MMM Steering Committee may have decided that the president couldn't come to our party, but that didn't stop the Michigan Million Mom Marchers from inviting the president and the first lady to theirs. Joy Livingston, who'd taken over the reins in Michigan from Spring Venoma, e-mailed the White House to invite the Clintons to their pre-march cocktail party at the Grand Hotel on the edge of Georgetown. In fact, Joy had the entire Michigan Million Mom March delegation bombard the White House with invitations.

Apparently, a very smart aide noticed the flurry of invitations coming in and took it as the opportunity to get the president airtime with the Million Mom March. Instead of having their invitation to a cocktail party accepted, the Michigan moms were invited to the White House for a pre-MMM rally for Sunday morning. I loved it that the grassroots moms didn't need to go through the official channels to get what they wanted. If the president can't make it to the mall, the Michigan moms thought, then the mall would come to him.

That week was filled with other tense moments, especially last-minute requests from staffers trying to get their bosses a moment in the sun (assuming there would be sun). The buzz was out—our stage was hot, and everybody was trying to secure a space on it. Vice President Al Gore wanted to speak, and though he didn't pose the same security risks as the president, our event manager, Rick Jasculca, advised us to keep high-profile politicians off the stage. They would speak too long, he cautioned, and they would wander off-message. The last thing we wanted was to turn this into a political convention. But Rick didn't want to be the one to deliver that news. Would I? No. I worried that if I turned Gore down, and he became president, I would surely be audited by the IRS. Instead, Andrew McGuire, from the Bell Campaign, told Gore's secretary that, though we were sorry, it would be impossible to have the vice president speak at our event. These sticky situations made it very clear to me that we needed a savvy political director to creatively involve Gore and other politicians who championed our cause. Since we didn't offer Gore an alternative form of involvement, he ended up babysitting his grandson on march day while Tipper and their daughter marched.

The phone was always busy at our national office, and volunteers packed three rooms that were clogged with tables and phones. The core of these volunteers were senior citizens—you couldn't have asked for a more dedicated, loyal, and productive group of grandmas and a few grandpas, too. These women were seasoned multitaskers. One of them in her eighties flirted between answering hundreds of calls and even managed to land two dinner dates. The troops were given a crash course in gun control by HCI's Connie Rucker. She ran a tight ship, and her seniors became very savvy very fast.

When people couldn't get through, they would just call my hotel, including Rosie, who tracked me down to say she wanted to march with Dawn Anna—the mother of the Columbine valedictorian who'd been killed in the massacre—and Sophie Newman, a 7-year-old activist from St. Louis who showed true grassroots spirit by writing to Rosie and getting herself invited to appear on her show to promote the march (something we moms had spent months trying to do ourselves!).

THURSDAY, MAY 11

Melissa Connor, our director of publicity, arranged a press conference on the National Mall. This was probably the fifth press conference we'd held on the mall since we announced the march in September. On this day, however, the staging was in place and huge Million Mom March banners dwarfed everything in sight. I was overwhelmed. This just didn't match up with the image I had held in my head for these months of our moms gathering in front of a soapbox, with speakers using megaphones to address the crowd. Now here I was, in front of not one stage, but two: One would be the main stage for our keynote speakers and invited guests (gun-violence victims and celebrities), and the second, which was set several blocks behind the first, would have a nonstop lineup of speakers, too. Rick Jasculca updated the crowd estimate from 50,000 to 150,000, but even that number was a little suspect. If it didn't rain, we might even double that. But rain was in the forecast for Sunday, Mother's Day.

I was feeling kind of cocky that day, as I remembered all of the second-guessing that had dogged us for most of the months leading up to this point. But before my head could swell too much, Deborah Kellye-Watkins took the podium and told the gathered reporters what it was like to lose a child to gun violence.

I started to cry. I don't know if it was Deborah talking about her son or the pressure of the last few months, including the problems with my marriage, but I began to cry and couldn't stop. Melissa caught my eye, and I could see that she was worried that her main spokesmom was on the verge of losing it. But my tears dried up as soon as I was hit with a barrage of rather hostile questions, such as how was it that I had contributed to Hillary Clinton's campaign but had failed to mention that. If I were more clearheaded, I would have responded, "Yeah, and I contributed to my Fire Island congressman Rick Lazio's (her Republican rival's) campaign, too." Of course, that's when the only issue I cared about was beach erosion.

At least some of the personal attacks made me seem more interesting than I really was, like the *Chicago Sun-Times* opinion that tried to paint me as a loony, leftist lesbian. (This investigative tidbit was based on the fact that I summered on Fire Island.) Only 2 of the 31 communities on

Fire Island are predominately gay and lesbian. The rest of the island is mostly twenty-somethings looking for a good time, or families. This fact was somehow lost on the *Sun-Times* guest columnist who described my Fire Island lifestyle as "hedonistic." Maybe he was referring to the time I went to the Seaview Market at 7 A.M. in my pajamas to satisfy a craving for a jelly doughnut. At the time, I was 7 months pregnant and pushing a 15-month-old in a stroller.

I found it amazing that the media found me so interesting. And I decided it would be best to just let the conservative pundits have their way with me.

Fox News's Brit Hume tried to give it a shot on his show *Political Grapevine.* He tried to make something of the "secret Democratic party operative" buzz about me, but he didn't get very far.

Brit Hume: More information you haven't heard from the rest of the media on Donna Dees-Thomases, organizer of that women's march for gun control here this weekend. *NBC News* says she's, quote, 'a mother who's never been politically active,' but, in fact, she once worked for retired Louisiana Democratic Senators Russell Long and Bennett Johnston. And the Media Research Center says she's been giving to Hillary Clinton's Senate campaign since last year.

Brit Hume: Let's talk a bit about this upcoming event which has generated so much attention, the Million Mom March. It's expected to not generate a million moms, maybe something like one-seventh of that, but there's a lot of excitement about it, a lot of publicity, and this character has emerged, Donna Dees-Thomases, who is leading it and is widely described in quite favorable media accounts as a mother who was simply there watching television at home one day, while tending to her children one presumes, and she saw horrible scenes of a shooting at a youth center where kids were killed, and she had to do this. So what are we to make of all this?

Fred Barnes, a conservative pundit who was Brit's guest, tried to write me off as a complete fraud.

Fred Barnes: Of course, all that's fakery. I mean, this is a woman who is a contributor to Hillary Clinton's Senate campaign. She's the

sister-in-law of Susan Thomases, who is a hardnosed liberal operative and one of Hillary's best friends. She's a New York City PR
woman who's worked for Dan Rather. I mean, this is not some stay-
at-home mom who's mad about Columbine.

Fred Barnes: It's just ridiculous, and, Brit, when you talk about all this
excitement over this thing, what there is is inordinate media attention, not because there's a huge groundswell against, in favor of, gun
control around the country. Far from that, it's because the media is
biased in a liberal direction, and they like this issue, so they're pretending like this thing is much bigger than it is.

What Fred Barnes and Brit Hume didn't know was that we were
underplaying our numbers, and there was a good chance we'd be well
over 250,000 strong come Sunday. Anyone who went to the National
Mall could have guessed at the kind of crowd we were really expecting
based on one thing alone: the number of portable toilets there. We
needed one for every 300 people expected. Deborah Wachspress, the
New Jersey state coordinator, went to the mall in the rain the night before the march and cried when she saw all the portable toilets. Brit and
Fred, it seemed, would eat their words—especially if the rain stopped.

The difference between a movement led by one person and a movement
of a million is that while the Right Wing was trying to discredit me,
moms across the country were popping up all over the place as media stars.
Take Tina Jackson, for example, yet another mother who'd lost a son to
senseless gun violence. She was a government census worker by day who
was a Million Mom Marcher in her spare time. She was direct, passionate,
and riveting when she spoke. No professional publicist could have dreamed
up the sound bites that were coming out of the mouths of real moms.

Tina scolded one reporter who questioned our confidence in thinking
we could push a bill through Congress when so many other skilled lobbyists had failed. "If we moms can push babies out of our bodies," Tina
said, "some with heads as big as bowling balls, then surely we can push
a bill through the halls of Congress!"

The day continued to be jam-packed. I stopped by to give a pep talk
to the Washington Hilton ballroom gathering of more than 1,000 volunteers for Sunday's event. Andrew McGuire of the Bell Campaign said
that this gathering technically became the second largest gathering of

gun-control advocates ever, the first being a rally to protest the NRA convention in Denver, Colorado, right after Columbine. Later, I would end up at the *ABC News* Washington bureau to go over the ground rules for the next day's scheduled broadcast from the White House. And before bed, I would finish half a dozen radio interviews set up for me by Melissa Connor.

FRIDAY, MAY 12

I returned to the White House once more that week, this time for a 2-hour live broadcast on *Good Morning America*. But by the time Friday rolled around, I was coming down with some bug (or maybe it was just too much coffee on too little sleep, a bad habit lately). I tried to wiggle my way out of going to the *GMA* production, hoping, maybe, that I wouldn't have to face the president *again*, but the producer—who had been very kind and accommodating until then—blew up at me when I suggested that I might back out.

I arrived at the White House feeling nauseous, but I managed to pull myself together—something I'd become good at lately. To add to my feeling unwell, there was a tremendous amount of tension among the scheduled guests, including Million Moms, representatives from the NRA, and a group of women who'd lost their kids to gun violence— the broadcast had everything but mud wrestling. Even the president wasn't in a great mood.

Meanwhile, another kind of victim of gun violence was getting a lot of media play. A state legislator named Suzanne Haupt was running around doing interviews about her own tragic story. Her parents were killed in 1991 in the Luby's Cafeteria massacre in Killeen, Texas. Suzanne's parents were among the 23 people shot and killed by George Hennard. Twenty others were injured. Suzanne believes that her parents would still be alive if she had brought her gun into Luby's with her, instead of leaving it out in the car. At the time, it was illegal to carry and conceal weapons in Texas. No one could argue with her that maybe the outcome of that massacre might have been different if she were able to shoot Hennard first. But it seemed to me that, rather than arm everyone, as she suggested, wouldn't it be better to stop mentally ill people from buying guns in the first place?

Both of Hennard's firearms were purchased legally in 1991 from

Mike's Gun Shop in Henderson, Nevada. Although he had a history of mental illness, Hennard was never committed by court order to a mental-health institution. Federal law prohibits firearms purchases by people who have been committed to a mental-health facility under court order only. Only the State of Connecticut has seen the insanity of allowing people with documented disturbed behavior to keep their guns. Connecticut now allows law enforcement to confiscate guns after threats are made from clearly disturbed people. It is the only state in the union that sees the wisdom in doing this.

Despite feeling so sick, I was whisked off to the National Press Club right from the *GMA* taping at the White House. Hazel Bradford, a volunteer PR person, handed me some copy to read to the press. I felt weak and shaky as well as blindsided and confused by some of the questions, particularly those implying that I still worked for *CBS News*, and wasn't that a conflict? I hadn't worked for *CBS News* in 7 years, a simple enough fact to check, and yet it continued to be an issue. Why wouldn't we let the Women's Shooting Sports Foundation—Shari LeGate's group—give away trigger locks on the mall? "Because the National Park Police said no," I said emphatically. Why were these questions so hostile? I wanted to ask right back at them. Who were these people? Then someone, a legitimate reporter, asked me the question that would haunt me for months and add tension to an already explosive mix of personalities and power within the movement: "After the march, then what?"

I started to say we were all just going to Disney World, but then thought better of it. In retrospect, it would have been a safer answer, but instead, I said something to the effect that after May 14, it would be "No more Mrs. Nice Mom." I claimed that the "oven mitts would come off, and we'd be working to elect better candidates to office." Of course, I also added that we'd be working with the existing state gun-control groups, but the damage had been done.

The story that came out on the wire was that the "Million Mom March will become a political organization," and although it was a bit of a misquote, I had messed up. I should have called the Associated Press to correct it right away, but I was just so tired, I let it go. And that tiny quote ended up causing an outcry in the whole gun-control movement—suddenly, everyone felt betrayed, as if the MMM had been planning all along to become a separate, political organization. Rebecca Peters called to yell at me, and Mike Barnes, the president of HCI, was extremely upset, because the MMM was now perceived as encroaching on his territory.

The NRA came at me with guns blazing after that. Conservative columnists started writing about my "hedonistic Fire Island lifestyle" (again!). Congressman Bob Barr put out a three-page press release "exposing" my political history as a Democratic operative—though he failed to mention that the pinnacle of my Capitol Hill career was my stint as "Yambassador."

SATURDAY, MAY 13

So much for there being a calm before the storm. Or a moment's peace before the water breaks. The Saturday before the march was crammed. From a rally over at Freedom Plaza organized by the D.C. moms, to a trip to Eastern Market to do a last-minute flier blitz to the southeast D.C. neighborhood, I was on the move.

Sometime in between, I was whisked over to *The Diane Rehm Show* on NPR for an hour-long interview on the Million Mom March. Pat Thomas joined me from the Bell Campaign by phone. And, in the studio, I was joined by Carole Price and the Reverend Jim Atwood, who was organizing the Interfaith Service to be held before the march. The Reverend Atwood, our spiritual midwife, is an avid hunter who has volunteered for years at the Coalition to Stop Gun Violence.

Of the four of us, two were mothers who'd lost sons: Carole, of course, and Pat, whose son Jerome was 19 when he was killed by a 15-year-old with a gun that couldn't be traced to its original owner because this country lacks national registration. Pat pointed this out on the show. Her son Jerome was not in a gang; he was from a good home.

The producer warned us ahead of time that the callers might skew male, because on yesterday's show, also devoted to the Million Mom March, the hostess was accused of taking calls from women who favored our position. We braced ourselves for the barrage.

The first caller was from Germantown, Maryland. He identified himself as an army small-arms specialist.

Diane Rehm: Brett you're on the air!

Oh, Lord, I thought, here it comes.

Brett: If we don't start registering guns and imposing stiffer penalties . . . if we don't start doing this now, then our kids should curse the ground we walk on.

Rev. Atwood: Bless him!

Diane Rehm: Let's go to Alexandria, Virginia, to David!

David: How can we volunteer to help on Sunday?

If this show was any indication of public sentiment, then the statistics were right. The majority of Americans were with us. Even a legal gun owner from New Haven, Connecticut, called in and contradicted the most right-wing contingent of the gun lobby that believes guns should be loaded and ready at all times. If you have kids, Mr. New Haven lectured, you have to lock your guns up in a vault or a safe. A mother of eight called in, identifying herself as a pheasant hunter, and I thought, here comes a Second Amendment Sister. But no, she said she was praying that people vote this issue.

Pheasant Hunter: As much as we love our guns, we love our children more!!

Diane had to interrupt and remind listeners that the callers were not prescreened to be pro–our cause. It was just working out that way. Then came along Don from Groton, Connecticut. Don was completely irritated that we expected gun owners to pay for a safety license. New guns would automatically be registered when they left the manufacturers, one of the reasons the manufacturers object (added cost plus diminished demand by criminals). But Don was irritated that he already had to pay $10 for a driver's license. And, damn it, he refused to do this for a gun license, he said.

Don: I should have to pay for this license and have to renew this every year? I should have to pay for this, like a driver's license?

The divisiveness of the gun issue seems to plant people firmly on one side or the other, and it is assumed that the line is drawn between liberal and conservative, Democrat and Republican. Alas, death is bipartisan, an equal-opportunity stalker—even death by gun.

Mary Leigh Blek is a staunch conservative; a lifelong Republican from the famously Republican bastion of Orange County, California. Mary Leigh is also one of the strongest voices in the crusade against gun violence. Like so many of us, she did not start out to be an activist. Mary Leigh was a stay-at-home mom, much like me, who lived in a nice, safe community, organized bake sales for the PTA, led a troop of Brownies, and loved her children. And like so many, her life was shattered at the speed of a bullet. In 1994, her 21-year-old son, Matthew, was shot on the streets of New York City by three 15-year-old boys who attempted to rob him. One of those boys wielded a Saturday Night Special. Matthew was Mary Leigh's firstborn, a gifted college student, a warm and caring young man. Not a day goes by that she doesn't think about him and mourn his loss.

She got involved in gun control shortly after Matthew's death, after attending the trial in New York of the boys who had shot and killed her son. A front-page story in the *New York Times* about her prompted people from all parts of the country to contact her with their own stories. This prompted Mary Leigh to learn more about the gun-safety issue. And the more she learned, the more outraged she became. The more outraged she became, the more she wanted to be a part of the solution. Her local Orange County organization was one of the pieces that ultimately became the Bell Campaign, a national victim-led organization whose mission was to prevent gun death and injury and to support victims and survivors of gun trauma. Mary Leigh discovered her own outspokenness quite by accident when, at a protest in Denver, Colorado, shortly after the

Pat Thomas: You feel this is too much trouble to save the life of a child?

Don: Yes, it is too much trouble!!!

This one man probably helped us more than all of the supportive calls we got combined. I jumped in and used the opportunity to plead with listeners to get involved. "If you disagree with Don, then please show up on Sunday and be counted," I begged.

Columbine massacre, she publicly declared to the NRA, "We love our children more than you love your damn guns."

The gun that killed Matthew was a cheap, junk weapon known as a Saturday Night Special, the kind of toylike handgun that was produced cheaply, distributed easily, and bought inexpensively around the country. At the time, 80 percent of these junk guns were produced in California. Mary Leigh and her husband, Charlie, joined others in California to establish minimal safety standards for domestic handguns, because there are no federal safety standards. "Matthew's old teddy bear and crib had consumer safety standards, but the gun that was used to kill him had none," she says. They succeeded in banning the production and sale of Saturday Night Specials in California, but with no federal safety standards, these guns will simply be produced in other states.

As a trained nurse, Mary Leigh's view of the epidemic of gun violence is very practical: She sees this as a public-health issue. And it is. "I strongly believe that public safety is a proper and necessary role for our national government, and we must rise above partisan politics to ensure the safety of our families," she said when addressing a congressional committee. "It is obvious that we are doing a terrible and shameful job of protecting our children. Please consider the fact that our firearm death rate for our children, 14 years and younger, is 12 times higher than for 25 other industrialized nations combined."

Mary Leigh was already the president of the Bell Campaign when I met her. The Bell Campaign was a true grassroots group, and she immediately saw the importance of harnessing our growing national attention with the strengths of their local and state level networks. Our ragtag band of mothers was growing at such a fast pace, we would need someone like Mary Leigh to keep us going after the march was over.

———

On Saturday, May 13, I stopped by the national office to be debriefed, and while I was there, Andy McKelvey called with some fantastic news: He wanted to help us keep the Million Moms alive after the march, and so he would invest another $2 million in us! This was on top of the million he had already invested in ads, Jumbotrons, bumper stickers—you name it—on the actual event.

The thought of $2 million to an inside-the-beltway nonprofit means more staff. To a grassroots organization like us, it meant we would finally be able to get materials to inner-city moms and to moms in rural areas. Two million meant more ads, better tech support—more of everything we needed.

I had no idea what Andy's promise to us would do to the rest of the movement, many members of which had been working on this issue for a very long time—some for the 30 years since the death of Bobby Kennedy (which unofficially marks the beginning of the gun-control debate in America)—with very little money. But I was too busy on the 13th to worry about all that. I needed to run out and buy a new pair of sneakers. I had lost my old ones at the MMM national office, where they had probably been thrown out with the trash.

Kimberly Rowland from the Bell Campaign offered to drive me to a store, and Judy Jasculca, wife of Rick, our project manager, offered to give me money to pay for them.

I went back to the Monarch Hotel and was pleasantly surprised to see that a few buses had lined up and were discharging passengers wearing Million Mom March T-shirts. I asked one of the passengers if she knew whether Spring Venoma had arrived. Yes, I was told, and she had already checked in to the hotel. The next few hours would be reunions with women I had never laid eyes on, including Spring, Dana Quist, and Rene Thompson. They were all here. And some of them even brought their husbands. Rene's husband, Stephen, was recruited by the MMM national office—by Connie Rucker, I'm sure—to stuff envelopes. Many dads came along to be honorary moms that weekend.

That night there was a series of parties. I tried to make the rounds, but Bonnie Berrie, who was acting as my handler, gave me the bad news that I was expected at the White House at 6 A.M. the next morning. Six A.M.!! I thought the president's premarch rally started at 10! For the thousand people expected to pass through security, we had to be there at 6 A.M.

I tried to go to bed shortly before midnight, but the sound of thunder and bursts of lightening kept me up. Not to mention the stray radio talk-show host who managed to get past the hotel operator and call me in my room.

What if no one showed up tomorrow? Well, at least I knew that a few of us would: Spring was there; so were the founding moms, Amy, Debbie, Robin, Alison, and Julie. Plus Dana Quist from Florida. Even Rene, our agoraphobic mom from Kentucky, got on a plane and came.

The only person I was really worried about was Rosie O'Donnell, who was supposed to fly in that afternoon from Disney World where she was taping the May sweep shows. Her plane and several others were rumored to be very, very late. I went to bed that night not sure if we would have an emcee in the morning. Or, more important, if the rain would ever stop and allow the ground a few hours to dry out before the crowds we hoped for arrived.

The pressure was enormous, and it was personal. The difference between the pressure I had faced in my career and the pressure I faced on the eve of the Million Mom March was that I didn't want to let the mom volunteers down. So I'd already asked the press secretary of the march to end any speculation about who I was or where I came from by putting out a one-page statement that Mary Leigh Blek of the Bell Campaign would officially be taking over as president for the MMM as of May 15, 2000. The change would be good for everyone, and I knew it would throw the NRA for a loop. It completely deflated their case against me—if I was leaving the day after the march, who could possibly care what my motives (however sincere) were for getting the MMM off the ground? This announcement wasn't just a ploy to outfox the enemy: I was also totally drained. I still had hopes of trying—one more time—to salvage what was left of my marriage. (After all, if I could help rally a million moms to fight for better gun-safety laws, surely I'd be able to convince the husband I adored to stay home.) Most of all, I really missed my kids and the mundane aspects of being a mom. Once I'd shepherded the march to life, it would be time to pass the baton.

DELIVERY

9

> "If we moms can push babies through our bodies, some with heads as big as bowling balls, surely together we can push a bill through Congress to protect those babies."
>
> — TINA JACKSON,
> WASHINGTON, D.C.,
> COORDINATOR

MOTHER'S DAY: MAY 14, 2000

5 A.M.

The clock-radio alarm cut through the only sleep I'd had all week, and I'd have thrown my new Reeboks at the snooze button if only I had the energy. After a measly 4 hours, I just wanted to roll over. I'd tried to get to sleep by midnight the night before, but every time I'd drift off, the phone would ring. I don't know how they managed to get through, but I got calls from all types throughout the night. There were the gun lovers who demanded, "Are you the (expletive deleted) lady trying to take my guns away?" (no, for the millionth time), and an intrepid radio talk-show host who asked, "So, you nervous that nobody is going to show up tomorrow, and you'll be the laughingstock of America come Monday morning?"

It was kind of tough to go back to sleep after that last call because, of course, the answer was a big, fat yes.

I was staying at the Monarch Hotel on the edge of Georgetown. Despite the name of the hotel, I felt more like a worn-out dishrag than royalty. I had been living on nothing more than coffee and adrenaline the past few days, and as I lay there in bed trying to catch a few more minutes of sleep, I found myself listening to the radio, waiting for the weather forecast. It had poured the night before, dampening our staging but not our spirits.

Some anonymous newscaster announced that we had raised our estimated attendance figures from 50,000 to 150,000. By now, in my heart, I truly believed this was lowballing it, but I realized it was better to be cautious at this stage of the game. I felt like our "raised" estimate was the same kind of news an obstetrician would deliver to his expectant patient when his stethoscope has picked up an extra heartbeat or two (or maybe even three). He can't be entirely sure without a sonogram, so he fudges it with "maybes" and "could be's," and even then he can't be 100 percent certain of what might be a bellyful of babies. He just knows it's not exactly what the mother has been preparing for, so he tries gently to brace her for some earth-rattling news.

At the crack of dawn on this particular morning, I felt like I was about to go into hard labor with triplets, and the hospital had just run out of anesthesia.

How in the heck, I wondered, did I let myself get into this condition?

6 A.M.

I stumbled around in the dark hotel suite, trying to comb the hair and brush the teeth of two very sleepy and cranky girls. After I got my daughters dressed, I threw on the only clean Million Mom March T-shirt I had left, the aquamarine one reserved for security detail, plus a pair of shorts and my sneakers. I threw open the curtains on the huge window in my hotel suite. It was a glorious day. The sun was out, and it was 75 degrees. I knew then that Mother Nature was a mom.

Originally, I wasn't due to be at the National Mall until at least 9 A.M., so I was going to treat myself to having my hair and makeup professionally done. Most of the media shots of me over the past 9 months had me without makeup, hair pulled hastily into a ponytail, and my uniform of T-shirt and ancient overalls. I thought I ought to at least try to upgrade my look for the big event. So much for wishful thinking. On Saturday night, I'd learned I'd have to be at the White House on Sunday morning at 6 A.M. for a pre-MMM rally. The hair and makeup people refused to come by that early, and so I got stuck with bed-head and a whopping cancellation fee. Even my mother, who had come up from Louisiana to help out with the kids a few weeks earlier, refused to get up that early. She gently reminded me that she often got up at 6 A.M. when I was a kid, but that that was a long time ago. Instead, she would meet us later on the mall. Off I went to the White House, with my sleepy, hungry kids and cranky husband in tow. At least we were clean.

And when we got to 1600 Pennsylvania Avenue, the Secret Service informed me that I could just take a seat on the curb. Through some bureaucratic snafu—of which I'd had plenty of experience these past months—I had not cleared security. My husband and kids, on the other hand, were welcome to walk right in.

As I sat there on the curb with my head in my hands, I thought about how President Clinton must have felt when I had to tell him earlier in the week that he couldn't speak on stage. Was this some kind of weird presidential revenge, I worried, or worse, was it an omen of what the day would bring?

Then some lunatic on the corner came over, and with his megaphone assured me that the curb was not such a bad place to sleep. Hmmm. Before I could give that some serious thought, he saw some other Million Mom Marchers breezing right past the Secret Service. He grabbed his megaphone and started shouting, "Don't go in there!! Women are not safe in there!!" This was not a good sign, I thought. Not a good sign at all.

9 A.M.

Even Carole Price, whose metal body-piercings set off every bell, whistle, and alarm, got cleared before I did. The Secret Service finally let me in, and it wasn't long before I wished I were back out on the street. My two ravenous, breakfast-deprived kids were on the verge of a major tantrum right there in the East Wing. I thought, mistakenly, that we were invited for breakfast. But only orange juice was served.

And to add insult to injury, my girls were informed by White House Presidential Secretary Bettie Currie that the most popular couple of the house wouldn't be available to greet them. Too busy, I suppose. I guess I shouldn't have bribed them with the promise of a private audience with Socks and Buddy, but I'd been desperate to get them excited to wake up at 5 A.M. Jeff, being a typical dad, was oblivious to the impending disaster, because he was busy chatting up the president. Luckily, the first lady—a mother—arrived dressed in hot colors, and I could tell she recognized on my face the look of a mother on the verge of some kind of breakdown.

What saved me was being introduced to Veronica McQueen, the mother of 6-year-old Kayla Rolland, who'd been shot by a 6-year-old boy in Flint, Michigan. Veronica thanked me profusely for giving her an opportunity to speak from the stage that day. I was stunned. She was thanking me? I was extremely grateful that she would speak out about her terrible tragedy.

Not only did she have to endure the loss of her child, but because her daughter's death made her a vocal gun-control advocate, she became, like me, a target for the gun nuts. It still saddened me, but I had discovered, over the course of the MMM journey, that it doesn't matter who you are or what you suffered, you will be attacked by gun nuts if you have the courage to speak out against the proliferation of firearms in this country. Despite this, people like Veronica McQueen refused to be silenced. This made her a hero in my book, and being around her gave me a fresh and much-needed boost of energy.

I looked over at my two girls, thankful that I had them safe and sound with me—even if they were not exactly on their best behavior at the moment. They were whispering to each other, conspiring to get into the kind of trouble only a 6- and a 4-year-old can manage while being surrounded by adults in a room full of historical artifacts they are not supposed to touch. A White House aide came in and said I was wanted outside on the front lawn for a live shot with *Meet the Press*. Seeing my kids restlessly eyeing the presidential sofa as a possible trampoline, Mrs. Clinton assured them that Socks and Buddy would be down momentarily, thereby freeing me to join my old nemeses, NRA leader Wayne LaPierre, for a media moment. Actually, I was more afraid of the host, Tim Russert, than Wayne. Tim and I had had a few encounters in the past, mostly wherein Tim would fire shots at his competitor, my then-boss, Dan Rather. I had dutifully acted as Dan's defender, and I was hoping Tim didn't remember me, or at least that he didn't hold a grudge of any kind, because I was in no mood to be Mrs. Nice Mom that morning.

I stood on the White House lawn awaiting my cue from the NBC production assistant. By this time, I must have had about 30 cups of coffee, and I was wired and jittery when the *Meet the Press* music came up.

Tim Russert: Our issues this Mother's Day: Moms march on Washington and across the country, calling for the licensing and registration of all guns. In favor: the march organizer Donna Dees-Thomases and a woman who was elected to Congress after this tragedy, her own husband shot dead on the Long Island Railroad, Democrat Carolyn McCarthy of New York. Against gun registration: Wayne LaPierre of the NRA and Republican Congressman Bob Barr of Georgia. The debate over gun control takes over Washington. Then, New York Mayor Rudy Giuliani copes with prostate cancer and marital strife.

Marital strife? My ears perked up.

Wayne LaPierre: . . . The NRA, we're the Red Cross of firearms safety. We put up a $1 million challenge to say: Let's put firearms education in every classroom in America. I mean, what makes kids safe— and moms know this—is teaching them to look both ways before they cross the street, teaching them not to touch a hot stove.

I didn't realize my mike was still hot, and I tried to answer this. I had to yell Tim's name about 10 times before he let me respond. Why hadn't somebody cut me off from all that coffee?

Dees-Thomases: Tim, you know, I do teach my children to look both ways before they cross the street. But I also expect the driver that's coming down the street to have a safety course, to have a license, to make sure that he knows he's supposed to stop at the stop sign and stop at the red light. And I also expect that the car's registered, so that if he hurts or injures someone on that street, that car can be traced. This is just common sense. And I think it's a ridiculous argument that the NRA is putting out. And we find it's laughable that they're putting out those big political ads saying that we're a political front. These are the guys that have been stuffing money down our congressmen's pockets for years, and they're really the political problem here. This is a public-health issue. We want to take the politics out of it, but they're the ones that are making it political.

LaPierre then accused the Democrats in Congress of playing politics with this issue, and my fellow guest, Carolyn McCarthy, became mad. Until her congressman refused to vote to ban assault weapons—like the one that killed her husband—Carolyn McCarthy was a registered Republican. I had met the congresswoman several times before now, but I had never heard her raise her voice. While I couldn't see her on the monitor, I could hear how angry she was.

McCarthy: If I hear one more time that I'm playing politics, I am going to scream! I didn't come to Congress to play politics. I came to Congress to reduce gun violence in this country.

Congressman Bob Barr, who is on the NRA board of directors, jumped in somewhere and accused me of being Dan Rather's publicist. Again, I hadn't been Dan's publicist for 7 years, but there wasn't time to correct this again. Our segment was over, but not before I got one last chance to plead for moms to come down to the mall that day to show their support. I was unmiked by NBC, then hooked up by CBS to tape a segment for *Face the Nation* with Bob Schieffer.

I felt I had screwed up a few times in these interviews, trying too hard to distance myself from the Democratic party, who were doing far more than their Republican counterparts to end gun violence in this country. It bothered me, in retrospect, that I had let the NRA's ridiculous assertion that I was a "secret Democratic operative" get to me.

I left the interviews feeling drained and inadequate, but only because I didn't want to let the mom volunteers down. I was, after all, representing them. And I wanted to make them proud of what we were accomplishing that day.

I wandered back into the White House to look for my family and found that everyone was outside on the South Lawn for the rally. Soledad O'Brien of the *Today* show was broadcasting live, and she interviewed Joy Livingston, the mom who had invited the president to the Michigan delegation cocktail party, and in turn, got 1,000 moms invited to the White House instead.

Soledad: Why are you marching today?

Joy: Because I want to be a mom forever. I don't want to be a mother who gets a phone call, that drastic phone call that something's wrong with my child. Anything anybody can do right now to stop the violence is so crucial to everybody.

I ran into Alison Hendrie, whom I hadn't seen since our Labor Day launch 9 months before.

Debbie Taffet was there. So were Julie Levi and Amy Putman and Robin Sheer. All of the original founding moms were gathered on the White House lawn. We spent a few minutes hugging and congratulating one another, and I could feel the incredible energy of the day gathering between us.

It was amazing, really, that we had all first gathered 9 months ago for a press conference at a clothing store on Columbus Avenue in New York City, and here we were, in Washington, just hours from the march. We had come a very long way in a very short time.

By the time the White House rally was over, my daughters were limp with hunger. Robin Sheer led Jeff and the girls to breakfast, while I headed over to the mall for another interview.

11 A.M.

I arrived just before the stroller march was scheduled to begin at 12th Street. The event planner had hired a golf cart and driver to take me to Constitution Avenue, a few blocks from the Capitol, where the stage was set up. The television show, *Sunday Today*, was preparing a live shot from the mall with Soledad O'Brien. This would be my last interview. Then the march would be out of my hands: Either people would come, or they would not.

I pulled up to the *NBC News* tent, with my fingers crossed that I'd run into a crowd. Instead, I watched a lone bus drop off its passengers on 4th Street, which wasn't at all where the buses were supposed to stop.

The women stepping off this rogue Greyhound were women dressed in purple and gold, not the Million Mom March hot pink. Were they at the wrong rally? Who were these people? Then I noticed that they were all carrying Jazz Funeral umbrellas decorated with Million Mom March paraphernalia. These were New Orleans moms! From my hometown!

Well, that explains the parking—in New Orleans we park anywhere we damn well please.

One of the Mardi Gras moms looked over at me and began to chant my name: Donna! Donna! Donna! I found myself looking over my shoulder, wondering who they were calling for. Then it dawned on me that it was me. I couldn't believe that they were here.

While the New Orleans moms managed to get to the mall in style, I couldn't even organize my own family that day: Jeff was now lost somewhere on the mall with our two daughters. At least I *hoped* he had the girls with him. By the time I arrived at the mall, the Interfaith Service was over. I was hoping somebody would have a video of the event so I could watch it later. Reverend Jim Atwood and Rabbi Marc Israel of the Religious Action Center had put their hearts into the program for months. They had done an incredible job uniting the religious communities of Washington, D.C. The service opened with an Islamic call to prayer and was followed by scripture readings from the Hebrew Bible and New Testament, and from the Hindu, Baha'I, and Sikh traditions.

THE STROLLER MARCH

When I finally had a good view of the mall and really looked around, I saw people bearing poster-size photographs of their children, mothers, fathers, sisters, brothers, and friends—all victims of gun violence. These portraits took my breath away. A contagious percussion beat erupted from the front of the crowd and an African drumming group from Richmond, Virginia, called Drums Not Guns led thousands toward the main stage. I stood and watched as a sea of bodies poured into the mall from all sides. This crowd stretched back for blocks and blocks and was marching in unison toward the mall.

Vibrant homemade signs colored the morning: "It's the Guns, Stupid!" (a takeoff on the 1992 presidential slogan, "It's the Economy, Stupid!"). Some advertised their business's support, "The White Dog Café in Philly says STOP THE VIOLENCE."

In the midst of this swirl of support and activity, I got lost—literally. I still hadn't found my family, and I'd even managed to lose my handler, Bonnie Berrie, whose assignment was to get me from one place to the next. I was a little panicked, looking through the throngs of people for someone, anyone, I recognized. But I ended up being swept along by the sea of marchers, and marching along anonymously, rather than arm-in-arm with the other founding moms or my own family. What an exhilarating feeling!

THE MAIN STAGE

The air was electric with purpose and with pride. Here we stood, hundreds of thousands strong, a force so determined I felt invincible, but more, I felt hopeful. Maybe we could get the politicians to listen. Maybe we could make a difference.

Rosie O'Donnell's plane had landed late the night before, and here she was, on stage, to serve as our emcee. Her enthusiasm set the perfect tone for the day: She, like the rest of us, was mad as hell and not going to take it anymore. Every speech that was made that day was electrified by both tragedy and possibility. There were no celebrities here today; only Americans with the will—and the guts—to make themselves heard.

Kerry Kennedy Cuomo spoke first. With the U.S. Capitol as her backdrop, she reminded the crowd that she was only 8 years old when Sirhan Sirhan walked up to her father in the kitchen of the Ambassador Hotel, raised a .22 caliber pistol, and killed presidential candidate Bobby Kennedy at the California primary in 1968. She noted the fact that the gun industry—a $2 billion business—is more about making money than protecting the constitution. She even gave this sobering statistic: There are more gun dealers in this country than there are McDonald's restaurants.

Then Alison Crozier, Kareen Turner, and Karen Scott—the Dunblane mums—took the stage. Up on the Jumbotron, the bright and shining faces of their kindergarten angels, Emma, Megan, and Hannah, beamed back at the crowd—precious young faces now frozen forever in time.

Karen Scott spoke for the trio. She told us that when their children were killed, they made Parliament listen, and in her beautiful Scottish brogue, Karen encouraged us: "We did it, and so can you!"

Wearing the Million Mom March T-shirts with their Scottish kilts, Ted Christopher's band then dedicated their ballad, "Throw These Guns Away," to America's children.

Jaime Foster Brown, publisher of *Sister2Sister*, an R&B hip-hop magazine, got up. "My son Randy is a great young adult today, a graduate of Brown University. He was shot [four times by a complete stranger] before the nation took notice that good kids get shot too—especially good black kids. It's not just the drug dealers and bad guys. But still we did nothing drastic to stop this trend. Gun manufacturers were making guns all the better to kill you with, more bullets, fire faster. Kids even developed a cool way of firing this gun. Turn it to the side when you pop a cap in his butt. This is a sexy way of killing. And we as adults continue to promote and foster this. Why? It's all for the love of the dollar. It sells records. It sells movies. We buy kids toy guns for Christmas, for Christ's sake. It's the American way. But I say today, America needs its butt kicked!"

Dana Quist, 4 months pregnant and suffering with a bad cold and morning sickness, had been up since 4:30 A.M. When she got to the mall, our logo, which had initially been so difficult to download and print, was EVERYWHERE. Dana pushed her young son Trent in a stroller and marched alongside Tipper Gore and Rosie O' Donnell. "I couldn't stop the river of tears rushing down my face," she later told me. We were all so moved by the culmination of so much work and blood, sweat, and tears. We were surrounded by a sea of souls who wanted exactly what we wanted: to protect our children from gun violence.

"WE ARE COLUMBINE!" read a massive sign held up by no fewer than seven Columbine mothers. Dawn Anna, the mother of Lauren Townsend, the Columbine valedictorian who was killed by 11 bullets while sitting in the library, spoke about her daughter's murder. "Eleven bullets" she repeated over and over as hundreds of supporters in the crowd wept quietly. "Eleven bullets pierced her thin body." She then spoke to her daughter, as any mother might do in the quiet of a cemetery: "Lauren, we are here, our arms are wrapped around you and the children of the nation."

Patty Nielsen, an art teacher from Columbine, spoke too. She was injured by a bullet while she tried to rescue her students. She was one of 23 injured that day. "It's time Congress showed some courage, too!" she shouted out.

Mindy Finkelstein, the teenage camp counselor who told her 5-year-old campers to "Run! Run!" as she lay struck by a bullet in Granada Hills, found the courage to take the stage. "My message to all of you today isn't that I am a hero, but I'm a victim. I am in pain. Emotionally and physically, I can still feel two bullets piercing my skin and blood gushing down my leg. I remember the instant shock to my body and the terrified feeling that I was going to die with all of my campers watching!"

Veronica McQueen, the mother of first-grader Kayla Rolland, told the marchers: "The gun that killed my daughter was a gun that could be loaded by a 6-year-old. It was a gun that could be concealed by a 6-year-old. And it was a gun that could be held and fired by a 6-year-old. Please don't ever forget that."

If there is such a thing as a star presence at an event such as this, it was Carole Price. By now, I had heard her story many times, but Carole told the crowd as if it were her first time. Joined by her husband, John, and children Carley and Michael, Carole described her 13-year-old son with a mother's tenderness. "He had big brown eyes," she said. "He was a friend to all. I remember him telling me, 'I love you, Mom' before he was killed." Carole continued in her beautiful but pained voice, telling the masses what it is like to get that terrible phone call or knock on the door. "Twelve mothers will cry themselves to sleep tonight. Twelve mothers will have to pick out a coffin and a headstone for the children they were certain would outlive them," she told us, her voice unwavering in its heartache.

Next a jolting public service announcement coproduced by Jann Wenner's organization, Ceasefire, and PAX was broadcast on the Jumbotron, showing a couple enjoying their "quiet" time as their kids play next door. The scene cuts to one of the kids finding a gun in the top drawer of the neighbor's house, and then we hear the sound of a gunshot. People in the crowd gasped.

I watched my husband Jeff, with whom I had been reunited in the crowd, brush away a few tears.

Mary Leigh Blek and Tina Johnstone spoke next. Mary Leigh spoke over the crowd, as if she were addressing the gun nuts who were lurking just beyond the Washington monument, where they were holding a "countermarch." "We love our children more than you love your guns!"

Probably one of the most passionate speeches was delivered by Rabbi Eric Yoffie, president of the Union American Hebrew Congregations.

Is the need for sensible gun control a religious issue? You bet it is.

The indiscriminate distribution of guns is an offense against God and humanity.

Controlling guns is not only a political matter, it is a solemn religious obligation. Our gun-flooded society has turned weapons into idols, and the worship of idols must be recognized for what it is—blasphemy. And the only appropriate religious response to blasphemy is sustained moral outrage.

Our legislators and the gun lobby want to blame everyone but themselves. The problem, they say, is media violence: violent action films, gory horror flicks, violent computer games. And this is a deeply troubling problem. There is far too much violent entertainment, and it is very bad for our children's souls.

But in Canada, Germany, and Japan, children watch the same movies and play the same computer games, and they don't kill anyone afterward. Their children are not more religious than our children, and their parents are not better parents than we are. What distinguishes us from them is the prevalence of our guns and the cowardliness of our politicians.

Some say that the problem is young people with violent fantasies. Oh, really? Young people everywhere have violent fantasies. Teaching teenagers to curb their angry impulses is a challenge for every parent and religious leader on the planet. But of all the developed countries, only in America is it possible for a disturbed teenager to get his hands so easily on such a terrifying array of weapons.

And so we come here today to counter the cheap platitudes of our political season and to help fill the moral void of our land.

We come here with a voice loud and strong, intent on shattering the complacency of our lawmakers and arousing their dormant conscience.

We are proud Americans, each and every one of us, and we know that we live in the greatest country on earth.

But are we proud of the fact that our murder rate is 12 times higher than any advanced country?

No! yelled the crowd.

Are we proud of the fact that too many members of Congress pontificate on morality and then do nothing while the carnage continues in our streets and our homes?

No! yelled the crowd.

Are we proud of the fact that there are too many handguns in too many trigger-happy hands, while politicians remain deaf to the frightened cries of children?

No! yelled the crowd.

Are we proud of the fact that the House and Senate are awash in NRA cash, while the voice of the average American gets lost in the halls of Congress?

No! yelled the crowd.

And so let's send a message today to those who represent us in Washington. And the message is this: We care deeply about this issue, and we will hold you accountable.

Yes! yelled the crowd.

We are ready for a knock-down, drag-out, no-holds-barred battle against the NRA, which is the real criminals' lobby in this country, and which is drenched in the blood of murdered children.

Yes! yelled the crowd.

True, we may not have the money of the NRA, but we've got savvy, grit, and passion. And we're going to find out who's getting NRA funds and benefiting from NRA ads, and we're going to vote for the other guy.

Yes! yelled the crowd.

Until now, our moral outrage has been too feeble and our sense of injustice too timid, but we look at the mothers of the murdered and the maimed, and we say: enough.

I, for one, am filled with a fresh spirit of hope. Yes, all of this may seem daunting, but the tobacco lobbyists once seemed invincible, and look what happened to them. The American people, I believe, are ready for a leader who will take on the fanatics and support sensible gun control. We are not prisoners of our past. We are not doomed to relive history. We are here today, in such great numbers, because we are, all of us, partners with God in shaping a better and more hopeful future for all of God's children.

Thank you.

The rabbi ought to run for office, I thought. Whew!

"We are giving birth to a movement," said Rosie O'Donnell, our indefatigable mistress of ceremonies. "We are now women and children demanding to be counted . . . We are the voice of the majority of Americans, and it is time we are heard . . . We have had enough . . . of the NRA and their tactics. Enough of the stranglehold the NRA has on the Congress and Senate. The NRA is buying votes with blood money."

"I stand here before you without any written words. I stand here before you, talking to you from my heart," cried Patricia Anderson, a Navajo Indian from Albuquerque, New Mexico, who came on behalf of her son who had been shot and survived. "Mothers, we have shed tears for our children. Let's make our tears a river . . . a raging river of votes [to] get our legislators out of office if they do not want stricter gun controls."

On stage, Laura Wallace and Renae Marsh Williams talked about their children, Wilson High School students Andre Wallace and Natasha Marsh, sweethearts slain on a District street in February. "I've been praying, 'Andre, give me the words,'" Wallace said.

Elsewhere on the mall, the march mood alternated between festive and somber: from the laughter and play at a "children's village" where clowns and games entertained, to the tears at the Conference of Mayor's memorial wall that listed the names of 4,001 victims of gun homicides.

Barbara Lee, a philanthropist, took the stage and recited the real meaning of Mother's Day as proclaimed by Unitarian activist Julia Ward Howe, who had organized it as a day for mothers (and others) to rally for peace.

From the bosom of the devastated earth, a voice goes up with our own. It says, "Disarm, Disarm!" The sword of murder is not the balance of justice! Blood does not wipe out dishonor nor violence indicate possession. As men have forsaken the plow and the anvil at the summons of war, let women now leave all that may be left of home for a great and earnest day of counsel. Let them meet first, as women, to bewail and commemorate the dead. Then let them solemnly take counsel with each other as the means whereby the great human family can live in peace. And each bearing after her own time the sacred impress, not of Caesar, but of God.

Go home and reclaim Mother's Day, Barbara urged us. Go home, roll up your sleeves, and demand action!

Reese Witherspoon, celebrating her first Mother's Day as a brand-new mom to baby Ava, took the stage next. But before she did, she went over to Mindy Finkelstein and said, "You are my hero." She probably hoped that Ava would have a camp counselor like Mindy in her life one day.

Off the stage and in the crowd, signs sometimes spoke louder than the voices echoing from our sound system. One said, "Make friends, not guns." Another: "We have the right to bear—and keep—children."

Journalists milled around, interviewing mothers. Adrienne Young, an African-American woman from Pittsburgh, held up a poster-size portrait of her son Javon Thompson and told a reporter, "He was a scholarship student at Carnegie Mellon, an award-winning young artist. He was shot to death on December 29, 1994. He was 18."

Every time Rosie came out onto the stage, the crowd cheered. "We are the voice of the majority of Americans, and it is time we are heard," she cried.

In a videotaped message, First Lady Hillary Clinton said: "We have had enough bloodshed, enough violence. When children are afraid to walk down their own blocks or walk to their own schools . . . or even visit neighbors, it is time to say, enough!"

Mieko Hattori had come to the rally from her home in Nagoya, Japan. She told the crowd that she is still grieving the death of her son

Yoshi, shot to death by a gun-wielding homeowner in Baton Rouge, Louisiana, nearly 8 years ago. The killer mistook the youth, an exchange student, for an intruder, when in fact he was just looking for directions.

"In Japan, only 30 people die each year from handguns, compared with 30,000 in America. I feel the great power of mothers here today. I want stronger gun laws. I can share the feelings of all these mothers here who have lost a child from gun violence." (I had met Mieko the night before at a reception by the Bell Campaign. She told me she felt sorry for the man who shot her son for he, too, she said, is a victim of America's gun culture.)

Sarah Brady took the stage with her husband, Jim, who was in his wheelchair. Sarah was wearing a bandana: She had lost her hair to chemotherapy. "If we can't get the lawmakers to change the law, then come November, we must change the lawmakers!"

The crowd cheered.

I walked the mall and saw two women from Alaska holding up a sign, "Alaskan moms support the Million Mom March." Alaska, another state with a frontier, gun-friendly culture, was not without its share of gun violence. In February 1997, a 16-year-old boy took a shotgun and a bag of shells to school in Bethel, Alaska, and killed the principal and a student and injured two others.

As Susan Sarandon took the stage, I walked to the tents set up behind the stage to check on the program. I ran into Rick Jasculca, the project manager for the day. He said that by walking the mall and counting the blocks of wall-to-wall people, plus the people lining up on the steps of buildings along Constitution Avenue, plus the fact that people were still coming up from the Metro stops, he was willing to raise the estimated attendance to 750,000, but for internal purposes only.

Why internal purposes only? Because, he explained, the press is trained to be skeptical about crowd estimates, and already the countermarch was claiming that we hadn't even reached our goal of 150,000. I didn't care what the press was going to report, and I cared even less that the gun lobby was trying to deny our numbers. I marched right over to Rosie's tent and gave her the new estimate— but, I added, the project manager advises that we sit on it. Rosie smiled devilishly. I smiled back. She got out of her chair, ran up the stairs, waited for Debbie Allen, who became famous with *Fame*, to finish her speech and took the stage. Although I hadn't heard it, Rosie must have given out the estimate of 500,000 earlier in the day.

Now I listened as Rosie shouted: "New estimate! Tomorrow you'll hear the NRA say that this many people were not here. But the fact is there are 750,000 people . . . 750,000 people. They said we couldn't do it; WE DID IT!"

How long ago it seemed that the professional gun-control advocates were trying to convince Rosie not to participate. It is going to fail! Nobody is going to show up! I might have gloated if I weren't so overwhelmed by the raw emotion surrounding our three-quarters-of-a-million marchers.

Antonia Novella—the former Surgeon General of the United States—waved her fist and pounded the podium. "Numbers don't show you a mother seeing her child shot as they walk in the zoo. Or a 6-year-old shot by a classmate, lying in a pool of blood. This is freedom? Freedom should not be built on the bodies of children shot on their front stoops. It must be built on common sense. Registering guns. Licensing gun owners. My friends, I need a license to use the tools that save lives. Why can't they get a license for the weapons that take them? Statistics do not bleed. We have to speak for the children who do!!"

Volunteer #154 caught my eye and made a beeline for me through the crowd. I braced myself for the barrage of venom I was sure would pour out of her mouth. It seemed that Volunteer #151—her buddy—was searching for ways to get into the VIP tent (reserved for major donors, corporate sponsors, the talent on the stage, and the state coordinators). She was running around trying to garner support for rushing the VIP tent to get in. Oh, brother. Those 151s were nothing if not dogged.

I couldn't get away from Volunteer #154 fast enough, but she grabbed the sleeve of my T-shirt and said, "I want to apologize." That stopped me in my tracks, and I turned to her. The tents, the stages, the program, she said. We could never have done this on our own, and I'm sorry. Until today, I just didn't get it, she admitted.

I appreciated her apology, but I reminded her that no matter how good our professional management team was, we never could have gotten the people there (the most important ingredient of the day) without the tireless efforts of the volunteers. What I had come to learn was how perfectly things would work if only we could all clearly identify what our talents were and then give selflessly. And that is why this day worked. In the end, people across the country just gave to us. They gave their time, their talent, their money, their energy. And one by one, we became the Million Mom March.

Dr. Michelle Erwin, a Washington, D.C., emergency-room doctor and mother of a 3-year-old, spoke tearfully of the 60 children who pour into the nation's emergency rooms every day with bullets in their bodies. She would welcome, she said, the decrease in her business that would come about if child-safety locks were installed on all handguns. "For the 60 children who will be shot today, they will be taken to an emergency room unless they are pronounced dead on the scene. The physician will then deliver the worst possible news a parent can hear . . ." Then she broke down and cried.

From the Jumbotron, a homemade sign was beamed out, showing the faces of Presidents Clinton, Carter, Ford, Reagan, and Bush with the caption, "Are they listening yet?"

A piano was wheeled out for Melissa Manchester, who sang a song she composed at an airport upon learning about Columbine. She called it "A Mother's Prayer."

Melissa Etheridge brought out her guitar and played a song she composed for her children called "Truth of the Heart." Emmylou Harris sang a song composed by Rosanne Cash who was there with her children. Tyne Daly, Bette Midler, Anna Quindlen, and a host of other celebrities shared their strength, along with a blessedly long list of other performers, policymakers, and religious leaders.

I made a pit stop at the VIP Tent to get Lili and Phoebe something to eat. I ran into Andrew McGuire from the Bell Campaign, and we high-fived. The day was almost over and nearly flawless to boot. I spotted billionaire Andy McKelvey, and I dragged Andrew McGuire and my kids in tow to say "thanks." Our benefactor was not as warm as I expected him to be, which struck me as odd, since he had promised to fund us to the tune of $2 million just yesterday. Lili, now sleepy, rubbed her eyes and got suntan lotion in one of them. Now she was screaming. I would have to worry about Andy's coolness later.

I took Lili up on stage to distract her. She felt better being up above the crowd, where she could rub elbows with Rosie, Elmo's friend.

Lynn BeBeaux, from the organization COPS, spoke of losing her husband, a police officer who lost his life while responding to one of the most dangerous calls a policeman gets—a domestic disturbance involving a gun. She had to break the news to her kids, ages 6 and 4, that daddy would never come home. "Somebody shooted my daddy?" her youngest would ask.

Police officers from around the country were in town for the next day's annual memorial on the Capitol steps—the same Capitol steps we were turned down for, since the Police Memorial permit had beaten us to the punch. The arriving officers were tooting their horns, giving us the thumbs up. The organizers of the Police Memorial had been gracious and had offered to share their space with us, since our events were a day apart. But now, looking out at the crowd, I realized what a lucky break it was to have lost out on that space, because surely the fire marshal would have shut us down for having too many people in such a confined area.

Joe Jaskolka, my 12-year-old friend from Delaware, who had promised to walk with us if we pulled off the march, managed to rise out of his wheelchair and take a few courageous steps. He also rang a 400-pound bell made of melted handguns. Joe was joined by 11 boys and girls who came up on stage one by one to ring the bell a total of 12 times, in symbolic remembrance of the 12 children who die by gunfire each day. Missy Jenkins, the brave young woman paralyzed from a bullet in the Paducah, Kentucky, massacre, rang the bell from her wheelchair, too.

Courtney Love took the stage. She had never spoken publicly about the suicide of her husband, Kurt Cobain, who was also the father of her daughter. "Suicide is a permanent solution to a temporary emotion," she said. She described the ease with which a felon had bought a gun and had given it to her depressed husband. "Three children will shoot themselves before the sun goes down," she warned. My mom, whom we had met up with earlier in the day, wandered off on her own. When she came back, she was sobbing. She had visited the Tapestry Wall of Hope, and I wished that I had told her to bring something of her sister Margaret's to tack onto the wall. My mother rarely spoke about her beautiful baby sister, who had killed herself with a gun, but I could tell from the anguish in her eyes that she was thinking about her today.

Schoolchildren filed though the crowd singing, "A, B, C, D, E, F, G, keep your guns away from me." Marchers wept on each other's shoulders in sympathy or danced in solidarity and celebration for the new movement they had given birth to.

The day was overwhelming and emotional. It was the culmination of so many long days and nights of dreaming, planning, cajoling, talking, reaching out, getting lost, and finding our way again. We were strong, we were huge, and we were united. On May 14, 2000, it seemed that the MMM would change the world.

The state coordinators finally took the stage. I couldn't believe it, but there was Rene, who a few months back doubted she would have the courage to leave her house, much less take the stage before 750,000 people. The Million Mom March started off with just two satellite marches: one in Portland, Oregon, organized by Lisa Laursen-Thirkill, and the one in Tulsa, organized by Dr. Jan Finer, Randee Charney, and Alice Blue. On May 14, 2000, Mother's Day, 73 satellite marches took place across the country, from Juneau, Alaska, to Jackson, Mississippi, putting our total number of Million Mom Marchers very close to a true one million. (And this doesn't include the more than five million visitors to the MMM Web site.)

The producers cued the playing of the recorded song, "Ain't No Stopping Us Now." This was a special request of Connie Rucker from Handgun Control Inc., who spent the last few weeks training hundreds of volunteers to answer phones in the national office.

I looked up at the stage and saw Henry Acosta, who organized the buses from Newark. I saw Stephanie Spicer, who organized the buses from Wisconsin. And Gail Powers. And Judy Harper from Georgia. One mom from New Jersey said, "This is the best Mother's Day I've ever had. It sure beats brunch!"

After a few hours, the event was officially declared over, but a huge swarm of people at the front didn't seem to want to leave. So I asked the producers to get the Dunblane band to play something for them. Once again, they played "Throw These Guns Away." A few women waved their arms in the air much like the crowd did at the beginning of the day.

I took the stage—the only time I did that day—to thank the National Park Police. Afterward, they asked if they could take a picture with me. How far we had come since that meeting in January, when I was too embarrassed to take my camera out of my bag and take *their* picture. I was thrilled. Yes! Yes! Let's take a picture together! It was a fine, sweet moment. Then I was escorted backstage to meet the press, who were waiting to get my impressions of the day.

Of course, one rarely exits such a stage gracefully. My daughters, whose patience with their mother had just about run out, marched up to me backstage at the postmortem press conference, each taking one of my hands and dragging me away. They looked the press right in their collective eye and declared loudly: "The march is NOW over!"

And for me, it was over. Finally. The press release had gone out announcing that Mary Leigh Blek of the Bell Campaign would be taking over the reins as president of the Million Mom March for the next year. And I would go home to try to patch up my marriage, go back to my job at the *Late Show*, and see if I could get my life back to normal.

———

At the end of the day, May 14, 2000, 12 mothers would end their Mother's Day by learning that their child had died at the end of a gun barrel. One of the children who died that day was B.J. Stupak, the teenage son of Congressman Bart Stupak. He committed suicide with a gun.

That night, hundreds of thousands of marchers got home safely, including those who came on the buses organized by Pennsylvania state coordinator Nancy Gordon—the organizer who feared she'd never be able to fill a single bus. In the end, she filled 100, the most buses to come from any one state.

On May 18, 4 days after the Million Mom March, the board of directors of the Bell Campaign voted to create a greater efficiency in the movement by merging with the ragtag Million Mom March. It also voted to change its name from the Bell Campaign to Million Mom March. But billionaire Andy McKelvey chose not to fund this new grassroots organization after all. Instead he put his $2 million into a new Washington, D.C.–based group called Americans for Gun Safety.

Also on May 18, 4 days after the

Million Mom March, the New Jersey State Senate overwhelming passed Ceasefire's Childproof Handgun Bill, which had languished in the state house for years. It would take another 2 years to get it passed by both houses and signed into law by Governor Jim McGreevey.

The institutionalized world of gun control bickered so much over money and minutiae during the summer of 2000 that it squandered the precious and fleeting moment when the Licensing and Registration Bill was to be introduced into Congress. Not only did this bill mysteriously disappear, but Congress also failed once again to close the gun-show loophole. Undeterred, grassroots activists in Colorado and Oregon pushed through referendums that closed this lethal loophole in both of those states despite the gun lobby's highly financed attempts to kill these referendums. In the end, the will of the majority of citizens in both states prevailed.

Also, that same November, thousands of Million Mom Marchers volunteered and campaigned for hundreds of local, state, and federal candidates who embraced the Million Mom March platform of sensible gun laws to save kids. As a result, some heavyweight NRA stalwarts were soundly defeated, including U.S. Senator John Ashcroft of Missouri, U.S. Senator Spencer Abraham of Michigan, and U.S. Senator Slade Gorton of Washington State, to name a few. For the presidential election, the NRA allegedly poured millions of dollars into the states of Pennsylvania, Michigan, Wisconsin, and Iowa to ensure a victory for its candidate, then-Gov. George W. Bush. Vice President Al Gore won all four. The NRA even failed to deliver Florida—Ralph Nader did that to now-President Bush. The one thing the NRA can claim credit for in the 2000 elections is a victory in spin. Their highly skilled publicists pumped out propaganda that it was Gore's stance on guns that cost him the election.

The Million Mom Marchers, being mostly mothers, did not know how to toot their horns and take credit for what they had accomplished. They put people in office—lots of them. But this was completely ignored by the Democratic Party, too.

In February 2001, overwhelmed with applications for Million Mom March chapters, but without the resources to respond, the Bell Campaign's national office collapsed. I was recruited by several of our funding foundations to return to the Million Mom March full-time to help rebuild it. With the help of key Bell Campaign board members, including Tom Vanden Berk, and under the new leadership of President Michael Barnes, Handgun Control Inc. merged with the Million Mom March. To honor Jim and Sarah Brady, the new organization is now called the Million Mom March United with the Brady Campaign to Prevent Gun Violence. The merger took effect in October 2001, shortly after the attack on the World Trade Center.

I moved back to New York City, safely above 14th Street, just a week prior to that attack. My husband and I attempted to reconcile our marriage off and on up until July 2003. We decided to amicably divorce later that year.

The 2002 election came and went without the Democrats embracing the issue. The only good news was that NRA board member and Republican congressman Bob Barr, who had publicly accused me of being a phony, was soundly defeated.

The Centers for Disease Control and Prevention in December 2003 revised its estimate that now only eight children die a day from gunfire. At the time of the Million Mom March, Mother's Day 2000, that number was as high as 12 a day. I'd like to think it has something to do with all of those mothers who now ask their neighbors if there's a gun in the home, and, if so, to please make sure it is locked up and unloaded, and that it has a high-quality trigger lock from a reputable source.

The trigger locks that Shari LeGate of the Women's Sports Shooting Foundation tried to force us to distribute on the National Mall were recalled by the Consumer Protection Safety Commission in the fall of 2000. Under certain conditions, these locks were able to be opened without the use of a key. The WSSF voluntarily agreed to replace its 400,000 giveaway locks with a better-made product.

That's the good news.

The bad news awaits us. Come September 2004, assault weapons such as AK-47s and Uzis will be legal again in America unless Congress votes to renew the ban put in place by President Clinton 10 years ago. Currently, U.S. Congresswoman Carolyn McCarthy, our working marcher, has introduced a bill that will not only renew the ban, but will strengthen it. House Leader Tom DeLay has vowed never to let that bill see the light of day. Unbelievable? Yes, but true. DeLay made that threat in May 2003. That's when we Million Mom Marchers resolved to go back to Washington, D.C., on Mother's Day 2004 to finish what we started in the year 2000.

Congresswoman Carolyn McCarthy also has a bill pending in Congress that would help law enforcement have access to data to prevent the sale of guns to people with a history of mental illness. The bill was named in memory of the two victims of a deadly shooting at Our Lady of Peace Catholic Church on Long Island, New York, in 2002.

Many in and outside of the movement believe we can never replicate the success of the Million Mom March 2000. I think they're wrong.

The stakes are even higher this time around. Call me crazy, but I believe that once American mothers realize that the same weapons used to mow down kids in a Stockton, California, schoolyard are about to become legal again, they will take action. When they understand that guns that can shoot hundreds of rounds in minutes might be on our streets again, they will come back to Washington, D.C.

I know I will be there. I hope you will be, too.

www.millionmommarch.com

POSTPARTUM DEPRESSION

If America's mothers fail to make themselves heard, then just around the time we're stocking up on back-to-school supplies next September, terrorists, drug lords, and the mentally unstable will be able to stock up on assault weapons that can wipe out a school yard full of kids in a matter of minutes. As mothers, we cannot let that happen.

Recipes for
a Revolution

Launching any kind of movement requires a few—but key—ingredients. We Million Mom March moms identified the need to have on hand the following ingredients.

- A Web site
- A solid grassroots organizational plan
- A plan for holding effective, dynamic meetings
- Tax-exempt status
- Grant money
- A comprehensive media plan
- The ability to organize a bus

And, most important:

- Common sense

SCOTT PALEY'S RECIPE
FOR BUILDING A WEB SITE

Our best chance for reaching the million moms we were seeking was to use the grassroots marketing power of the Internet to spread the word. Abstract Edge Web Solutions, an interactive marketing agency, built our successful Web site for us. In doing so, they taught us a number of crucial things.

Be clear. One of the keys to creating a successful Web site is to give clear, articulate direction to the Web designers. Identify your goals, and polish your message before you hand it off to the Web site developers. In this regard, simplicity must rule: A scattered, unfocused message will lead to a scattered, unfocused Web site and is probably more indicative of an organization that is scattered and ill focused rather than the Web designer.

Our Web site was for recruiting. The other gun-control sites were mainly to disseminate information and to raise money, and although ours evolved over time, we needed it up before our Labor Day news conference to begin recruiting a million moms. We also needed to be easy to reach and didn't have the money for a fancy database system, so instead, we put up a couple of e-mail addresses. (This was both a good thing and a bad thing. We were inundated by gun nuts, but thousands of legitimate marchers would contact us over the next few months with our simple little Web site.)

Make it easy. Not only must you motivate your target audience, you must make participation as easy and painless as possible. Our Web site, for example, had to capture moms the first time they visited because they were unlikely to return otherwise.

Create a user-friendly site that makes the visitor's engagement with the organization simple, empowering, and compelling. Offer a subtle series of questions to identify the visitor's intent—for example, with the MMM, visitors were able to identify what type of constituent they were (i.e., interested bystander, marcher, organizer, donor, or spoiler).

Once your user self-identifies, make all the necessary tools to navigate the site readily available. On our site, for example, marchers could book a hotel in Washington and sign up for transportation, while bystanders could join our mailing list for information updates, and donors could make donations with their credit cards, etc.

Make an emotional connection. Nonprofit organizations frequently make the mistake of thinking that their cause itself is enough to motivate the masses but the *way* a message is delivered can be just as important as the message itself. Make an emotional connection, and carry that theme throughout your site.

The Million Mom March Web site was intentionally inviting and noncontroversial—how could anyone be against mom and apple pie, or against the notion of mothers protecting their children? Robin Toner wrote in the *New York Times* that the Web site was "warm and fuzzy" and made "an appeal based on the moral authority of women as mothers."

This was particularly true with our online fundraising. Rather than simply make an appeal for contributions—which wasn't very successful—we introduced two features that directly communicated our primary motivation and goal: protecting our children. First, "Tapestry of Woven Words" provided a public forum for people to express their thoughts and feelings about gun violence, with a high percentage of postings from people who had lost a family member to gun violence. This element proved to have unintended benefits by allowing us to create an excellent database of respondents who, through this emotional dialogue, opened themselves up and became quite literally an online family whom we counted on for their involvement. The tapestry was, in fact, a pioneer Web log (or "blog"), and we were pioneer bloggers.

On the same page was the "Registry of Protected Children." As people read the heartrending stories on the tapestry, they were given the opportunity to make a donation in the name of a child.

Make your cause their cause. A thriving, large-scale grassroots movement takes advantage of the unique talents and capabilities, passion, and energy of its constituents.

People are much more likely to get involved when the message comes from a friend than from an organization, and the role of an organization in such an exchange is to act as a catalyst by providing tools that empower these organizational advocates. Provide a variety of materials, information, and ideas on how to disseminate the message, and then get out of their way!

Word of mouth and word of e-mail played huge roles in the success of the Million Mom March, and some of the most creative ideas came from people who were not directly affiliated. Several Web site features, such as the tapestry, were managed by volunteers who were themselves brought into the fold through word of mouth. The site presented a forum for people to find each other and provided items such as T-shirts for purchase, and posters, bumper stickers, and other materials for download.

While your site should help guide people in terms of steps they can take to become active in your movement, try not to dictate how materials will be used, how the message should be told, or who could tell it.

Be flexible. Your Web site can and should be updated as you move forward, but don't dilute your message with everybody's suggestions. Stick to the key points, and while you may be flexible, your vision should always remain steady.

DANA QUIST'S RECIPE
FOR GRASSROOTS ORGANIZING

• First, create a database of your friends and family, particularly those who are doctors, lawyers, teachers, clergy, and most important, people with clerical skills.

• Next, organize a coffee get-together in your home with your friends and family. Set a simple agenda. (See Hilary Wendel's Recipe, page 209.)

• Keep expanding outward. Your next meeting should be the friends of your friends and family. Delegate small tasks and set realistic deadlines.

As soon as you have a core group of three to five volunteers, expand outward again.

• Post fliers everywhere a mom goes: to the local kid's shoe store, to your pediatrician. Put your e-mail address, Web address, and national phone number on the fliers. (If you can afford a separate number from your home phone, you won't have to worry about your kids pretending to take messages.)

• For follow-up meetings with new recruits you are not familiar with, make sure you meet in a public place, and ask for security if you are concerned. New agenda items should include:

(a) Find volunteers for small business sponsorship.

(b) Find endorsing organizations, such as the local PTA, churches and synagogues, YMCA, YWCA.

(c) Make a list of local media (TV, radio, print).

(d) Make a list of local celebrities. Ask volunteers who may know them to contact them. Ask them to attend a local rally or lend their name in support.

(e) Form coalitions with organizations who have a similar mission and already have solid statistics, data, talking points. Some may already have legislation in the State House. Work together.

• Network, network, network.

• Keep your materials with you at all times—wherever you go, your fliers go. Keep them in the car, in your purse, in the diaper bag or briefcase. Make distributions part of your daily life—when you're grabbing coffee at Starbucks, tack up a flier, when grocery shopping, stick one in the store.

• Spoon-feed your volunteers. If you want them to call their congressman, provide the phone numbers for the congressman; if you want them to attend a meeting or a rally, provide a map to the event, complete with parking details and public transportation. By shortening the steps, you will transform your volunteer from an apathetic couch potato to an activist.

• And, most important, every 2 weeks or so, write an upbeat, enthusiastic letter congratulating and thanking the volunteers for their help. And solicit comments and concerns on how to move forward to the next level.

HILARY WENDEL'S RECIPE
FOR EFFECTIVE, DYNAMIC MEETINGS

Find a location. Not so easy, because many public organizations are nervous about being associated with what they see as a political cause. Don't use your own home, because you have no idea what kind of strange people might show up. (I was able to get a regular conference room at the Jewish Community Center by persuading them that this was a cause they should get involved in, particularly with memories of the JCC shooting in California still fresh).

Get people to come. Look to your friends first, and ask them to invite at least two other people to attend. (I had to beg some friends to come, which they did, and this really helped my first meeting, because I knew them and they were warm bodies.)

Make your meeting fun. The last thing anyone wants is another dry, boring talkfest, so make your meeting welcoming, homey, and lively. You don't need to go overboard on making it a party, but serving refreshments, handing out name tags, having people introduce themselves and maybe share a reason for attending will break the ice. (I tried to have cookies and juice and make it just a little social, but with so many people from different places in their lives—young, old, politically active, not at all active—there wasn't too much of this).

Make your meeting useful and efficient. Socializing aside, it is a meeting and should be run as such.

• Use a whiteboard or easel with paper. Allow the group to help you brainstorm even though you should already have a good idea where you want the discussion to end up.

• Take control of the discussion; don't allow the group to discuss a certain point for too long, or you will run out of time. People not involved in the discussion will tune out and you will lose them. Don't be afraid to say "Okay, sorry, I have to cut this discussion off, because we are running out of time." You might get a few discouraged people, but it must be done to stay on track.

• Get people to commit to all "To Do's" at the meeting.

• Make a list of organizations beforehand to assign tasks during the meeting—schools, churches, associations.

• Make a list of neighborhoods, and designate neighborhood coordinators.

• Make a list of large local businesses to contact, and assign names to each business.

• Make a schedule of setting up tables for flier distribution.

• No one should be allowed to leave the meeting without committing to create or print fliers; pass around a hat to pay for the first round of printing.

Get the word out so people will attend. It is crucial that local people become aware of your organization.

• Put fliers announcing your meeting in as many store windows as possible. Don't include the location, but your e-mail or cell phone number. Take names and contact information for anyone who responds, to create a master list, and ask respondents to please bring three friends (usually not too hard since most people don't want to attend alone).

• Get exposure, exposure, exposure. Call your local parenting newspapers and magazines, send to local PTA and schools for inclusion in their newsletters, try to list your meetings in local papers (be sure to check deadlines, which are often far in advance), make a little noise.

• Contact your local television station to see if they will do a human-interest story on your group at one of your meetings. (Being in New York, we stood outside the windows of the *Today* show holding signs!)

• Advertise yourself with an organizational T-shirt (or even a home-made one), and become a walking billboard. (I wore my MMM T-shirt all the time, and since my child was still in a stroller, we walked the streets of Manhattan a lot. My T-shirt was responsible for getting a few new bodies.)

Recognize the types of people who come to the meeting. You'll find that the people who come to your meetings fall into several categories.

• **The passionate ones.** The truly passionate are the ones that seek YOU out. They are the ones you can get to work for you; they are the PERFECT CATCH.

• **The newly converted.** They believe in the cause, but not enough to do much to get others involved. They may or may not come to your final march or event; your job is to not LOSE them.

• **The not-so-useful ones.** Their hearts are in the right place, but they tend to be more disrupting than contributing. Try to ignore them politely and not allow them to dissuade normal people from getting involved.

You never know when that certain someone is going to appear, the one who will carry the movement with a great force, so every contact that comes your way, whether through the MMM Web site, through a flier, through a friend of a friend, or through seeing an MMM T-shirt on someone, you need to welcome them and give them a chance to show their true colors. Some people don't even realize what they can offer until you help them find it out!

Get other organizations involved in your meeting. This is an excellent way to increase your ranks significantly.

• **Churches, synagogues, etc.** The way to get a church or synagogue involved is through a congregation member or personal contact. Blindly calling someone rarely works, because they aren't receptive, unless you get lucky and the head of the religious organization is a "passionate one." Some religious organizations are used to organizing themselves for this sort of thing, which is great, because then you can leave them be and just help them periodically when they ask you for help. Other organizations need a bit more guidance, and you need to play a more active role in helping them along.

• **Professional organizations.** There are many professional groups who seek out cause-oriented activities and might welcome your organization. You can offer to host a meeting at an upcoming gathering or at least hand out information to the constituency about your own meetings.

JEFF BERGER'S RECIPE
FOR IRS TAX-EXEMPT STATUS

Ingredients: Name of organization, purpose and specific activities, names and addresses of board members, financial statements and budgets (actual or proposed), and an explanation of fundraising methods.

Prepare your countertop. Get IRS Publication 4220, "Applying for 501(c)(3) Tax Exempt Status," and IRS Forms SS-4 and 1023. All are available on the IRS Web site at www.irs.gov/eo.

Preheat the IRS oven. Use IRS Form SS-4 to obtain a Federal EIN (Employer Identification Number), an identifying number for all federal tax purposes, regardless of whether you have employees. NOTE: This number does not, in any way, indicate whether or not your organization is exempt from tax!

Vary proportions to taste. When formulating your board, try to have some community representation, and keep the size to a manageable number, generally between 5 and 13 members. The board may create any number of committees on which others may participate to perform specified functions or activities.

Sift all ingredients into a large bowl. Apply for exemption on IRS Form 1023. You must describe all of the above ingredients on the form as indicated. Many states also require nonprofits to register and/or make other state-level filings. Be sure that you photocopy everything you send to the IRS, because documents can be lost, and certified mail is recommended. NOTE: Your exemption application and any supporting documents as well as your annual federal tax return will be open to public inspection.

Add ¼ cup gold leaf. The IRS charges a "user fee" to apply for exemption, which is $150 for organizations whose gross receipts have averaged, or will average, not more than $10,000 per year, and $500 for larger organizations. Other costs might include incorporation filing fees, charitable solicitation, state or local registration fees, and professional fees for lawyers and accountants.

Use spice judiciously. The IRS generally will not grant 501(c)(3) status to nonprofits that participate in political campaigns or engage in more than an insubstantial amount of legislative lobbying. These restrictions should not prevent grassroots organizations from obtaining exempt charitable status provided they are careful as to how they go about their activities. An experienced tax advisor can help navigate the complex rules that apply. Political organizations may qualify for exemption under other provisions of the federal tax code, but additional restrictions and reporting obligations are imposed.

Avoid excess sweeteners. A 501(c)(3) organization must avoid conferring excess benefits on its founders and other insiders. While tax law permits the payment to insiders of reasonable compensation for goods or services actually rendered, it is a good idea to fully document the board's decision-making process when any kind of payment will be made to an insider.

Bake for 120 days. It takes an average of 120 days to process an application, although expedited handling may be available under certain circumstances. Roughly a quarter to a third of the applications the IRS receives do not require further work and are processed in 6 to 10 weeks. If the IRS returns your application for clarification or additional information, respond promptly in writing, and ensure that all documents are returned so as not to delay your application.

Present finished product to donors. Your exemption will be effective as of the organization's date of formation if the Form 1023 is filed within 15 months of formation and ultimately approved. An automatic 12-month extension to the 15-month period is generally available. Contributions to your organization made after the *effective date* of 501(c)(3) status generally will be deductible by the donor.

SEANA ZIMMER'S RECIPE FOR GRANT WRITING

Decide what needs funding. Whom you look to for money for a public-awareness campaign will be different than whom you look to for a new computer.

Locate potential funders. Use The Foundation Center (www. fdncenter.org), state directories, and government resources.

Call the foundation. Request Grant Guidelines and an Application AND any other materials they offer regarding their foundation, like an annual report. Be prepared to discuss your project with them.

Follow their guidelines TO THE LETTER. If you have any questions, call the foundation program officers—they're nice people, and it's their job to help make sure it's a good match. If they ask for an attachment, but it's not applicable to you, insert a page saying: "Attachment 4—Proof of Building Ownership—not applicable, since we rent."

Submit your proposal 2 weeks in advance, when possible. Send it via UPS, FedEx, or other courier, requiring the foundation to sign for it—unless otherwise instructed.

Expect a response . . . someday. Turnaround time on grants can vary from 2 weeks to 9 months. Check the guidelines, because they may tell you when the board or committee meets, and you should hear within 2 weeks after that meeting. Call the foundation if there's no word after 1 to 2 months.

If the grant is awarded, send a thank you! Add the foundation to your mailing list, so they get your newsletter. Thank the foundation publicly when appropriate—newsletter, media, public event. Follow their guidelines for reporting (6 months, annually, etc).

If your proposal is rejected, ask to speak with someone to review your proposal. Find out why it didn't make it and if you can resubmit later in the year.

BOB KAPLAN'S RECIPE
FOR KEEPING THE BOOKS

Although accurate financial records are not the mission, they are essential for any organization to function efficiently and legally. Financial records are necessary to plan, operate, and report both to the membership and the government. Furthermore, keeping records for a chapter is not difficult.

Ingredients: One computer, one financial software program like Quicken (or at least a spreadsheet program like Excel), one checking account, and a healthy dash of common sense.

1. Obtain a tax ID number from your organization's headquarters to open a nonprofit account.

2. Select a convenient bank, and pick up forms to open a tax-free account. Most banks will provide a no-fee account.

3. Select signers for the account at your next board or executive meeting (signers will typically be the officers) to fill out forms and resolutions. Two signatures should be required on all checks.

4. Unless you expect a large amount of activity, you can use the check register as a general ledger.

5. Record all receipts and disbursements in the register with the date, recipient or payee, and reason. To the greatest extent possible, all disbursements should be done by check. Keep a separate file for backup receipts for disbursements, labeled by check number; this includes expense reports, which should have receipts for all items.

6. Keep a separate list for membership receipts.

7. Reconcile the register promptly after receiving each monthly statement.

8. Fill out the quarterly reports promptly.

9. If the total income is less than $25,000 per year, there is no need to file any IRS reports. However, you should have the books (check register and subsidiary files) reviewed each year by an accountant; there is probably a member who will do it pro bono.

10. Finally: DO NOT COOK THE BOOKS.

DONNA DEES-THOMASES' RECIPE FOR MEDIA PLANNING

• Identify your target audience, and research the media outlets that best reach this audience. Make a list of appropriate media outlets, including television, radio, newspapers, and magazines.

• Identify several spokespeople who can address different aspects of your issue to offer for interview.

• Identify three to four key topics you wish to get across during each interview: overview of your issue, date of your planned event, phone number, and Web site for recruiting and fundraising, and be sure your spokespeople deliver these points every time.

• A kickoff news conference can generate immediate media attention for your issue. Plan an event for a weekday midmorning at a location convenient to the majority of the media.

• Have a specific agenda in mind, including who will speak and what will be said. Think visually—what kind of backdrop or prop would look good on television or in a newspaper photo?

• Maintain contact with key media people, and offer your spokespeople to discuss your issue or any current events that touch on your issue, on a regular basis.

• If you are planning a rally or other big event, keep the media apprised of your scheduling, agenda, and other interesting topics so they are well aware of your efforts and will be prepared to attend and cover it.

• Finally, keep your wits about you at all times—and your caffeine to a minimum.

SUZI ROBINSON'S RECIPE FOR HOW TO ORGANIZE A BUS

Organizing a bus is the single most important thing a person can do if she doesn't want to bother becoming a policy expert overnight. And it happens to be one of the most important volunteer positions in any activist organization.

Booking a group on a bus is the most cost-effective way to travel to and from any march, protest, or activist event. Bus captains—so critical to the success of the Million Mom March—help to coordinate logistics, recruit passengers, and make sure that many people from your community go to your event. People should reserve buses immediately upon finalization of your event date.

Bus Captain Checklist

• Determine who has buses to lend or rent in your area. Call religious congregations, civic groups, schools, childcare centers, senior centers, and others for in-kind donations or to borrow their bus. Find out about special rates.

Contact major busing lines to check rates, book buses, and elicit discounts (Greyhound is 800-454-2487; Peter Pan Trailways is 800-343-9999, to name two). Make reservations with local bus or van rental companies, and secure them with deposits. Develop a transportation budget. Calculate per-person costs.

• Recruit riders. Keep an organized, updated record of confirmed and potential bus, train, or plane riders. Register all participants as soon as you get them. In case you have a last-minute family emergency, a complete list of registered names will help the national office refer them to other buses in the community.

• Develop maps, directions, and a travel schedule to give to the carpools. Estimate travel time to and from your destination. Determine the departure place and time. Working with the national office of your organization, determine where the bus will drop and meet riders at the event site. Determine what time the bus will leave the site and arrive back at your community.

• Arrange with a local bakery or deli to provide coffee and bagels or donuts to marchers as they meet for the bus ride. You may be able to negotiate this at a nominal fee or even as a donation in exchange for the publicity and goodwill generated. This is valuable for many local businesses; for example, we had several local florists donate their leftover Mother's Day bouquet flowers and were able to hand out a flower to each of our marchers.

• Invite clergy members from a range of religions to bless the buses before departure.

• As your event day approaches: Collect riders' share of the expenses for their seats on the bus (don't forget to figure in a tip for the bus drivers), and if you want, stock a cooler for the ride.

Hand out any pertinent information as provided by your national office (agenda, itinerary, local maps/subway lines) so riders can plan their time.

• Arrive at the bus at least 1 hour before the riders are scheduled, to handle any last-minute details, coordinate any media coverage, and greet the inevitable early birds and people who want to come but don't have a reservation.

• Make sure bus drivers (if more than one bus) know each other and have a plan for stopping while en route. This will keep stops to a minimum and all the buses together.

Be sure to have a contact number to reach the bus company manager or president at 4 A.M. on a Sunday morning—that was probably the most important thing I had in my possession!

• Make sure riders know where to meet the bus after the event for the trip home. Help resolve riders' problems as they arise.

Important Bus Captain Responsibilities

1. Since there may not be actual tickets for the bus, make sure you have the names of everyone on the bus, either by checking them off on a preexisting list, making a list as the marchers board the bus, or passing out 3 × 5 cards and having marchers fill out information. You'll need this to check attendance before returning home. Also, get the name and number of an emergency contact for each marcher, if you don't already have one.

2. Try to make sure that any last-minute additions have paid for their seats.

3. Make sure every marcher gets a name tag with their name, the name of their group, the bus number (if possible), and their emergency contact information. Parents of small children should make sure that their child's ID is securely fastened and includes the name of the accompanying adult.

4. Make sure everyone understands where the bus will pick them up following the event and at what time. The bus captain should have a cell phone and make sure everyone has the number so they can call if they can't make it back to the bus on schedule or run into other problems.

5. If the bus company has given you any special instructions (such as whether food is permitted) make sure everyone is aware of them.

On the return trip:

1. Check to make sure you have everyone who came down (and no extra people!).
2. Be sure to thank everyone for their efforts.
3. Collect a few extra dollars from everyone to tip the bus drivers.

Parking: If you are marching on Washington, D.C., the area has a genuinely safe, fast, and cost-effective underground transportation system—the Metro. Using the Metro to get to the U.S. Capitol is highly encouraged, and parking near metro stations is available in suburban southern Maryland, northern Virginia, and the outskirts of D.C. Shuttling to the Capitol via the Metro from the most distant station should take less than an hour. For Metro parking or transit information, call the Metro customer service center at (202) 637-7000, or visit them on the Web for maps at www.wmata.com.

A few weeks before the event, and rarely sooner, bus captains will receive information about reserved lots for bus parking. Those with disabilities who need special arrangements should contact your national office to make appropriate parking allocations.

COMMON SENSE—OR LITTLE THINGS MEAN A LOT

- Get to know the names of your volunteers, particularly the ones with whom you are in closest contact.
- Return telephone calls and e-mail messages as quickly as possible—if you cannot do this yourself, have another volunteer handle them.
- Check in with your volunteers on a regular basis. Once you've recruited someone, reach out every so often to see how they're doing, if they need something, are overwhelmed, or need more to do—or just the sound of a friendly voice saying "good job."

• Don't be afraid to delegate—it will free you up to stay focused and make volunteers feel as if they are contributing.

• Write a newsletter, even a short one, to keep everyone who is involved in your organization up to speed. Try to include miniprofiles on individuals involved, for added moral support.

• Be sure you have a mechanism in place to send your newsletter and all messages out promptly. Enlist more than one person to cover any gaps and to prevent dumping too much onto one person's shoulders—including your own.

Just the Facts, Mom:

A Gun-Issue Primer

SENSIBLE GUN LAWS FOR SAVING KIDS

The Million Mom March United with the Brady Campaign to Prevent Gun Violence works to enact sensible gun-control legislation in the United States but does not seek to ban guns.

Not only do opponents of gun control, chief among them the National Rifle Association (NRA), whip up hysteria by defining gun control as a campaign to storm the homes of law-abiding gun owners and confiscate their weapons, but they also argue that U.S. citizens are stifled by "thousands of federal, state, and local gun laws," which place an unnecessary burden on firearm ownership and use. Neither claim is true.

The guns laws that we currently have are antiquated and riddled with loopholes. Most Americans are shocked to learn that there are only SIX FEDERAL gun-control laws that are designed to keep handguns out of the wrong hands. These include:

1. **The National Firearms Act of 1934**, passed in response to the fierce gun violence and gangsterism of the prohibition period and an attempt to assassinate President Franklin D. Roosevelt, placed a tax on such dangerous weapons as sawed-off shotguns and machine guns and required background checks for purchasers of them.

2. **The Federal Firearms Act of 1938** made licensing of gun makers and dealers mandatory and made it illegal to sell guns to known criminals.

3. **The Gun Control Act of 1968**, which was the first comprehensive federal gun law, was passed partly in response to the assassinations of Martin Luther King and Robert Kennedy earlier in the year. The law placed additional restrictions on who could buy a gun, barring purchases by:

- convicted felons
- fugitives from justice
- the mentally ill
- expatriates
- illegal aliens
- dishonorably discharged ex-soldiers
- anyone younger than 21 (to purchase handguns)
- anyone younger than 18 (to purchase long guns)

The law also banned the mail-order sales of all firearms and ammunition, such as the rifle used by Lee Harvey Oswald to shoot President John F. Kennedy, set standards for gun dealers and age guidelines for gun purchasers, and prohibited the sale and manufacture of new fully automatic civilian machine guns.

While the 1968 law was the foundation for today's system of gun regulation, the law's effectiveness was undermined because gun sales operated on an "honor system." Prospective gun buyers were only required to sign a statement vouching that they were not legally forbidden to buy a gun. In most states, no follow-up was conducted to make sure the statements were true.

4. **The Brady Handgun Violence Prevention Act**, signed into
law in 1993, addressed these holes in the nation's gun-control
safety net. Named for James Brady, press secretary to Ronald
Reagan, who was partially paralyzed in the assassination attempt
on the president in 1981, the Brady Law replaced this so-called
"lie-and-buy" system with one in which background checks are
performed before guns can be purchased. Under this system, gun
dealers are required to contact a government agency (either the
FBI or a local agency, depending on the state) to determine if the
buyer is legally allowed to purchase a firearm.

Since the Brady Law took effect, more than 600,000 gun sales have
been stopped because the records check revealed a felony or other prohibiting condition in a prospective buyer's background.

5. **The Violent Crime Control and Law Enforcement Act of
1994**, or **Assault Weapons Ban**, places a ban on the manufacture,
sale, and possession of 19 types of semiautomatic assault weapons
and copycat models, including duplicates of any of these assault
weapons, and the manufacture of guns with more than one of the
features commonly found on assault weapons.

The 1994 law also outlawed magazines holding more than 10 rounds
of ammunition and juvenile possession of a handgun or handgun ammunition, made it a crime to sell or give a handgun to anyone 18 or
younger, toughened requirements for obtaining gun dealer licenses, and
barred firearm possession by anyone subject to a restraining order because of threats of domestic violence.

It is illegal to hunt animals with more than 10 rounds of ammunition—rendering the weapons useless for sport—so what is the purpose,
other than to kill another human being? Assault weapons were used to kill:

• 5 children and wound 29 others in a Stockton, California, schoolyard in 1989. The AK-47 held 75 bullets.
• 8 people and 6 others at a San Francisco law firm in 1993. Two
TEC-9s with 50-round magazines were used in the massacre.
• 2 CIA employees and wound three others outside the CIA's
Langley, Virginia, headquarters in 1993.

• 4 ATF special agents and wound 16 others at the Branch Davidian compound in Waco, Texas, when the officers were attempting to serve warrants on the cult in 1993.

6. **The Domestic Violence Offender Gun Ban** of 1996 is the most recent federal gun law, which prohibits anyone convicted of domestic violence crimes from buying or owning a gun.

WHAT IS THE MEANING OF THIS?
(A GLOSSARY)

When dealing with an issue as complex as gun safety, it's essential to know some of the lingo.

An automatic weapon, or machine gun, fires continuously while the trigger is pressed and ammunition remains in the magazine.

A semiautomatic weapon fires one round and then instantly loads the next round with each pull of the trigger.

Assault weapons are usually equipped with some or all of the following combat hardware.

• Large-capacity ammunition magazines, enabling the shooter to continuously fire dozens of rounds without reloading. (Standard hunting rifles are equipped with no more than three- or four-shot magazines.)
• Folding stocks on rifles or shotguns, which enable guns to be stored in smaller spaces and make them more mobile
• Pistol grips on rifles or shotguns, which make it easier to shoot from the hip, enabling shooters to spray-fire the weapon
• Barrel shrouds, which keep the gun barrel cool enough to allow multiple shots in rapid succession without overheating
• Threaded barrels, which can be used to attach silencers or flash suppressors, both of which allow shooters to remain concealed or fire their weapons undetected
• Barrel mounts designed to accommodate a bayonet

A handgun is a firearm that is concealable and originally designed to fire a projectile from one or more barrels when held in one hand.

Handguns include pistols and Saturday Night Specials, semiautomatic handguns, machine pistols, revolvers, and derringers.

Licensing would require that an applicant be fingerprinted and pass a background check to ensure that the potential buyer meets legal gun-purchasing criteria (which exclude conviction for any violent misdemeanor, any gun-related crime, or history of domestic violence). Like a driver's license, the gun license would require the applicant to pass a test demonstrating thorough knowledge of safety and proper operation of a firearm.

Registration creates accountability for gun owners, requiring gun owners to claim responsibility for each gun they buy or own. Again, like licensing drivers and registering vehicles—you wouldn't hand over your car keys to a felon preparing to rob a bank, after all—this system places the responsibility in the gun-owner's hands and would thereby increase the ability of law enforcement to identify illegal possessors and to take unregistered guns out of circulation.

Conceal/carry is confused frequently with licensing and registration; some states permit an individual to not only own a gun for the home, but to carry it on his or her person hidden from view. This is like giving somebody gasoline and matches to carry around and becomes a self-perpetuating cycle of violence: If your crazy neighbor is carrying a gun around, you're going to feel the need to carry one, too. Unfortunately, most people who have permits to carry concealed weapons, other than law-enforcement officers, have limited training and yet erroneously believe they, and those around them, are safer should a dangerous situation arise. (Ironically, the NRA forbids its own members from carrying guns into the NRA's national convention).

Background checks provide a critical opportunity for law enforcement to stop criminals from owning guns by tapping into a database that shows whether a buyer is a convicted felon, has a history of mental instability, an outstanding restraining order, or other potentially dangerous background that would prohibit him or her from buying a gun.

Waiting periods serve a dual purpose: to provide ample time for background checks to be completed and to serve as a cooling-down period between purchase and possession of a gun. Too often, a gun is bought in a fit of passion, and the waiting period might alter the buyer's state of mind, allow family or friends to recognize and diffuse a potentially dangerous situation, and give law-enforcement officers ample time to track down criminal behavior frequently missed in the instant background checks conducted by dealers.

Instant background checks, also known as the National Instant Criminal Background Check System (NICS), were an NRA-inspired provision that ended the Brady Bill's 5-day waiting period for purchasing a gun. Background checks using this federally maintained database are less thorough, and the database is missing many records, including those from state prisons, criminal asylums, and terrorist watch lists.

Childproofing guns is a commonsense way to prevent kids from shooting a gun. Most handguns have so little trigger resistance that they can be fired by a 3-year-old or too easily discharge when dropped on the floor by clumsy little hands. Many popular semiautomatic handguns lack magazine safety disconnects or load indicators, meaning that children have no way of knowing that a gun that appears unloaded actually has a bullet in the chamber. There are a couple of ways to childproof guns, including:

- Smart technology—refers to a nonmechanical device that prevents the discharge of a firearm by someone other than the owner or authorized user. This would include a microchip, fingerprint detector, password, or other similar system.
- Trigger locks—mechanical locks that prevent the trigger of a firearm from being pulled. The lock may or may not have been locked onto the firearm but must be the appropriate type and size for that particular gun.

These childproofing tools are only as good as their users, however, and just mandating a trigger lock but not mandating its usage is like giving the new owner of an auto a pair of seatbelts and suggesting he or she install them. Without installation being mandatory, even those with the best of intentions probably wouldn't do so.

THE DEADLY GAME OF LOOPHOLES

There are several significant loopholes in the six federal gun-control laws in place in the United States, diluting their usefulness and impact.

The gun-show loophole. Under federal law, firearms can be sold at gun shows without background checks on the buyers. Since there are roughly 5,000 gun shows attended by more than 5 million people every year in the United States, according to the National Association of Arms

Shows, this significantly undermines the effectiveness of federal gun regulations. (The students responsible for the Columbine High School shootings bought their firearms, which included two shotguns, a rifle, and a 9mm pistol, at a gun show.)

The Internet loophole. Because the Brady Bill was enacted in 1993 before the boom in Web use, it has no provisions for Internet regulations. As a result, the Internet loophole allows gun sales to take place over the Internet without any background checks on buyers. And the numbers of Internet gun sales appears to be growing. GunBroker.com, for example, which claims to be the Internet's largest firearms auction site, boasts over $1 million in sales every month.

The secondary sales loophole. Gun purchases from licensed dealers are known as primary, or initial, purchases and are subject to the federal background check. However, a secondary gun sale is the reselling of a gun by a private individual (not a licensed gun dealer) and is not subject to background checks nor often regulated by state law. It's no wonder there are so many untraceable guns flooding our streets and in the wrong hands.

The newspaper loophole. An offshoot of the secondary sales loophole. Guns can be legally sold through newspaper classified advertisements—with no questions asked. The newspaper loophole allows those prohibited by law from buying or possessing firearms to buy guns with no background check, no record of sale, no regulation whatsoever.

CLOSING THE LOOPHOLES

Pro–gun-control factions in Congress are working to write new legislation aiming to close some of these dangerous loopholes, including **The Gun Show Accountability Act**, introduced in the House and the Senate in 1999. This act would have required gun show vendors to register with the federal government and maintain clear records of sales, while also requiring background checks for gun-show buyers. Unfortunately, although passed in the Senate, the proposal failed in the House of Representatives—2 short months after Columbine.

How did your Congressman vote? See the chart on pages 228 and 229. A Yes vote says to me that my elected official is in favor of stopping kids from buying guns through a loophole. A No vote is a cowardly cop-out, in essence saying, "Go ahead kids, head on out to the gun show. There's a sale going on!"

(continued on page 230)

SENATE
Republicans in roman; Democrats in italic

Yes		No	
State	Senator	State	Senator
Arkansas	*Lincoln*	Alabama	Sessions, Shelby
California	*Boxer, Feinstein*	Alaska	Murkowski, Stevens
Connecticut	*Dodd, Lieberman*	Arizona	Kyl, McCain
Delaware	*Biden*	Arkansas	Hutchinson
Florida	*Graham*	Colorado	Allard, Campbell
Georgia	*Cleland*	Delaware	Roth
Hawaii	*Akaka, Inouye*	Florida	Mack
Illinois	*Durbin, Fitzgerald*	Georgia	Coverdell
Indiana	*Bayh,* Lugar	Idaho	Craig, Crapo
Iowa	*Harkin*	Iowa	Grassley
Louisiana	*Breaux, Landrieu*	Kansas	Brownback, Roberts
Maryland	*Mikulski, Sarbanes*	Kentucky	Bunning, McConnell
Massachusetts	*Kennedy, Kerry*	Maine	Collins, Snowe
Michigan	*Levin*	Michigan	Abraham
Minnesota	*Wellstone*	Minnesota	Grams
Nebraska	*Kerrey*	Mississippi	Cochran, Lott
Nevada	*Bryan, Reid*	Missouri	Ashcroft, Bond
New Jersey	*Lautenberg, Torricelli*	Montana	*Baucus,* Burns
New Mexico	*Bingaman*	Nebraska	Hagel
New York	*Moynihan, Schumer*	New Hampshire	Gregg, Smith
North Carolina	*Edwards*	New Mexico	Domenici
North Dakota	*Conrad, Dorgan*	North Carolina	Helms
Ohio	DeWine, Voinovich	Oklahoma	Inhofe, Nickles
Oregon	*Wyden*	Oregon	Smith
Rhode Island	J. Chafee, *Reed*	Pennsylvania	Santorum, Specter
South Carolina	*Hollings*	South Carolina	Thurmond
South Dakota	*Daschle, Johnson*	Tennessee	Frist, Thompson
Vermont	*Leahy*	Texas	Gramm, Hutchison
Virginia	*Robb,* Warner	Utah	Bennett, Hatch
Washington	*Murray*	Vermont	Jeffords
West Virginia	*Byrd, Rockefeller*	Washington	Gorton
Wisconsin	*Feingold, Kohl*	Wyoming	Enzi, Thomas

HOUSE OF REPRESENTATIVES
Republicans in roman; Democrats in italic; DNV = did not vote

Yes

State: Representative

Arizona: *Pastor*

Arkansas: *Berry, Snyder*

California: *Becerra, Berman,* Bilbray, *Brown* (DNV), Campbell, *Capps,* Condit, *Dixon, Dooley, Eshoo, Farr, Filner,* Horn, *Kuykendall, Lantos, Lee, Lofgren, Martinez, Matsui, Millender-McDonald, Miller, Napolitano,* Ose, *Pelosi,* Rogan, *Roybal-Allard, Sanchez, Sherman, Stark, Tauscher, Thompson, Waters, Waxman, Woolsey*

Colorado: *Degette,* Udall

Connecticut: *DeLauro, Gejdenson,* Johnson, *Larson, Maloney,* Shays

Delaware: Castle

Florida: *Brown, Davis, Deutsch,* Diaz-Balart, *Hastings, Meek,* Ros-Lehtinen, Shaw, *Wexler*

Georgia: *Lewis, McKinney*

Hawaii: *Abercrombie, Mink*

Illinois: *Blagojevich, Davis, Evans, Gutierrez, Jackson, Lipinski, Rush, Schakowsky*

Indiana: *Visclosky*

Iowa: Ganske, Leach

Kansas: *Moore*

Louisiana: *Jefferson*

Maine: Allen, *Baldacci*

Maryland: *Cardin, Cummings,* Gilchrest, *Hoyer,* Morella, *Wynn*

Massachusetts: *Capuano, Delahunt, Frank, Markey, McGovern, Meehan, Moakley, Neal, Olver, Tierney*
Michigan: *Bonior, Conyers, Kildee, Kilpatrick, Levin, Rivers, Stabenow, Stupak,* Upton
Minnesota: *Luther,* Ramstad, *Sabo, Vento*
Mississippi: *Thompson*
Missouri: *Clay, Gephardt, McCarthy*
Nebraska: Bereuter
Nevada: *Berkley*
New Jersey: *Andrews,* Franks, Frelinghuysen, *Holt, Menendez, Pallone, Pascrell, Payne, Rothman,* Roukema, Smith
New Mexico: *Udall*
New York: *Ackerman,* Boehlert, *Crowley, Engel,* Forbes, *Hinchey,* King, *LaFalce,* Lazio, *Lowey, Maloney, McCarthy, McNulty, Meeks, Nadler, Owens,* Quinn,

Rangel, Serrano, Slaughter, Towns, Velazquez, Weiner
North Carolina: *Clayton, Price, Watt*
North Dakota: *Pomeroy*
Ohio: *Brown, Hall, Jones, Kaptur, Kucinich, Sawyer*
Oregon: *Blumenauer, DeFazio, Hooley, Wu*
Pennsylvania: *Borski, Brady, Coyne, Doyle, Fattah,* Goodling, Greenwood, *Hoeffel, Klink*
Rhode Island: *Kennedy, Weygand*
South Carolina: *Clyburn, Spratt*
Tennessee: *Ford*
Texas: *Bentsen, Doggett, Edwards, Frost, Gonzalez, Hinojosa, Jackson-Lee, E. B. Johnson, Reyes, Rodriguez*
Vermont: Sanders (Independent)
Virginia: Bateman, Davis, *Moran,* Scott
Washington: *Dicks, Inslee, McDermott*
Wisconsin: *Baldwin, Barrett, Kleczka*

No

Alabama: Aderholt, Bachus, Callahan, *Cramer,* Everett, *Hilliard,* Riley
Alaska: Young
Arizona: Hayworth, Kolbe, Salmon (DNV), Shadegg, Stump
Arkansas: Dickey, Hutchinson
California: Bono, Calvert, Cox, Cunningham, Doolittle, Dreier, Gallegly, Herger, Hunter, Lewis, McKeon, Gary Miller, Packard, Pombo, Radanovich, Rohrabacher, Royce, Thomas (DNV)
Colorado: Hefley, McInnis, Schaffer, Tancredo
Florida: Bilirakis, *Boyd,* Canady, Foley, Fowler, Goss, McCollum, Mica, Miller, Scarborough, Stearns, *Thurman,* Weldon, Young
Georgia: Barr, *Bishop,* Chambliss, Collins, Deal, Isakson, Kingston, Linder, Norwood
Idaho: Chenoweth, Simpson
Illinois: Biggert, Crane, Ewing, Hastert (DNV), Hyde, LaHood, Manzullo, Shimkus, Weller
Indiana: Burton, Buyer, *Carson* (DNV), *Hill,* Hostettler, McIntosh, Pease, *Roemer,* Souder
Iowa: *Boswell,* Latham, Nussle
Kansas: Moran, Ryun, Tiahrt
Kentucky: Fletcher, Lewis, *Lucas,* Northup, Rogers, Whitfield
Louisiana: Baker, Cooksey, *John,* McCrery, Tauzin, Vitter
Maryland: Bartlett, Ehrlich
Michigan: *Barcia,* Camp, *Dingell,* Ehlers, Hoekstra, Knollenberg, Smith
Minnesota: Gutknecht, *Minge* (DNV), *Oberstar, Peterson*
Mississippi: Pickering, *Shows, Taylor,* Wicker
Missouri: Blunt, *Danner,* Emerson, Hulshof, *Skelton,* Talent
Montana: Hill
Nebraska: Barrett, Terry

Nevada: Gibbons
New Hampshire: Bass, Sununu
New Jersey: LoBiondo, Saxton
New Mexico: Skeen, Wilson
New York: Fossella, Gilman, Houghton (DNV), Kelly, McHugh, Reynolds, Sweeney, Walsh
North Carolina: Ballenger, Burr, Coble, *Etheridge,* Hayes, Jones, *McIntyre,* Myrick, Taylor
Ohio: Boehner, Chabot, Gillmor, Hobson, Kasich, LaTourette, Ney, Oxley, Portman, Pryce, Regula, *Strickland, Traficant*
Oklahoma: Coburn, Istook, Largent, Lucas, Watkins, Watts
Oregon: Walden
Pennsylvania: English, Gekas, *Holden, Kanjorski, Mascara, Murtha,* Peterson, Pitts, Sherwood, Shuster, Toomey, Weldon
South Carolina: DeMint, Graham, Sanford, Spence
South Dakota: Thune
Tennessee: Bryant, *Clement,* Duncan, *Gordon,* Hilleary, Jenkins, *Tanner,* Wamp
Texas: Archer, Armey, Barton, Bonilla, Brady, Combest, DeLay, Granger, *Green, Hall,* Sam Johnson, *Lampson, Ortiz,* Paul, *Sandlin,* Sessions, Smith, *Stenholm,* Thornberry, *Turner*
Utah: Cannon, Cook, Hansen
Virginia: Bliley, *Boucher, Goode,* Goodlatte, *Pickett, Sisisky,* Wolf
Washington: *Baird,* Dunn, Hastings, Metcalf, Nethercutt, *Smith*
West Virginia: *Mollohan, Rahall, Wise*
Wisconsin: Green, *Kind, Obey,* Petri, Ryan, Sensenbrenner
Wyoming: Cubin

• The Firearms Safety and Consumer Protection Act, proposed in 2003, would require firearms to be subject to the same standards as all other products made in America. (Currently, gun makers are exempt from federal heath and safety requirements.)

• The Child Handgun Injury Prevention Act, proposed in 2001, would have allowed the Homeland Security Chief to regulate (or encourage) the design and manufacture of safety products like trigger locks that are vital in preventing the accidental firing of handguns.

• The Internet Gun Trafficking Act, proposed in 1999, is an effort to prevent the unlawful sale of guns on the Internet. The act would have made it illegal to operate a Web site that sells guns unless the Web site is licensed by and registered with the federal government. NRA opposition helped to quash the bill.

• The NICS Improvement Act (or Our Lady of Peace Act) introduced by Rep. Carolyn McCarthy is an effort to more strictly enforce the 1968 Gun Control Act by requiring states to automate and provide information to the FBI regarding any individual who is banned from having a gun for which the states maintain the records. Because background checks can easily miss histories of criminal or mentally ill behavior that are not logged into the system, too many people who are barred from owning guns slip through the cracks—to deadly results. The name, Our Lady of Peace Act, refers to the church in McCarthy's New York district where a man with mental illness shot and killed a priest and parishioner in March 2002.

A GUN IS NOT A TOY—CHILDREN AND ACCESS TO GUNS

Toy guns are far more stringently regulated than the real thing.

• An estimated 35 percent of homes with children have a firearm present. In half of those homes, guns do not have trigger locks and are not stored in a locked location (*American Journal of Public Health*, 2000).

• Two-thirds of the 41 students involved in 37 school-shooting incidents since 1974 got their guns from their own home or from a relative (U.S. Secret Service).

• Florida was the first of 17 states to enact a child access prevention (CAP) law in 1989, making it illegal to leave a loaded gun within the reach of a minor. If a child gains access to a gun, the owner is held responsible.

Similar laws were passed in California, Connecticut, Delaware, Hawaii, Illinois, Iowa, Maryland, Massachusetts, Minnesota, Nevada, New Jersey, North Carolina, Rhode Island, Texas, Virginia, and Wisconsin.

- In addition, the cities of Elgin and Aurora, Illinois; Houston, Texas; and Baltimore, Maryland, have passed laws making it a crime to leave a loaded firearm where it is accessible by children.

NRA MYTHS VERSUS REALITY

The NRA's fierce opposition to gun control often leads it to make outlandish and unfounded claims about the effectiveness of current gun regulations. Some of these phony claims include:

NRA MYTH:

The Brady Bill is ineffective.

FACT:

The Brady Bill has had a major impact by reducing crime and keeping guns out of the hands of criminals.

- Since implementation of the Brady Law, there has been a significant drop in the percentage of violent crimes committed with a firearm.
- The number of all aggravated assaults since 1994 has fallen by 12.5 percent, but the number of aggravated assaults with a firearm since 1994 has fallen by 31.4 percent.
- A similar trend can be seen for robberies. The number of all robberies since 1994 has fallen by 27.8 percent, but the number of robberies committed with a firearm since 1994 has fallen by 33.7 percent.
- The same trend applies to homicides. The number of all murders since 1994 has fallen 23.4 percent, while the number of murders committed with a firearm has fallen 29 percent.
- Some criminologists think the decrease in the use of firearms during robberies and aggravated assaults may help explain the overall decline in the murder rate during the same time period.

• The Brady Law also reduced levels of illegal gun trafficking by establishing a uniform standard for background checks nationwide. Previously, guns were often illegally shipped from states without background check requirements to states that had them.

NRA MYTH:

Background checks mandated by the Brady Bill aren't being performed.

FACT:

Background checks under the Brady Law have been effective.

• The Brady Law does not require that police forces conduct background checks. In fact, the law requires federally licensed firearm dealers to check with state agencies for background checks before selling firearms.

• Currently, 15 states have full-time agencies that conduct background checks on handguns and long guns, and 11 states have part-time agencies that perform background checks for handgun purchases, while the FBI processes checks for long-gun purchases.

• In states that have no agencies, firearm dealers contact the FBI, via a toll-free telephone number, to request a background check before selling a gun.

• State agencies and the FBI *are* conducting background checks: Since the Brady Law took effect, more than 600,000 gun sales have been stopped because the background check revealed a felony or other prohibiting condition in a prospective buyer's past.

NRA MYTH:

The Assault Weapons Ban is ineffective and should be repealed.

FACT:

The banned firearms are very dangerous and must remain off the streets.

• An assault weapon is a firearm with certain features that make it easier to shoot many bullets across a wide area in a short time.

• There are 19 different weapons on the list of banned firearms.

• Most assault weapons are semiautomatic guns very much like machine guns designed specifically for the military. Assault weapons include the Uzi, AK-47, and TEC-9 as well as long guns like the AR-15 rifle or the Street Sweeper shotgun.

• These assault weapons are very different from those weapons *not* on the banned list. The guns that are not banned are smaller, nonautomatic pistols and handguns.

- Studies have shown that the ban has been effective. Gun traces are one of the best measures of gun usage in crime. In 1999, the National Institute of Justice reported that trace requests for assault weapons in the 1993–95 period declined 20 percent in the first calendar year after the ban took effect, dropping from 4,077 in 1994 to 3,268 in 1995.
- This same study also reported that the number of assault weapons traced in St. Louis and Boston declined 29 percent and 24 percent respectively.
- Also, a study by the Brady Center found that, in Maryland, the number of assault pistols recovered by Baltimore police fell by 45 percent in the first 6 months of the ban.

GUNS AND SUICIDE

In the United States, nearly 60 percent of all persons who die by suicide use a gun to kill themselves. Experts believe that most suicidal individuals do not want to die; they just want to end the pain they are experiencing. Experts also know that suicidal crises tend to be brief.

In part because of the cultural stigma associated with suicide, this aspect of gun violence has largely gone unnoticed among the wider population. However, statistics show that, contrary to popular belief, factors like depression or even suicidal thoughts are not the best predictors to determine the likelihood of a person committing suicide. The decisive factor is gun ownership.

GUNS AND SUICIDE: STATISTICS

- Roughly 180,000 people used guns to kill themselves between 1988 and 1997 in the United States, according to the Centers for Disease Control and Prevention.
- Guns are used at higher rates in suicides among young people and minorities. For males ages 15 to 19, guns were used in 70 percent of suicides, and for males ages 20 to 24, they were used in 64 percent of suicides.

ACCESS TO GUNS: MAKING SUICIDE MORE LIKELY

- Suicide is the leading cause of death among buyers of handguns within a year of purchase (*New England Journal of Medicine*, 1999).

• The high rate of suicide among young African-American males—the third leading cause of death from ages 15 to 24—is tied to firearm accessibility in urban environments.

• The connection between guns and suicide led the surgeon general, in his 1999 report on suicide, to describe gun access as a public-health issue.

GUN OWNERSHIP AND SUICIDE

• Gun owners were 16 times more likely to use a gun to commit suicide than people who do not own guns (University of Pennsylvania's Firearm Injury Center study, June, 2003).

• Harvard researchers have found that there is a "robust" correlation between gun ownership and the likelihood of committing suicide, but the same connection is not seen between lifelong depression or suicidal thoughts and suicide.

• The Harvard study also revealed that the highest rates of suicide were found in the regions of the country with the highest gun-ownership rates, while regional rates of depression did not show any statistical relevance to suicide likelihood.

• Many doctors believe that by providing an immediate lethal force conveniently located within the home, guns are the great facilitators of suicide.

SOLUTIONS

• Waiting period for gun purchase. This commonsense strategy can help prevent firearm suicides because suicidal persons are at particularly high risk in the days immediately following the purchase of a gun, with one study showing firearm suicide was 57 times higher in the week after buying a gun than the overall suicide rate nationwide.

• Increased data collection can help law enforcement and health officials find out how suicide victims obtained access to guns, how long they owned them, and where they acquired them. Some experts believe that by tracking the types of guns most often used in suicides, design improvements could be developed.

• Services are available in our community for the assessment and treatment of suicidal behaviors and their underlying causes.

Contact the American Association of Suicidology, (202) 237-2280, 4201 Connecticut Avenue, NW, Washington, D.C. 20008, www.suicidology.org.

THE SECOND AMENDMENT: A BRIEF OVERVIEW

The Second Amendment has become a major point of contention in the 20th century as efforts to deal with gun violence have encountered opposition from gun advocacy groups like the NRA.

To fully understand today's debate over the Second Amendment, it's necessary to go back to the days of the nation's founding, when James Madison wrote the amendment in part to placate political forces of the day who argued that the new constitution placed too much power in the hands of a centralized government, especially if the new government were to create a standing army. At the time, standing armies in most European countries quashed uprisings and dissent, repelled invasions, and were often used as instruments of oppression.

Of course, the types of arms that were in use at that time were a far cry from the dangerous, technologically advanced weaponry available today.

Over the years, conservatives have taken the view that the Second Amendment is a prohibition of any and all gun control, creating a right to bear arms that belongs in the private realm, rather than the public.

But the mainstream of American political opinion has taken the view that the amendment does not create an individual right to possess a firearm and that the language of the amendment should be strictly adhered to. The "well-regulated militia" clause affords only definite, organized militias, like the National Guard, the right to arms.

The U.S. Supreme Court has consistently interpreted the Second Amendment as a means to "assure the continuation and render possible the effectiveness" of state militias, a precedent ruling that means, as the ACLU has stated, "The question is not whether to restrict arms ownership, but how much to restrict it."

Gary Wills, the well-known writer and academic, is critical of modern-day gun-control opponents, arguing that their view ignores the actual meaning of the words of the Second Amendment. "To bear arms," explains Wills, "is, in itself, a military term. One does not bear arms against a rabbit." In European language, "arms" is synonymous with waging war. It does mean, in either English or the Latin derivative, "guns."

The NRA protests that if gun ownership is restricted too much, ultimately only the federal government will have guns, giving it the opportunity to abuse power and oppress its constituency. (Even though the nation's history has consistently shown that the best guarantor of individual civil liberties has been the federal government, not local authorities.)

The Million Mom March United with the Brady Campaign to Stop Gun Violence's stance on gun control is aligned with the mainstream position on the issue, respecting the right to gun ownership but advocating regulations that promote safety and minimize gun crime and violence.

Underscored page references indicate boxed text.